T0313997

Videogame Formalism

Games and Play

Games and Play in Contemporary Culture and Society is a new international and interdisciplinary book series dedicated to game and play research. Its primary focus is on the aesthetic, cultural and communicative aspects of games and play in our contemporary society. The series provides scholars with a peer-reviewed forum for their theoretical, analytical as well as historical contributions to the ongoing discussions on games and play. The series is not limited to digital games; it includes play phenomena, both digital as well as non-digital; and it covers social-scientific, humanities, as well as industry and design approaches. The proposed books should help readers understand the 'ludic' aspect of games and play–the 'gameness' of games and the 'playfulness' of play–without reducing games and play to mere applications or illustrations of other ideas or issues.

Series editors
Clara Fernández-Vara, New York University, USA
Jeroen Jansz, Erasmus University Rotterdam, the Netherlands
Joost Raessens, Utrecht University, the Netherlands

Videogame Formalism

On Form, Aesthetic Experience, and Methodology

Alex Mitchell and
Jasper van Vught

Amsterdam University Press

The publication of this book is made possible by the Utrecht Center for Game Research (one of the focus areas of Utrecht University; gameresearch.nl) and the Open Access Fund of Utrecht University.

Cover image: Studio Fantail

Cover design: Coördesign, Leiden
Lay-out: Crius Group, Hulshout

ISBN	978 94 6372 066 3
e-ISBN	978 90 4855 423 2
DOI	10.5117/9789463720663
NUR	670

Every effort has been made to obtain permission to use all copyrighted illustrations reproduced in this book. Nonetheless, whosoever believes to have rights to this material is advised to contact the publisher.

Table of Contents

List of Figures and Tables

Acknowledgements

We would like to thank the Utrecht University Focus Area: Game Research and the Utrecht University Library for kindly providing the funding to make this book available as an open access publication.

Portions of chapters 1 and 2 previously appeared in:
Van Vught, Jasper. 2021. "What Is Videogame Formalism? Exploring the Pillars of Russian Formalism for the Study of Videogames." *Games and Culture* 17 (2): 284–305. Copyright © 2021 The Author. DOI: https://doi.org/10.1177/15554120211027475.

Table 2.1, Poetic Gameplay Categories and Devices, previously appeared in:
Mitchell, Alex, Liting Kway, Tiffany Neo, and Yuin Theng Sim. 2020. "A Preliminary Categorization of Techniques for Creating Poetic Gameplay." *Game Studies* 20 (2). http://gamestudies.org/2002/articles/mitchell_kway_neo_sim

Illustrations:
Figure 3.3: Screenshot of *Akrasia* from http://gambit.mit.edu/images/loadgame_akrasia_03.jpg. Copyright © 2012 the Massachusetts Institute of Technology ("MIT"), used by permission of the Massachusetts Institute of Technology ("MIT").

Figure 5.17: Johnny and Junebug appear on WEVP-TV's "Night Noise with Rita," used by permission of Cardboard Computer.

Figure 5.18: "The Evening Broadcast," in-game version (left) and live-action version (right), used by permission of Cardboard Computer.

Figure 5.21: The triangle rule in the landscape design of *BotW*. Image taken from Schnaars (2021, 123), used by permission of Cornelia J. Schnaars.

Alex Mitchell:
This book is the culmination of ideas that I've been developing over the past decade, so there are many different sources of inspiration that I feel I should acknowledge. My early thoughts about defamiliarization, and my first exposure to some of the ideas that led to my work on poetic gameplay patterns, came from conversations with Kevin McGee. I also had a chance to explore some of these ideas when taking a graduate level class on interactive

media art with Lonce Wyse. I would like to thank my colleagues in the Department of Communications and New Media for listening to my ideas during several research talks, ideas that may not be familiar to them but hopefully encouraged some reflection and meaning-making as part of that process of defamiliarization. Much of the work that led to this book would not have been possible without the support and collaboration of the many undergraduate and graduate students that took part in the Narrative and Play Research Studio over the years, in particular Evelyn Chew, Liting Kway, Tiffany Neo, and Yuin Theng Sim, whose work directly relates to the ideas developed in this book. I literally could not have done this without you. I would also like to thank Jasper van Vught, "that Dutch guy you've been bumping into during the past couple of DiGRA gatherings," for reaching out to me and suggesting that we write a book based on our overlapping interests in Neoformalist approaches to game studies. It's been a great experience working together, and I'm so happy that I agreed to your suggestion.

Finally, thank you to my family, and in particular thank you to Karen for putting up with my late nights writing this book. Your support is what makes it all worthwhile. Thank you.

Jasper van Vught:
It is only befitting that I'm writing these acknowledgements from a camp-ground in New Zealand, since some of the core ideas in this book were conceived at this end of the world at the University of Waikato. While there are many people to thank for their support at that time, I particularly want to highlight the inspiring talks I had with Ted Nannicelli who steered me in the direction of Neoformalist film theory. This allowed me to draw on my time studying literary criticism in Groningen, from which I can still vividly remember Professor van Baak's explanation (and pronunciation) of "literaturnost!"

I would also like to thank the students and my colleagues in the depart-ment of Media and Culture Studies at the University of Utrecht which have formed a wonderfully warm and intelligent support network which has certainly allowed for ideas in this book to flourish. I specifically want to thank Joost Raessens for his selfless and oftentimes strategic advice, and my dear friend and colleague René Glas with whom I have done wonderful projects over the past years which have partly ended up in this book. I'm hoping there will be many more of those projects to come.

And of course, I need to especially thank my co-author Alex Mitchell who has been amazing at bringing things together in this book, while I was off wandering in *Breath of the Wild* or some New Zealand or Australian countryside. Thanks for agreeing to write this book with me, Alex, I could not have done this without you.

Finally, my greatest thanks go out to my loved ones and particularly my partner Willemijn and our two kids Mads and Evi who are currently reliving old New Zealand memories with me. Thank you for your unbridled support when there was writing to be done at unreasonable hours or in unsuitable places (like this campground). But thank you most of all for always giving me better things to do.

Preface

This book brings together ideas about defamiliarization and poetic gameplay that I have been exploring for some time but had not clearly grounded either historically or theoretically. Although my thinking about how gameplay can be made strange and unfamiliar drew inspiration from the work of Victor Shklovsky (2012a), I had not traced the connections from this early work on defamiliarization through either the later work of the Russian Formalists, or that of the Neoformalist movement in film studies. I certainly had not explored in detail the various ways that game studies have viewed (and critiqued) formalism in its various forms. That is why, for me, when Jasper approached me to write this book together, I felt it provided the perfect opportunity to rethink my work on poetic gameplay patterns, and also bring in the strong foundations in the history of this approach that Jasper had been exploring in his own work.

Although I say that my work before embarking on this book was not strongly grounded in theory or historical context, what I am happy about is that it was firmly based on both the player's (my) aesthetic experience of the various works I have analysed, and in those works themselves. As Jasper and I worked to articulate our understanding of our videogame formalism, I was pleased to realize that yes, what I have been doing, namely starting from what intrigued me about these works and my particular aesthetic experience, and then working through and identifying specific ways in which that experience was defamiliarized, thus identifying the various poetic gameplay devices, actually aligned with much of what we were developing in the book. Where I found the most useful insights, both as a critic and as an author of this book, was the way that using the dominant as a means to focus the analysis and find the connections between the various devices, really seemed to strongly connect to what I had been seeing in my work, but had not had the vocabulary to directly articulate. This, plus the extension of the notion of devices beyond the purely ludic, which had previously been my main focus, felt like a major step forward in terms of my own thinking about these concepts. For this, if nothing else, I am thankful to have worked on this book. I hope that for you, the reader, you find similar insights and inspiration!

Alex Mitchell
Singapore, December 2022

While I had worked on developing a formalism in game studies before, drawing from the tradition of Neoformalist film theory (van Vught 2016), I am glad I decided to let those early ideas simmer for some years before developing them into a book. This not only allowed me to further explore the Russian Formalist heritage that Thompson (1981; 1988) draws from in her work, it also forced me to reconsider some core tenets of the videogame formalism I thought I had figured out pretty clearly at the time.

In this earlier work on videogame formalism, I had basically done away with the whole idea of defamiliarization, thinking of it mostly as a nuisance that risked turning an otherwise useful and broadly applicable, systematic methodology into a highly narrow, evaluative theory of good art or, in my case, good games. However, once I had come across Alex's work on defamiliarizing poetic gameplay devices (Mitchell 2016), I gained a renewed appreciation of the usefulness of the concept and started delving back into the theory to see where my thinking had taken a wrong turn. I started realizing that by doing away with defamiliarization I had inadvertently hollowed out much of the approach even though I was still of the opinion that the concept was too often used for a study of games as art.

This is where my thinking was when I asked Alex to join me in authoring this book. And over the course of the past year and a half, this thinking has matured significantly in the back-and-forth between him and me. The approach has now evolved away from its useful but oftentimes abstract theoretical underpinnings into a much more practical set of methodological considerations. This is probably what I feel proudest of and where I think our book offers the greatest contribution.

Having done quite a bit of work with my colleague René Glas on the challenges of teaching students to analyse games as texts (e.g., van Vught and Glas 2018), I am happy to be able to offer my students sections from this book that will take them through the more practical considerations of doing the analysis. I hope they will experience this book as an inspiring, comprehensible and helpful source.

Jasper van Vught
New Zealand, December 2022

References

Mitchell, Alex. 2016. "Making the Familiar Unfamiliar: Techniques for Creating Poetic Gameplay." In *Proceedings of the First International Joint Conference of DiGRA and FDG 2016*. Dundee: Digital Games Research Association.

Shklovsky, Victor. 2012a. "Art as Technique." In *Russian Formalist Criticism: Four Essays*, edited by Lee T Lemon and Marion J. Reis, 2nd ed., 21–34. Lincoln: University of Nebraska Press.

Thompson, Kristin. 1981. *Eisenstein's "Ivan the Terrible": A Neoformalist Analysis*. Princeton, New Jersey: Princeton University Press.

Thompson, Kristin. 1988. *Breaking the Glass Armor: Neoformalist Film Analysis*. Princeton, New Jersey: Princeton University Press.

Vught, Jasper van. 2016. "Neoformalist Game Analysis: A Methodological Exploration of Single-Player Game Violence." PhD Thesis, University of Waikato.

Vught, Jasper van, and René Glas. 2018. "Considering Play: From Method to Analysis." *Transactions of the Digital Games Research Association* 4 (2).

1. Introduction

Let's start this book with a brief thought experiment and some probing questions to establish your academic situatedness. Consider the following game:[1] *Stray* (BlueTwelve Studio 2022c) is a "third-person cat adventure game set amidst the detailed neon-lit alleys of a decaying cybercity and the murky environments of its seedy underbelly" (BlueTwelve Studio 2022b). Released on the PlayStation 4 and 5 and Windows platforms, *Stray* is marketed as an adventure game in which you play from the perspective of a stray cat in a "strange city populated only by robots" (BlueTwelve Studio 2022a). Gameplay involves exploring the city, befriending robots, and working together with a "drone" companion to solve environmental puzzles and uncover the mystery of what happened to the human population in the city.

Now think about how you would study this game. What would you focus on? (How) would you play it? On what grounds would you consider the various elements of the game to be important, interesting, or valuable? Should you consider the gameplay? The ways that the framing of the game as an "adventure game" places it within a specific genre and in the context of a long history of previous adventure games? The choice of a cat as protagonist, and the emphasis on the realistic portrayal of the cat's physical behaviours? The choice of setting the game in a "strange city" which is explicitly modelled after the Kowloon Walled City, a place that the "BlueTwelve Studio co-founders have always been fascinated by" (BlueTwelve Studio 2022a)?

It is safe to assume that the answers to these questions will differ considerably from person to person. That is, of course, because when we think, talk, or write about videogames, we always do so from our own particular social, cultural, and academic situation. For those of us unfamiliar with or new to the academic field of game studies, that situation may largely consist

---

1 Note that this book presents a proposal for a *videogame* formalism. As such, when we use the term "game," we generally mean "videogame" unless we explicitly state otherwise. While acknowledging the complexity of the different uses and (questionable) interchangeability of these two terms (Aarseth 2017; 2019), for simplicity we use the term "videogame," largely due to its general acceptance both in industry and academia. We will return to the term, and the limitations its use may place on the methodology laid out in this book, in chapter 6.

Mitchell, A. and J. van Vught, *Videogame Formalism: On Form, Aesthetic Experience, and Methodology.* Amsterdam: Amsterdam University Press, 2024

DOI 10.5117/9789463720663_CH01

of specific repertoire knowledge (the games we have played), the value we attribute to games in our society (why a game deserves academic scrutiny), and the (oftentimes normative) language we have learned from videogame reviews and videogame culture. For those of us more embedded in the academic field, that situation is likely to also be made up of assumptions about what our reality is and what videogames are like (ontology), what we think the corresponding valid knowledge of videogames consists of (epistemology), and what procedures we think can provide this knowledge when we study them (methodology). Oftentimes, these assumptions are not stated explicitly in academic writings about videogames, but they are always there. In fact, as Silverman and Marvasti have put it, even those researchers trying to grasp reality independent of such guiding assumptions are simply "oblivious to the theory dependent nature of their research" (2008, 106).[2]

There are of course myriad valid ways to study a videogame, all of them based on their own ontological, epistemological, and methodological assumptions. For example, it could be that you answered the above questions from a (transcendental) phenomenological perspective where the game is considered to be actualized in the player's consciousness and therefore knowledge of the game can only be gathered from subjective "lived experiences." For example, in *Stray* the player takes on the role of an unnamed stray cat. The player views the cat from a third-person perspective, and much of the game involves solving environmental puzzles designed based on the cat's size and physical abilities. This raises questions such as: What is it like, experientially, to play a game as a cat? Does this impact how much the player feels a connection to the player character? How realistic is the simulation of the cat? Is this something that the player is concerned about, and how does it impact the gameplay experience? These questions may then lead you to use stimulated recall methods on other players (Pitkänen 2015) or to play the game yourself with your actions executed to cue bracketed experiences of characters and the game world, allowing you to then reflect on these issues of embodiment, presence, or player-character identification (Keogh 2015a).

On the other hand, a background in cultural studies, feminism or critical theory may have you consider the game to be part of a socially and discursively constructed reality in which certain power structures are reflected, reproduced, or resisted. This may have you adopt the methodology

---

2   As Silverman and Marvasti argue, scholars seeking an understanding independent of theoretical assumptions still implicitly (and perhaps unknowingly) adhere to a theory of naturalism.

of discourse analysis to study the meanings in and around the game as text to see how these meanings linguistically, audio-visually, or procedurally reflect these power structures (Ensslin and Balteiro 2019). In the case of *Stray*, the game is set in a post-apocalyptic version of the Kowloon Walled City in Hong Kong, a historical location that provided much of the visual inspiration for the game's design. There are also particular choices that the designers made regarding representation, such as the portrayal of robots wearing conical rice hats, which "have a troubled history within the Asian diaspora community. They're used as a racial shorthand to indicate Asian origins, regardless of the actual context" (Jiang 2022). This invites discussion of issues surrounding cultural appropriation, colonialism, and representation. To what extent, for example, did the developers consider the actual cultural history of their source material? Is any of this reflected in the game, or is the "oriental" setting simply used, as is often the case in cyberpunk, simply to create an "exotic" locale? Have these issues been written about in the popular press and online? And how have players responded both to the game and to the discourse surrounding it?

Or finally, to give one more example, you may have answered these questions from a more positivist perspective, assuming that the game and its elements exist outside of our experience of them and that we can only gain knowledge about them from value-free and reproducible sensory data. In that case, you may prefer to employ a quantitative content analysis of the game to study the representation (e.g., screentime or relative number) of something like violent acts or female characters (a kind of Bechdel test)[3] in cutscenes or the main questline (Schmierbach 2009). Taking this approach with *Stray*, you may want to perform a content analysis on the frequency of use of Japanese and Chinese text in locations around the city, or the number of times and in which circumstances the conical rice hats mentioned earlier appear in the game.

These approaches (and many more) all have their merits. Yet, all of them are also bound by their underlying assumptions, which steer the types of insights that can be gained into the game under investigation. So, while phenomenologists can employ a variety of introspective procedures, they cannot rely on observation of play behaviour alone, nor would it make

---

3   The Bechdel test is a gender diversity measure for a work of fiction that first appeared in a cartoon from Allison Bechdel in 1987. A work of fiction passes the test if it 1) has at least two female characters that 2) talk to each other about 3) something other than a man (see https://en.wikipedia.org/wiki/Bechdel_test). The test is mostly meant to raise awareness of the poor state of gender equality in popular culture.

much sense to embark on something like a formal analysis of the game's source code (Willumsen 2018a). These methods simply don't fit with how phenomenologists assume valid insights into a game can be gained and employing them would make the analysis self-contradicting. So, by laying bare and examining the assumptions of an approach we minimize the risk of a random or self-contradicting analysis and thereby make the analysis more rigorous, consistent, and convincing.

That is exactly what we aim to do in this book. Here, we historicize and further develop one specific set of assumptions which we relate to and file under the label *videogame formalism*. Drawing from Russian Formalist literature theory and Neoformalist film theory, we understand videogame formalism as an approach to studying videogames as texts or systems with assumptions about how videogames work aesthetically, the types of responses players can have to them, and how they relate to the world around them. By specifically situating videogame formalism in the context of these literary and film criticisms, we aim to separate this videogame formalism from other uses of the term, many of which have been criticized for being too reductive and selective in their approach to games (see below for a discussion on the anti-formalisms in game studies). While this videogame formalism still allows for a variety of methods that can be adjusted according to the game under investigation (we do not provide a recipe that you can follow to the letter), the underlying assumptions are still carefully and thoroughly developed thereby confining the analyses to a clear set of focus points and practical, methodological considerations.

By more explicitly outlining videogame formalism as an approach to doing game analysis, this book targets two types of audiences. On the one hand, this book offers methodological pointers to students and those relatively new to the field of game studies who wish to engage in a textual analysis of games from a formalist perspective. For them, the book shows what insights the formalist approach can generate, it explains the analytical focus points that come with it, and it provides instructions on its methodological considerations. On the other hand, this book invites fellow videogame scholars to reconsider some of their preconceptions about formalisms and engage more in-depth with the heritage and core principles of the approach. For them, this book takes a position in a longer running academic debate about the value or disvalue of a formalist approach to videogames, it points out some common misconceptions about the approach, and it lays the foundations for a formalist approach to videogame analysis by drawing extensively from well-established formalisms in literature studies and film studies.

A Hotchpotch of (Videogame) Formalisms

If you're new to the field of game studies, this may be the first time you come across formalism as a critical approach. But many others reading this book will have at least a cursory understanding of what formalism is. Chances are, however, that those understandings will be widely different once we move beyond formalism's central principle of focusing on the work's formal elements (rather than authorial intent or the reception process). This is because, as Medvedev already noted in the 1920s: "there are as many Formalisms as there are Formalists" (1928, 97, quoted in Steiner 2014, 18). For some, formalism consists of a set of shared artistic principles to strive for when creating modern art (Seiferle 2012; Greenberg 1971) or poetry (Academy of American Poets 2014; Gioia 1987). Here, formalism is considered an art movement, a shared practitioners' mantra that, for instance, emphasizes and values interesting relationships of a work's compositional elements (colour, line, and textures) over its subject matter. For others, formalism looks for the nature of an artwork, sometimes judging its artistic merits in line with some core artistic principles (Dowling n.d.). Here, formalism is a philosophy of art or aesthetics that functions as an analytical directive for defining (and sometimes evaluating) the artfulness of a work on the basis of its intrinsic values alone (cf., l'art pour l'art) (see Dowling n.d.). For yet others, formalism is a set of analytical procedures and focus points for the study of literature (New Criticism, Russian Formalism) or film (Neoformalism). Here, formalism is a methodology or research approach that provides a range of close reading techniques and considerations to analyse a work without having to rely on the fallacies of authorial intent (Wimsatt and Beardsley 1946) or a work's affective results (Wimsatt and Beardsley 1949).

These three broad strands or schools of formalism (formalism as an art movement, aesthetic formalism, and analytical formalism), identified here for categorical convenience, of course fail to do justice to the many different types of formalism out there.[4] In fact, we can identify fickle nuances within and between these three. For example, while abstract expressionist painters like Pollock (who is generally associated with a formalist approach – see Seiferle 2012) shunned subject matter to focus on experimentation with form,[5] the New Formalist movement in poetry also

---

4   For a much more thorough disentangling of the many types of formalism out there, see Brinkema's chapter on form in *Wiley Blackwell Concise Companion to Visual Culture* (2020).
5   Pollock famously went from naming his paintings to numbering them to do away with any potential references to subject matter.

emphasized the importance of narrative, next to elements like rhyme and metre (Academy of American Poets 2014). Also, while certain strands of aesthetic formalism like Zangwill's moderate formalism (Dowling n.d.), were mostly interested in categorizing the aesthetic properties of an artwork (as formal or non-formal), other strands, like Bell's more extreme formalism (ibidem) grew much closer to art criticism, using ontological claims on the formal nature of art for a normative judgement of beauty or artfulness.[6] And finally, while for instance some analytical strands of formalism like New Criticism remained firmly committed to close reading the artwork divorced from its context, Neoformalist film theory and late Russian Formalist works do away with this strict separation and have the critic study the work within its social-historical context and in relationship to a changing system of norms (Thompson 1981, 16–17).

We can also find this range of different formalisms within game studies. Willumsen (2018b), for example, identifies three broad schools of game formalisms: an *aesthetic game formalism* identified with those scholars looking for a "narrativeness" in games (Murray 1998); a *game essentialism* identified with those scholars interested in finding the "gameness" in games (e.g., Juul 2003); and finally a *formalism as a level of abstraction* identified with design scholars or content analysts interested in mapping the constituting elements in games (e.g., Lankoski and Björk 2015). Roughly speaking, these schools map onto the second and third category of formalism we identified above. Here, Lankoski and Björk's work (2015) corresponds to our category of analytical formalisms and, while Willumsen is of course completely right in identifying the differences between Murray (1998) and Juul's work (2003), the two would correspond to our aesthetic formalism since they are both looking for defining properties of the work, or, as Willumsen puts it, the "x-essence or x-ness" (gameness or narrativeness) in games (2018b, 141).

However, on top of these academic formalisms, you will not be hard-pressed to also find the practitioners' formalist perspective uttered by game scholars (since many game scholars are also practitioners, after all). For example, in (online) discussions on the pros and cons of formalism, the term has been used for a design philosophy which values (experimentation with) interactive form over attention given to audio-visual "content" (Lantz 2015c; 2015b). Here we also find different crossovers between these strands of formalism, when for instance Keogh (2015b) and others respond to Lantz's practitioner stance from a more aesthetic formalist perspective,

---

6   E.g., Bell's claim that an artwork's aesthetic properties were solely formal – lines, colours, relations – has him value abstract art over other forms of art (Dowling n.d.).

outlining how such design preferences also feed into (and are in fact often articulated as) value judgements on what constitutes the gameness of games (see below for a more elaborate discussion on (the criticism voiced against) this perspective).

This brief overview makes clear that this book comes in amongst a hotchpotch of different formalisms both inside and outside of game studies. So, to prevent confusion, it is imperative that we find a focus. We need to explain what academic tradition we draw from and for what purpose we are advancing the videogame formalism presented in this book. These three strands of formalism, however reductive, offer a preliminary framework for positioning our formalism. In line with these strands, our videogame formalism is best grouped amongst the analytical types of formalism in the tradition of Russian Formalism and Neoformalist film theory.[7] While there is certainly overlap between this formalism and many other types of formalism in game studies, this heritage also helps to distinguish our videogame formalism in terms of some core assumptions (e.g., on the role of the critic) and analytical procedures (e.g., focus on form and content). Furthermore, we purposefully position our formalism as an analytical formalism, so as not to confuse analytical focus with practitioner's preferences or prescriptive claims on what counts as proper form and thereby as "real games" (cf., Consalvo and Paul 2019). This should also go some way towards tackling many of the anti-formalist sentiments in game studies, which is what we will delve into now.

Anti-formalisms in Game Studies and Beyond

Over the years, formalisms have been at the receiving end of much criticism in game studies. In the wake of the 2015 online discussion, alluded to above, between academics, critics and developers,[8] in which the exclusionary foci and politics of certain formalisms were even associated by some commentators with the horrors of #GamerGate (most vehemently by Howe (2015)), Juul (2015a) wrote a blog post identifying a total of eight(!) different

---

7   We realize that Willumsen aligns ludology's game essentialism with Russian Formalism due to Russian Formalism's focus on the literariness or essence of the work. However, as we'll discuss in the next chapter, Russian formalists used the concept of literariness as a methodological starting point rather than as the result of an ontological enquiry.

8   Most of the discussion is summarized in (Howe 2015), which is a response to (Lantz 2015c), which generated a lot of backlash (kunzelman 2015; Keogh 2015b; Errant Signal 2015), to which Lantz (2015a) responded again.

anti-formalisms in popular and academic discourse. While some of those anti-formalisms have existed for close to a century (more on that below), many of the ones identified by Juul are exclusive to our field and related areas like game design and game criticism. When we zoom in on those specifically, a couple of core sentiments can be distinguished.[9] These anti-formalisms accuse formalism of 1) preventing experimentation by erecting stifling definitions of games, 2) looking at game rules to the detriment of story or representational elements, and 3) focusing on game design and excluding a consideration of players and player experiences (Juul 2015a). We will unpack these sentiments here to help understand which (preconceived) formalist ideas they are based on, we will identify the ideological underpinnings of many of the charges brought against formalism, and we will acknowledge the long tradition of anti-formalist sentiments that they are part of. This not only further advances our idea of what a formalist approach has meant in game studies, it also allows us to steer clear of the apparent pitfalls of the approach when constructing the videogame formalism that we present in this book. We will follow up on these sentiments in the next chapter once we start historicizing and outlining the core principles of our videogame formalism.

Formalism as Preventing Experimentation through Stifling Definitions of Games

The first anti-formalism listed above identifies one of the most common concerns people have with the approach. Here, formalisms are put on par with game definitions and thereby cue concerns that come with the inherent limitations of any definition. Especially in the first decade of the twenty-first century, during a period in which Aarseth (2001) famously declared the emergence of the new academic field of game studies, several attempts were made to identify the constituting elements that define games (Wolf 2002; Costikyan 2002; Salen and Zimmerman 2004; Juul 2005; Frasca 2007; Myers 2009; Waern 2012) or videogames specifically (Tavinor 2008; Karhulahti 2015). These definitions served important analytical, explanatory, and institutional purposes by building a shared terminology, and exploring the boundaries of

---

9   While Juul finds some more nuances in the different anti-formalisms, connecting each to one or two key sources, we decide here to group several of those arguments and (accompanying sources) together in these three strands of anti-formalism due to their overlapping themes (e.g., Juul's anti-formalisms #4 and #8 both deal with the problem with definitions, and #6 and #7 both focus on an insufficient acknowledgement of an active player).

our objects of study and by extension our field. However, in their function as boundary-work, definitions are always exclusionary, fitting specific phenomena and unfitting other ones. As such, any definition is always going to fall short of accounting for the great variety of entertainment phenomena that the videogame industry has been squeezing out of a rapidly developing new digital technology, thereby inherently generating more and more borderline cases (Juul 2015b).

Although the shortcomings of definitions are not necessarily problematic in themselves (Juul 2015b), they become problematic once these definitions are taken as normative or prescriptive. In other words, once definitions start to dictate what phenomena count as "good" or "real" games, they are inherently going to cause backlash. It is this backlash to the (implicit or explicit) value judgement that comes with what counts as games and what not, that Juul identifies as an anti-formalism. For Juul, this anti-formalism mostly centres around Koster's (2012) polemically voiced ideas about what a game is, especially the backlash that came from his statement that *Dys4ia* (Anthropy 2012), an autobiographical game about gender dysphoria and feminizing hormone therapy, "could be built in PowerPoint and *isn't a game*" (emphasis in original).[10] Although Koster explicitly states this is not a value judgement (implying this is more a matter of taxonomy for him), his hostile, dismissive phrasing still contributes to, as Consalvo and Paul put it, "which games get centred as real and which get marginalized as something else [...] [which in turn] shapes what games we are likely to see more of" (2019, 125). This is the prevention of experimentation that Juul's anti-formalism pushes back against, but the spill over of this boundary work is arguably much greater. Consalvo and Paul also show how legitimizing some phenomena as games and marginalizing others, contributes to "who gets imagined as a player and is welcomed into a community of fellow players" (125), and which scholarship is valorized (xxv–xxvi). Many of these sentiments can indeed be read in the arguments against this formalism online (e.g., Howe 2015).

Formalism as Focusing on Rules to the Detriment of Story or Representation

The second anti-formalism outlined above does not criticize formalism on matters of ontology (what are the essential existing properties of games) but on matters of epistemology (what counts as valuable knowledge) and design focus (see Fernández-Vara 2019; Fullerton 2019). Here, formalism

---

10   For backlash against (Koster 2012) see (Hernandez 2013; Howe 2015).

is denounced for valuing and focusing on games as rule-based systems first and representations second. As Lantz, who is considered to be one of these formalists, puts it, a formalist is "someone who tends to be primarily interested in a game's underlying structure of choice and action [...] [and is] less focused on things that could be considered 'content' – audio-visual components, narrative, theme and setting, etc." (Lantz 2015c). Lantz (2015c), like Koster (2014), enters this discourse with a focus on practice rather than analysis, advocating a specific type of "deep games, games that have surprising emergent properties, games that allow for player learning and mastery" (Lantz 2015c). As such, the formalism that these scholars-practitioners support is best grouped under the formalism as an art movement identified above. However, a similar argument has also been made from an aesthetic or analytical formalist perspective, propagating a specific understanding of what games are, resulting in a specific analytical focus. This, of course, takes us back to one of the founding (and more frustrating) debates in our field: the ludology vs. narratology debate (Frasca 2003). Without wanting to dig up those old demons, it is fair to say that early ludologists saw the gameness of games in their configurative components and consequently viewed a game's audio-visual output in the form of stories or fictional worlds as "secondary" (Konzack 2002, 95) or "coincidental" (Aarseth 2004, 48) in the process of analysing games. Or even, as Eskelinen (2001) famously put it, as "just a waste of time and energy." Instead of favouring specific types of games, which Lantz and Koster do, this formalism makes claims about the nature of games and favours a specific type of game scholarship.

While this formalism does not always draw ontological conclusions from its research and/or design preferences, the exclusionary approach to what counts as interesting about games feeds anti-formalist sentiments similar to those identified as the first anti-formalism. Responding to Lantz's dismissive attitude towards "pretend worlds and childish make-believe" (Lantz 2015c), this anti-formalism came from people who felt that more narrative driven games and those who play them (e.g., the Twine community) deserved the same amount of respect, especially given the misogynistic context of #GamerGate that formed the backdrop against which this online discussion took place. Beirne, for example, accuses Lantz of being a ludo-fundamentalist for downplaying the importance of "non-ludic parts" (2015), and Howe (2015) and Walker (2015) both identify similarities with the cultural gatekeeping done by #GamerGaters. Similarly, the academic discussion concentrated on how a sole focus on ludic functionalities makes light of the complexity and expressive potential of games and laid bare the academic gatekeeping that comes with an exclusionary formalism that (de)legitimizes certain scholarship. Murray, for example, accuses Aarseth (2004) and Eskelinen (2001) of being formalists with a "mind of winter" because they are "able to look at highly emotive, narrative, semiotically charged objects and see only their abstract game function" (Murray 2013). And Vossen's (2018) auto-ethnographic account of being a game scholar with an interest in the "wrong topics" (221) or in the "wrong games" (223) makes painfully clear how the academic boundary work by early ludologists made it increasingly difficult for some to feel a sense of belonging in the field.

Formalism as Focusing on Game Design, Not Players and Player Experience

The last anti-formalist stance returns us to a more classic analytical dispute in line with the structure-agency debate (O'Donnell 2010). Here, formalism is criticized for focusing too much on the game and insufficiently accounting for the important role of the player. We find this game/player problem (cf., Juul 2008) being articulated on an ontological (aesthetic formalism) and a methodological (analytical formalism) level. On a methodological level, Sicart (2011) famously criticized Bogost's (2007) work on procedural rhetoric (Sicart sees proceduralists as a "class of formalists") by arguing how the "meaning of a game cannot be reduced to its rules, nor to the behaviours derived from the rules, since play will be a process of appropriation of those rules, a dialogue between the system and the player." In other words, Sicart argues that we cannot study what a game means if we focus on the game's formal elements alone and only see players "as *activators* (emphasis in original) of the process that sets the meanings contained in the game in motion" (Sicart 2011). At an ontological level, Malaby (2007) condemned formalism in game studies by emphasizing the processual nature of games. According to Malaby, "Every game is an ongoing process. As it is played, it always contains the potential for generating new practices and new meanings, possibly refiguring the game itself" (2007, 102). Consequently, "any attempt to formalize games by defining them essentially in terms of their rules or through a taxonomy of types falls short" (2007, 103). Here, similar to the first anti-formalist sentiment, formalism is criticized for boiling down an inherently complex (and continuously changing) range of phenomena to a few essential formal features like rules and representational elements. Although Malaby's argument is focused on what games are, proposing a new game definition that accounts for the contingency of the human play practice, it obviously comes with the methodological consequence that a focus on the object's form should be shunned when analysing games (Malaby 2007, 101).

Both Sicart (2011) and Malaby (2007) emphasize a player whose behaviour, meaning-making, and general experience cannot be determined by the game. As such, both authors ascribe to what Smith (2006) has identified as "the active player model" in game studies. As Smith explains, works within this perspective show a clear preference for "player creativity" and highlight "the unexpected, the complex and the resistant" (2006, 33). This focus on player agency in the form of subversive play is also ideologically charged. After all, instead of approaching play as submitting to the ideology embedded in the game system, play is now considered to be an act of resistance, of challenging dominant power structures. So, according to this argument, formalism's presumed focus on the game as object rather than the game as process, makes it unable to account for this emancipatory potential of playing games, consequently making the approach conservative or even reactionary.

Formalism as Conservative

The three anti-formalisms identified here are articulated against the three different strands of formalism identified earlier. As such these sentiments come from different videogame related fields (academia, design, journalism), focus on different levels of the research process (ontology, methodology), and emphasize different shortcomings of the approach (insufficient ac-knowledgement of/attention to the player, representational elements, less conventional games). However, they all also share a similar ideological agenda, criticizing formalism for containing (or at least accommodating) a conservative agenda. This makes the criticism of formalism not just a matter of academic disagreement but also a political power struggle for inclusion and equality. Considering that much of the criticism of formalism was articulated during or in the wake of #GamerGate's socio-political climate of hostility and fear, this is understandable. For example, after acknowledging how ludology's focus on games as rule-based systems did not offer the tools to study the representation or position of marginalized groups in games and game culture, Mäyrä summarizes much of the academic criticism of formalism as follows: "formalism was also not able to provide game scholars any solid foundation for responding to the #GamerGate attacks, as they moved to target feminist and cultural studies game scholars, in addition to female game designers, players, and game journalists." (2020, 21) Therefore, the reasoning amongst anti-formalists appears to be that pushbacks against some of these formalisms were needed for our field to become more inclusive in the games we study, and thereby legitimize the scholarship we value, and the games and game culture we are getting in the process of doing so.

This criticism of formalism being uncommitted to social change falls into a familiar tradition. In historicizing anti-formalist sentiments, Juul (2015a) already identifies a couple of early twentieth century examples, many of which are articulated from a Marxist/Communist perspective and therefore combine accusations of political conservatism with charges of elitism. First of all, the 1948 decree by the Soviet Union's Committee for Artistic Affairs accused several Soviet composers, amongst whom most famously Shostakovich, of creating "decadent and formalistic music" (Central Committee of the All-Union Communist Party 1948). These "complex forms of instrumental music" were said to lower "the high social role of music" and were therefore considered "anti-popular," "bourgeois," and "anti-democratic" (1948). Secondly, Juul also implicitly refers to the l'art pour l'art movement of early aesthetic formalism which holds that an artwork should be judged on the basis of its intrinsic formal qualities rather than any reference to the world around it, let alone its social usefulness (Dowling n.d.). This aesthetic formalism has therefore also been accused of "political and ethical quietism" and an affinity with "the political right, which tends to preach acceptance of the social status quo" rather than social change (Seiferle 2012). Finally, we also find similar charges brought against the literary theory of Russian Formalism (which lies at the basis of the videogame formalism outlined in this book). Here, Russian Formalism was seen in strong opposition to Marxism (and later the aesthetic movement of Socialist Realism). The disagreement mostly centred on the (early) Russian Formalists' claim that literature (and art in general) should be seen as separate/divorced from everyday life while Marxists saw "literature as a weapon in the class struggle, as a potent means of 'organizing the social psyche'" (Erlich 1980, 99). This resulted in several polemic attacks from Marxist scholars in the early twentieth century, most famously Trotsky himself who spends an entire chapter in his book *Literature and Revolution* (2005, 138–53) dissecting the formalist theory, calling it "reactionary" and "superficial" (2005, 138).

As you can see, there is criticism aplenty of formalism, most of which homes in on its political conservatism or quietism. While we may not necessarily agree with all of these criticisms, we do not take them lightly either. Instead, these criticisms function as important warning signs for our exposition of videogame formalism in this book. First of all, they make us cautious not to advocate a videogame formalism that can easily be (mis)used to draw a line between what counts and does not count as a real or interesting game, proper game scholarship, or who count as fellow game players. Although we can never rule out an instrumentalization for political ends, we hope to make this more difficult by positioning videogame formalism first and foremost as a set of methodological considerations rather than an evaluative framework for games (as art) (see chapter 2). Secondly, we hope to steer clear of advocating a formalism that looks at form or systems to the detriment of content or representational components by advancing the Russian Formalist idea of the dominant, the idea that all devices (rules-based, narrative, or stylistic) are equally important in triggering our play experiences and thus equally deserving of our academic scrutiny (see chapters 2 and 4). Thirdly, the videogame formalism we put forward here also carefully moves on from the early – more fundamentalist – Russian Formalist idea to completely separate the object of study from its context, instead placing a game firmly in relationship to prevalent social, technical, and cultural norms in its time and their movement over time. This also allows for a consideration of a game's meaning/content as social commentary, instead of only its form as challenging dominant technological and cultural conventions (see chapters 2 and 4). Fourthly and finally, while our videogame formalism's focus remains squarely on the game as system, we still acknowledge and extensively explore the important role of the player-critic whose experience forms the departure point of the poetic analysis and whose different play strategies are capable of yielding different insights into the game under investigation (see chapters 2, 3 and 4) while being careful, as Smith reminds us, to do so without "explicitly claiming that this behaviour is the norm in a statistical sense" (2006, 31).

A Videogame Formalism Based on Russian Formalist Literature Theory

By choosing to anchor our videogame formalism in the tradition of Russian formalist literary criticism and by extension Neoformalist film theory, we argue for a very specific understanding of formalism that hopefully tackles many of the potential pitfalls of the approach outlined above. As we mentioned above, Russian Formalism and Neoformalist film theory can roughly be placed amongst the more analytical schools of formalism which have little ambition to demarcate art from non-art (or literature from non-literature) or evaluate the artfulness of a work (see chapter 2). But there are two other reasons for drawing from these traditions specifically.

First of all, as Myers (2010) rightfully notes, Russian Formalism is "one of the clearest and most influential statements of formalism in the arts" (40) and has consequently been the one most explicitly taken up in our field (e.g., Myers 2010; Mitchell 2014; 2016; Mitchell, Sim, and Kway 2017; Pötzsch 2017; 2019; Willumsen 2018b; Chew and Mitchell 2020; Mitchell et al. 2020). Myers (2010), for example, gives an extensive overview of the Russian formalist tradition with the aim of positioning it within semiotics and as "the initial step in establishing a relationship between aesthetics and cognition" (2010, 48). Willumsen (2018b) delves into the literary tradition of Russian Formalism and gives a great explanation of the difference between material and form referencing Aristotle's different causes in order to point out different formalisms in game studies. And Pötzsch (2017; 2019) and Mitchell (2014; 2016) and his co-authors (2017; 2020; 2020) explore the Russian Formalist idea of ostranenie (defamiliarization) for the study of (an aesthetic experience) of games. Furthermore, works by film scholars such as King and Krzywinska (2002; 2006a; 2006b) and Wolf (2002) are situated within a Neoformalist paradigm (which itself builds on the literary tradition), using much of the language and tools of this approach to study stylistic devices like camera work (King and Krzywinska 2006a, 115–18) and narrative devices for the triggering of suspense (King and Krzywinska 2006b, 105).

This extensive game studies library of work on Russian Formalism and Neoformalist film theory not only provides us with useful foundations to build on, but it also tells us that further exploring these traditions for our videogame formalism is potentially fruitful. To expand on this work, we identify a few areas in which previous adoptions and adaptations of these literary and cinematic formalisms fall short. First of all, in some cases (e.g., King and Krzywinska 2002; 2006a; 2006b), these approaches simply remain unmentioned and unexplored backdrops for ideas rather than a thoroughly explored guiding set of assumptions and procedures. While this is not necessarily problematic in itself, not engaging with these traditions also keeps these approaches from building on a set of core assumptions (on what constitutes form, engagement with the artefact, and the relationship of the artefact to the world around it) which, as we noted above, risks them becoming unfocused, inconsistent, and even self-contradictory (see also Thompson 1988, 3). Secondly, in some of these cases, the discussion of these traditions is put in service of other aims than establishing a more focused and more fine-grained videogame formalism, which risks moulding these formalist approaches in such a way that they no longer reflect their core assumptions. Myers, for instance, draws from Russian Formalism to develop a videogame semiotics even though Russian Formalism can be considered at odds with semiotics if we consider early Russian Formalism's focus on form over meaning or late Russian Formalism's consideration of meaning as merely one formal element to evoke aesthetic effects (see chapter 2). Similarly, Willumsen (2018b) draws from Russian Formalism to define her formalist strand of game essentialism even though Russian Formalism is better considered a functionalism (focusing on what the artwork is for) rather than an essentialism (what an artwork is) with any claims about essential qualities of art mostly being used for methodological convenience rather than ontological claims (see chapter 2). Thirdly, much of the work in this tradition (e.g., Pötzsch 2017; Mitchell 2016) remains limited to an exploration of defamiliarization (or ostranenie) which, although an important component of the approach, is only one part of it. This leaves us guessing how other components of the tradition could be applied in a formalist toolkit for the study of games.

Another reason for drawing from these traditions specifically, is that Russian Formalism, and by extension Neoformalism, provide a highly flexible toolkit capable of guiding research into aspects of form without predetermining their relevance or their functioning. As the Russian Formalist Eichenbaum (2012) puts it: "We posit specific principles and adhere to them insofar as the material justifies them. If the material demands their refinement or change, we change or refine them" (81). Similarly, Bordwell, following Eichenbaum, explains how Neoformalism deploys "hollow categories" since the approach has "no set point of arrival, [is] committed to no *a priori* conclusions [...] [and uses] concepts that will be refined through encounter with data" (1989, 381). As such, the approach is also not necessarily medium-specific and can be (and has been) moulded to study games as well as literature or films (as others have already shown).

However, (partly) due to this flexibility, Russian Formalism in particular is also known as a highly heterogeneous approach. Its theorists were subdivided into two different geographically dispersed schools of thought which approach their objects of study from slightly different perspectives. In St. Petersburg, scholars such as Shklovsky, Eichenbaum, and Tynianov formed The Society for the Study of Poetic Language (OPOJAZ) and approached their objects as literary historians. As such, their interests lay mostly in those devices that distinguished art from non-art or literature from non-literature. On the other hand, Jakobson and Thomashevsky as members of the Moscow Linguistic Circle, approached their objects as linguists. As such, they were interested in how the word in literature functions aesthetically. This means that rather than theorizing about what constituted literature (at a given time), the Muscovites theorized about the functioning of language and approached literature as a testing ground for these theories (Erlich 1980, 94). This heterogeneity also showed within the schools themselves, where consensus on methodological or epistemological issues was rarely reached. In fact, Steiner (2014) spends his entire book outlining the nuanced differences between formalist theories in an aim to find commonalities in different formalist models, only to admit that the only real agreement in formalism seems to be the "implicit agreement to disagree" (221). Similarly, Erlich (1980) shows how formalism evolved significantly over the years, changing from a polemic approach emphasizing the self-valuable word and a strict separation between art and life into a more nuanced poetic semantics interested in both sound and meaning and recognizing the connection between literature and other overarching systems.

The notorious heterogeneity of Russian Formalism therefore forces us to direct attention to a specific interpretation of the approach. Here, Neoformalism comes in handy because, contrary to Russian Formalism, Neoformalism builds on a more solid foundation of only a few works from two main authors. First developed by Thompson (1981; 1988) and later Bordwell (1989; 1991), Neoformalism translates Russian Formalism's core ideas around defamiliarization, motivations and techniques (such as mise-en-scéne, narrative, editing techniques or sound), and the dominant to the study of film.[11] As such, Neoformalism not only brings focus and clarification to the heterogeneous school of Russian Formalism, it also shows how a literary theory can be transposed for the study of another medium. On top of that, the Russian Formalism compendia by Steiner (2014) and Erlich (1980) also allow for an overview of the core pillars of the approach and prevent us from getting bogged down in the details and different translations of often contradicting and evolving perspectives.[12] Steiner and Erlich's books are milestones in the study of Russian Formalism that outline both the establishment and historical development of the movement within the Russian socio-political and cultural landscape of the time, as well as its main analytical tenets and contributions to the field of literature studies.

These key sources help to historicize our approach and direct our attention to three core pillars. These pillars consist of ideas around 1) the *object* as a

11   It should be noted here that Neoformalism focuses exclusively on the literary approach and discards the Russian Formalists' own works on film. In fact, Thompson is very adamant in her dismissal of the work by Russian Formalists on film, arguing it was too much focused on exploring the parallel between cinema and language, which Thompson sees as an incorrect and unconstructive way of looking at cinema (1981, 31).

12   See, for instance, Pötzsch's (2017) excellent but very detailed analysis of the different translations of Shklovsky's essay *Art as Technique*.

machine which directs our attention to how games work rather than on what games mean, 2) the aesthetic experience of the *process* of defamiliarization which functions as a methodological starting point for the analysis, and 3) the importance of historical *context* for identifying the (norm changing) points of interest in a game. This is what we'll delve into in detail in the next chapter.

Formalism as a Methodology for Studying Games as Texts

As mentioned above, we are approaching our version of videogame formalism as a form of textual analysis. This aligns with the approaches taken by, for example, Bizzocchi and Tanenbaum (2011), Tanenbaum (2015), Carr (2009; 2014; 2019), and Fernández-Vara (2019) who all adopt a "close reading" methodology. Carr (2009) views the game as a "text" that is actualized through reading or playing. For Carr, analysis involves applying three overlapping "lenses": structural, textual, and intertextual. The structural lens involves looking at the elements that make up the game and how they relate to each other. This can be seen as similar to our notion of viewing the game as an *object*. The textual lens involves "a focus on the game as actualized during play" (2019, 710), corresponding to our approach to games as a *process*. Finally, drawing from Bennett and Woollacott's (1987) reading formations, Carr proposes the third, intertextual lens, which acknowledges that the "context, subjectivity, and lived experience" (2019, 711) of the player-as-analyst inevitably impact the resulting interpretations. This corresponds to our inclusion of the *context* of both the game and the analyst.

Our approach to formalism as a methodology for studying *games as texts* draws from these ideas. In particular, as we will discuss in chapter 4, we focus on the ways in which the game as an object, when put in motion through the process of play, creates an aesthetic experience against the backdrop of both the context of production and the context of consumption. This requires looking at the game itself, but also at our own play experience, carefully paying attention to when, how and by whom the game was created, where and when it was initially played, and what we bring to the process because of our own background and context of play.

As an example, consider the game *Stray* (BlueTwelve Studio 2022c) that we introduced at the start of this chapter. To undertake an analysis of this videogame from a formalist perspective, we first consider what it is about the game that intrigues us and keep that in mind as we play the game for the first time as a player. We raised a number of questions about the game at the start of this chapter, including the choice of a cat as the protagonist, the focus on the realistic behaviour of the cat-as-playable-character, the choice of setting, and the framing of the game as an adventure game. These can all be kept in mind by the player critic during their first playthrough, but the focus should be on experiencing the game. From this initial play-through, some aspects of the game as an *object* will stand out: the visuals, the narrative structure, the level design, and so forth. At the same time, elements of the game as experienced through the *process* of play will draw attention to themselves: the behaviour of the playable character as a cat, the presence of spatial puzzles that make use of this behaviour, and the introduction of the drone companion B-12 which alters the focus of the game mechanics. Finally, particularly during subsequent analytic playthroughs, the player critic will need to think carefully about their own positionality with respect to the game, and how this impacts their analysis. This should be considered in relation to the original production and play *context* of the game. The analysis will, as we will discuss in the following chapters, be informed by a focus on how the various *materials* that make up the game relate to each other and perform specific functions. Some of these materials will be *foregrounded* as a result of their violation of player expectations. These foregrounded materials, or *devices*, work together or against each other and the other materials in the game to create a particular aesthetic experience. As part of a formalist analysis, the critic will attempt to identify the organizing principle behind this tension, or the *dominant*, and use this to focus further analysis, iteratively refining and revising their understanding of the materials, devices, and resulting dominant.

This example demonstrates how our formalist approach starts from the aesthetic experience of play, and then focuses on the way that experience emerges from the game as an object, set in motion as a process, in a particular context. As discussed at the start of this chapter, this enables our approach to interrogate the way that the form of the game, when played, creates a particular experience, grounded in context. It does not tell us anything about, for example, the player's psychological responses to the game, how the game's source code impacts the play experience, or whether the way that journalists have written about the game had any impact on its sales. These are just examples of questions that are outside the scope of this approach. Throughout this book, we encourage the reader to keep both the strengths and limits of our methodology in mind, as they consider whether or not to adopt this approach as part of their toolkit when carrying out an analysis. This is something we will return to in the final chapter.

Chapter Outline

Now that we've outlined why it is important to examine the core assumptions of this (or any) approach to studying videogames, where (or amongst what hotchpotch) our videogame formalism comes in, what pitfalls to watch out for when advancing the approach, and finally, which academic tradition we draw from, it is time to get out hands dirty and start fleshing out the approach.

In *Chapter 2: On Videogame Form* we flesh out the approach's core assumptions on form. We discuss the Russian Formalist notion of the work as a machine, and how this allows for a movement away from authorial intent and instead supports a focus on the how the player's aesthetic experience emerges from the defamiliarization of form. Here we draw on Shklovsky's notion of *devices* and Thomashevsky's notion of *motivation* and adapt these concepts to videogames. We examine the differences between form and material, and our consideration of meaning as an integral part of the work's form. Finally, we argue for the importance of considering context in establishing where a work defamiliarizes and discuss the usefulness of the concept of the *dominant* as a methodological strategy to focus on a core set of defamiliarizing devices.

We follow up on this in *Chapter 3: On Aesthetic Experience* by turning to the question, not of what games mean, but how they can trigger an aesthetic experience. Here, we emphasize the importance of the process of defamiliarization and foregrounding, but in the context of a lived experience by players. This builds on the foundation laid in chapter 2, exploring in detail how foregrounding and defamiliarization can lead to an aesthetic experience. We build on Mitchell et al.'s (2020) work on poetic gameplay devices, rethinking and restructuring them through the lens of motivation as developed in chapter 2. We ground this discussion in an analysis of several games: *Lim* (k 2012), *Getting Over It with Bennett Foddy* (Foddy 2017), *Akrasia* (Team Aha! 2008), and *Shadow of the Colossus* (Team Ico 2005).

Building from this discussion of aesthetic experience, in *Chapter 4: On Methodology* we explore the considerations that a formalist critic should keep in mind when applying this approach to videogames. Building on the notions of form developed in chapter 2, and the resulting player experience discussed in chapter 3, we argue that a focus on the game as an object, the process of experiencing the game as a player, and the context both of production and consumption, is essential for understanding how games work. This is followed by a detailed discussion of methodology, explaining with specific examples from the games *Paratopic* (Arbitrary Metric 2018) and *A Short Hike* (Robinson-Yu 2019) how the formalist method can be applied to games.

Following from this discussion of methodology, *Chapter 5: Applying Formalism* takes the concepts developed throughout the book and applies them in an extended fashion to the analysis of two games: an "art" game (*Kentucky Route Zero* (Cardboard Computer 2013)) and a "mainstream" game (*The Legend of Zelda: Breath of the Wild* (Nintendo 2017)). Here, we deliberately choose two very different games, going beyond the traditional notion that defamiliarization can be best applied to games that consistently violate player expectations, and instead can be applied to any videogame.

Finally, in *Chapter 6: Conclusion*, we step back and reconsider the videogame formalism presented in this book, suggesting possible limitations, and areas where this approach can be developed further.

References

Aarseth, Espen. 2004. "Genre Trouble: Narrativism and the Art of Simulation." In *First Person: New Media as Story, Performance, and Game*, edited by Noah Wardrip-Fruin and Pat Harrigan, 45–55. Cambridge, MA: MIT Press.

Aarseth, Espen. 2017. "Against 'Videogames': Epistemic Blindness in (Video) Game Studies." In *Extended Abstract Presented at DiGRA 2017 International Conference*.

Aarseth, Espen. 2019. "Game Studies: How to Play – Ten Play-Tips for the Aspiring Game-Studies Scholar." *Game Studies* 19 (2).

Academy of American Poets. 2014. "A Brief Guide to New Formalism | Academy of American Poets." 2014. https://poets.org/text/brief-guide-new-formalism.

Anthropy, Anna. 2012. "Dys4ia [Flash Game]." Newgrounds.

Arbitrary Metric. 2018. "Paratopic [MacOS Game]." Arbitrary Metric.

Beirne, Stephen. 2015. "Why I Said Ludo-Fundamentalism and Not Something Else." *Normally Rascal* (blog). January 13, 2015. https://normallyrascal.wordpress. com/2015/01/13/why-i-said-ludo-fundamentalism/.

Bennett, Tony, and Janet Woollacott. 1987. *Bond and beyond: The Political Career of a Popular Hero*. London: Macmillan International Higher Education.

Bizzocchi, Jim, and Teresa Jean Tanenbaum. 2011. "Well Read: Applying Close Reading Techniques to Gameplay Experiences." In *Well Played 3.0. Video Games, Value and Meaning*, edited by Drew Davidson, 262–90. Pittsburgh: ETC Press.

BlueTwelve Studio. 2022a. "A Spoiler-Free Introduction to Stray." Playstation. Com. 2022. https://www.playstation.com/en-sg/games/stray/a-spoiler-free-introduction-to-stray/.

BlueTwelve Studio. 2022b. "Stray." Playstation.Com. 2022. https://www.playstation. com/en-sg/games/stray-englishchinesekoreanjapanese-ver.

BlueTwelve Studio. 2022c. "Stray [Microsoft Windows Game]." Annapurna Interactive.

Bogost, Ian. 2007. *Persuasive Games*. Cambridge, MA: The MIT Press.

Bordwell, David. 1989. "Historical Poetics of Cinema." In *The Cinematic Text: Methods and Approaches*, edited by R. Barton Palmer, 369–98. Cambridge, MA: Harvard University Press.

Bordwell, David. 1991. *Making Meaning: Inference and Rhetoric in the Interpretation of Cinema*. Cambridge, MA: Harvard University Press.

Brinkema, Eugenie. 2020. "Form." In *A Concise Companion to Visual Culture*, 259–75. Hoboken, New Jersey: John Wiley & Sons, Ltd.

Cardboard Computer. 2013. "Kentucky Route Zero [MacOS Game]." Annapurna Interactive.

Carr, Diane. 2009. "Textual Analysis, Digital Games, Zombies.' In *Proceedings of the 2009 DiGRA International Conference: Breaking New Ground – Innovation in Games, Play, Practice and Theory*. London: Digital Games Research Association.

Carr, Diane. 2014. "Ability, Disability and Dead Space." *Game Studies* 14 (2).

Carr, Diane. 2019. "Methodology, Representation, and Games." *Games and Culture* 14 (7–8): 707–23.

Central Committee of the All-Union Communist Party. 1948. "Against Formalistic Tendencies in Soviet Music." *Sovetskaia Muzyka* 1: 3–8.

Chew, Evelyn C., and Alex Mitchell. 2020. "Bringing Art to Life: Examining Poetic Gameplay Devices in Interactive Life Stories." *Games and Culture* 15 (8): 874–901.

Consalvo, Mia, and Christopher A. Paul. 2019. *Real Games: What's Legitimate and What's Not in Contemporary Videogames*. Cambridge, MA: MIT Press.

Costikyan, Greg. 2002. "I Have No Words & I Must Design: Toward a Critical Vocabulary for Games." In *Proceedings of the Computer Games and Digital Cultures Conference, Finland*, edited by Frans Mäyrä, 9–33. Tampere: Tampere University Press.

Dowling, Christopher. n.d. "Aesthetic Formalism." In *Internet Encyclopedia of Philosophy*. Accessed December 7, 2022. https://iep.utm.edu/aesthetic-formalism/.

Eikhenbaum, Boris. 2012. "The Theory of the 'Formal Method'." In *Russian Formalist Criticism: Four Essays*, edited by Lee T. Lemon and Marion J. Reis, 2nd ed., 78–104. Lincoln: University of Nebraska Press.

Ensslin, Astrid, and Isabel Balteiro, eds. 2019. *Approaches to Videogame Discourse: Lexis, Interaction, Textuality*. New York: Bloomsbury Academic.

Erlich, Victor. 1980. *Russian Formalism: History, Doctrine*. 4th ed. The Hague: Mouton & Co.

Errant Signal, dir. 2015. *Errant Signal – The Debate That Never Took Place.* https://www.youtube.com/watch?v=xBN3Rom31bA.

Eskelinen, Markku. 2001. "The Gaming Situation." *Game Studies* 1 (1).

Fernández-Vara, Clara. 2019. *Introduction to Game Analysis.* 2nd ed. New York: Routledge.

Foddy, Bennett. 2017. "Getting Over It with Bennett Foddy [Microsoft Windows Game]." Bennet Foddy.

Frasca, Gonzalo. 2003. "Ludologists Love Stories, Too: Notes from a Debate That Never Took Place." In *Proceedings of the 2003 DiGRA International Conference: Level Up*, edited by Marinka Copier and Joost Raessens, 92–99. Utrecht: Utrecht University.

Frasca, Gonzalo. 2007. "Play the Message: Play, Game and Videogame Rhetoric." PhD Thesis, IT University of Copenhagen.

Fullerton, Tracy. 2019. *Game Design Workshop: A Playcentric Approach to Creating Innovative Games.* 4th ed. New York: CRC Press (Taylor and Francis).

Gioia, Dana. 1987. "Notes on the New Formalism." *The Hudson Review* 40 (3): 395–408.

Greenberg, Clement. 1971. "Necessity of 'Formalism'." *New Literary History* 3 (1): 171–75.

Hernandez, Patricia. 2013. "It's Time We Put the Bald Space Marine Away. It's Time to Make Games for More People. " *Kotaku*, January 8, 2013. https://kotaku.com/its-time-we-put-the-bald-space-marine-away-its-time-to-5973806.

Howe, Austin C. 2015. "Haptic Feedback: On The Ghost of Formalism." *Haptic Feedback* (blog). January 31, 2015. http://hapticfeedbackgames.blogspot.com/2015/01/on-ghost-of-formalism_62.html.

Jiang, Sisi. 2022. "Stray Falls into the Usual Orientalism Pitfalls of the Cyberpunk Genre." *Kotaku*, July 25, 2022. https://kotaku.com/stray-game-annapurna-interactive-cat-cyberpunk-1849328820.

Juul, Jesper. 2003. "The Game, the Player, the World: Looking for a Heart of Gameness." In *Level Up: Digital Games Research Conference Proceedings*, 30–45. Utrecht: Utrecht University.

Juul, Jesper. 2005. *Half-Real: Video Games between Real Rules and Fictional Worlds.* Cambridge, MA: MIT Press.

Juul, Jesper. 2008. "Who Made the Magic Circle? Seeking the Solvable Part of the Game Player Problem." In *Philosophy of Computer Games Conference 2008*. Potsdam.

Juul, Jesper. 2015a. "A Brief History of Anti-formalism in Video Games." *The Ludologist* (blog). February 11, 2015. https://www.jesperjuul.net/ludologist/2015/02/11/a-brief-history-of-anti-formalism-in-video-games/.

Juul, Jesper. 2015b. "What Is a Game Redux." *The Ludologist* (blog). June 10, 2015. https://www.jesperjuul.net/ludologist/2015/06/10/what-is-a-game-redux/.

k, merritt. 2012. "Lim [Browser Game]." merritt k.

Karhulahti, Veli-Matti. 2015. "An Ontological Theory of Narrative Works: Storygame as Postclassical Literature." *Storyworlds: A Journal of Narrative Studies* 7 (1): 39–73.

Keogh, Brendan. 2015a. "A Play of Bodies: A Phenomenology of Videogame Experience." PhD Thesis, RMIT University.

Keogh, Brendan. 2015b. "Some Quick Thoughts on Videogame Form off the Top of My Head." Tumblr. *Tumblr* (blog). January 13, 2015. https://ungaming.tumblr.com/post/107969280935/some-quick-thoughts-on-videogame-form-off-the-top.

King, Geoff, and Tanya Krzywinska. 2002. *Screenplay: Cinema/Videogames/Interfaces*. London: Wallflower Press.

King, Geoff, and Tanya Krzywinska. 2006a. "Film Studies and Digital Games." *Understanding Digital Games*, 112–28.

King, Geoff, and Tanya Krzywinska. 2006b. *Tomb Raiders and Space Invaders: Videogame Forms and Contexts*. London: IB Tauris.

Konzack, Lars. 2002. "Computer Game Criticism: A Method for Computer Game Analysis.' In *Proceedings of the Computer Games and Digital Cultures Conference, Finland*, edited by Frans Mäyrä, 89–100. Tampere: Tampere University Press.

Koster, Raph. 2012. "Two Cultures and Games." *Raph's Website* (blog). July 6, 2012. https://www.raphkoster.com/2012/07/06/two-cultures-and-games/.

Koster, Raph. 2014. "A New Formalism." *Critical Proximity* (blog). March 16, 2014. https://critical-proximity.com/2014/03/16/a-new-formalism/.

kunzelman. 2015. "On Video Games, Content, and Expression." *This Cage Is Worms* (blog). January 22, 2015. https://thiscageisworms.com/2015/01/22/on-video-games-content-and-expression/.

Lankoski, Petri, and Staffan Björk. 2015. "Formal Analysis of Gameplay." In *Game Research Methods: An Overview*, edited by Petri Lankoski and Staffan Björk, 23–36. Pittsburgh: ETC Press.

Lantz, Frank. 2015a. "Parley." *Game Design Advance* (blog). January 1, 2015. https://gamedesignadvance.com/?p=2794.

Lantz, Frank. 2015b. "TwitLonger – When You Talk Too Much for Twitter." January 13, 2015. http://www.twitlonger.com/show/n_1sjugos.

Lantz, Frank. 2015c. "More Thoughts on Formalism." *Game Developer* (blog). January 20, 2015. https://www.gamedeveloper.com/design/more-thoughts-on-formalism.

Malaby, Thomas M. 2007. "Beyond Play: A New Approach to Games." *Games and Culture* 2 (2): 95–113.

Mäyrä, Frans. 2020. "Game Culture Studies and the Politics of Scholarship: The Opposites and the Dialectic." *G|A|M|E Games as Art, Media, Entertainment* 1 (9). https://www.gamejournal.it/game-culture/.

Medvedev, Pavel N. 1928. *Formal'nyj Metod v Literaturovedenii: Kritieskoe Vvedenie v Sociologieskuju Poetiku*. Leningrad: Proboj.

Mitchell, Alex. 2014. "Defamiliarization and Poetic Interaction in Kentucky Route Zero." *Well Played: A Journal on Video Games, Value and Meaning* 3 (2): 161–78.

Mitchell, Alex. 2016. "Making the Familiar Unfamiliar: Techniques for Creating Poetic Gameplay." In *Proceedings of the First International Joint Conference of DiGRA and FDG 2016*. Dundee: Digital Games Research Association.

Mitchell, Alex, Liting Kway, Tiffany Neo, and Yuin Theng Sim. 2020. "A Preliminary Categorization of Techniques for Creating Poetic Gameplay." *Game Studies* 20 (2).

Mitchell, Alex, Yuin Theng Sim, and Liting Kway. 2017. "Making It Unfamiliar in the 'Right' Way: An Empirical Study of Poetic Gameplay." In *Proceedings of the 2017 DiGRA International Conference*. Melbourne, Australia: Digital Games Research Association.

Murray, Janet H. 1998. *Hamlet on the Holodeck: The Future of Narrative in Cyberspace*. Cambridge, MA: MIT Press.

Murray, Janet H. 2013. "The Last Word on Ludology v Narratology (2005)." *Janet H. Murray* (blog). June 28, 2013. https://inventingthemedium.com/2013/06/28/the-last-word-on-ludology-v-narratology-2005/.

Myers, David. 2009. "The Video Game Aesthetic: Play as Form." In *The Video Game Theory Reader 2*, edited by Bernard Perron and Mark J. P. Wolf, 45–64. New York: Routledge.

Myers, David. 2010. *Play Redux: The Form of Computer Games*. Ann Arbor: University of Michigan Press.

Nintendo. 2017. "The Legend of Zelda: Breath of the Wild [Nintendo Switch Game]." Nintendo.

O'Donnell, Mike. 2010. *Structure and Agency*. London: Sage Publications.

Pitkänen, Jori. 2015. "Studying Thoughts: Stimulated Recall as a Game Research Method." In *Game Research Methods: An Overview*, edited by Petri Lankoski and Staffan Björk, 117–32. Pittsburgh: ETC Press.

Pötzsch, Holger. 2017. "Playing Games with Shklovsky, Brecht, and Boal: Ostranenie, V-Effect, and Spect-Actors as Analytical Tools for Game Studies." *Game Studies* 17 (2).

Pötzsch, Holger. 2019. "From a New Seeing to a New Acting: Viktor Shklovsky's Ostranenie and Analyses of Games and Play." In *Viktor Shklovsky's Heritage in Literature, Arts, and Philosophy*, edited by Slav N. Gratchev and Howard Mancing, 235–51. Lanham: Rowman & Littlefield.

Robinson-Yu, Adam. 2019. "A Short Hike [MacOS Game]." Adam Robinson-Yu.

Salen, Katie, and Eric Zimmerman. 2004. *Rules of Play: Game Design Fundamentals*. Cambridge, MA: MIT Press.

Schmierbach, Mike. 2009. "Content Analysis of Video Games: Challenges and Potential Solutions." *Communication Methods and Measures* 3 (3): 147–72.

Seiferle, Rebecca. 2012. "Formalism in Modern Art: Definition Overview and Analysis." The Art Story. 2012. https://www.theartstory.org/definition/formalism/.

Sicart, Miguel. 2011. "Against Procedurality." *Game Studies* 11 (3).

Silverman, David, and Amir Marvasti. 2008. *Doing Qualitative Research: A Comprehensive Guide.* London: Sage Publications.

Smith, Jonas Heide. 2006. "Plans and Purposes How Videogame Goals Shape Player Behaviour." PhD Thesis, The IT University of Copenhagen.

Steiner, Peter. 2014. *Russian Formalism: A Metapoetics.* Geneva: Sdvig Press.

Tanenbaum, Teresa Jean. 2015. "Identity Transformation and Agency in Digital Narratives and Story Based Games." PhD Thesis, Simon Fraser University.

Tavinor, Grant. 2008. "Definition of Videogames." *Contemporary Aesthetics (Journal Archive)* 6 (1).

Team Aha! 2008. "Akrasia [Microsoft Windows Game]." Singapore-MIT GAMBIT Game Lab.

Team Ico. 2005. "Shadow of the Colossus [Playstation 2 Game]." Sony Computer Entertainment.

Thompson, Kristin. 1981. *Eisenstein's "Ivan the Terrible": A Neoformalist Analysis.* Princeton, New Jersey: Princeton University Press.

Thompson, Kristin. 1988. *Breaking the Glass Armor: Neoformalist Film Analysis.* Princeton, New Jersey: Princeton University Press.

Trotsky, Leon. 2005. *Literature and Revolution.* Chicago: Haymarket Books.

Vossen, Emma. 2018. "On the Cultural Inaccessibility of Gaming: Invading, Creating, and Reclaiming the Cultural Clubhouse." PhD Thesis, University of Waterloo.

Waern, Annika. 2012. "Framing Games." In *Proceedings of the 2012 Nordic DiGRA.* Tampere: Digital Games Research Association.

Walker, Austin. 2015. "The Long Game: Subterfuge, Formalism and Interactivity." *Pastemagazine.Com*, January 28, 2015. https://www.pastemagazine.com/games/the-long-game-subterfuge-formalism-and-interactivi/.

Willumsen, Ea Christina. 2018a. "Source Code and Formal Analysis: A Reading of Passage." *Transactions of the Digital Games Research Association* 3 (2).

Willumsen, Ea Christina. 2018b. "The Form of Game Formalism." *Media and Communication* 6 (2): 137–44.

Wimsatt, William K., and Monroe C. Beardsley. 1946. "The Intentional Fallacy." *The Sewanee Review* 54 (3): 468–88.

Wimsatt, William K., and Monroe C. Beardsley. 1949. "The Affective Fallacy." *The Sewanee Review* 57 (1): 31–55.

Wolf, Mark J. P., ed. 2002. *The Medium of the Video Game.* Austin: University of Texas Press.

2.   On Videogame Form

Abstract: In this chapter, we focus on the notion of *form* as distinct from material and intertwined with content. Following Russian Formalism and Neoformalism, we first discuss how considering the work as a machine enables a shift from focusing on authorial intent to a focus on how the work evokes an aesthetic experience in the player through the defamiliarization of form. In this broader aesthetic response meaning is put on equal footing with other formal devices, all of which work together in different motivational categories to form the *dominant*, the organizing principle underlying the work. To get to this dominant, we stress the importance of context which allows the critic to see where the work challenges not just technical and cultural norms, but also social, political, and/or economic norms.

Keywords: form, material, meaning, content, aesthetic experience, context

One of the more common understandings of formalism is that, according to this approach, form equals material, and that, in the case of games, material equals rules. As we have seen in the previous chapter, this leads to charges against formalism accusing the approach of being essentialist (demarcating games from non-games on the basis of some essential material properties) and/or being ludocentrist/ludofundamentalist (preferring a game's ludic over its representational components for analytical or design purposes). In this chapter we aim to rescue the term from these understandings and show how, in line with formalist traditions in literature studies (Russian Formalism) and film studies (Neoformalism), form resides in the functioning of material to cue an aesthetic response rather than in the material itself. This not only makes our videogame formalism in this book more functionalism than essentialism, but it also opens up discussions on what the form of videogames is, so as to do away with the artificial opposition of form versus content or form versus meaning.

More specifically, this chapter is divided into four main sections. In the first section, we emphasize formalism's focus on form over authorial

Mitchell, A. and J. van Vught, *Videogame Formalism: On Form, Aesthetic Experience, and Methodology*. Amsterdam: Amsterdam University Press, 2024
DOI 10.5117/9789463720663_CH02

intent. We show how formalism arose as a reaction against romantic literary criticisms of the late nineteenth and early twentieth century to focus on the work rather than the life and love of an author. Following Shklovsky (2012a; 2012b), we argue that the machine metaphor allows for a focus on how the game works, which already sets our formalist analysis apart from a materialist analysis and puts meaning on equal footing with other formal components. These characteristics distinguish our videogame formalism from other formalisms in game studies.

In the second section, we further disentangle form from material and consider videogame form in terms of different "poetic gameplay" devices (Mitchell 2016) which can be considered to have different "motivations" for being there. These devices and motivations turn our attention towards the ways in which a game, through the processes of making things strange (defamiliarization), can trigger our aesthetic play experiences and thereby function as a useful analytical starting point for those wanting to perform a textual analysis of a game. We'll therefore pick up on these devices and motivations in the next two chapters when we delve into the aesthetic experience in more detail and provide a few methodological considerations for doing a formalist analysis.

In the third section of this chapter, we'll tackle the form vs. content dichotomy. We'll show how early Russian Formalism indeed eschewed a focus on "the what" of an artwork (content or meaning) in favour of an analysis of "the how." However, we also show that Russian Formalists have always opposed a clear form-content divide by arguing against a communications model of art, and how later stages of the approach (and subsequently also Neoformalism) reintroduce meaning as a formal element. By letting go of the strict separation between form and content and relying on the later stages of Russian Formalism, a formal analysis of videogames can then focus on the ways in which the things represented in games (i.e., its social-cultural message) become defamiliarized, making way for those scholars interested in representational elements of games. Here we also discuss the importance of beginning an analysis from the player's aesthetic experience as a way to understand how the formal devices in the work evoke that experience. This provides the basis for our more detailed discussion of the relationship between form and aesthetic experience in chapter 3.

Finally, in the fourth section we discuss the ways in which a game's formal devices become foregrounded, making those devices the focus points of the analysis. Here, we introduce the idea of the *dominant* which functions as a heuristic strategy to systematically tease out the interesting devices in a game by comparing them to other devices in games of the same historical context. This also shows how our videogame formalism does not tear the work from its context, instead using the technical, social, economic, and cultural norms of the time of its creation to establish where the work challenges these norms.

Form vs. Authorial Intent: The Machine Metaphor

If formalism as an analytical approach is known for one thing, it is probably the fact that it eschews a romantic concentration on the artist and instead aims to shift the focus to the work itself. Aligning with the mid twentieth-century formalist school of New Criticism in the US, Wimsatt and Beardsley, for instance, argued against the "intentional fallacy" which they saw as a remnant of the romanticism that still permeated much of literary criticism and education to that day (Wimsatt and Beardsley 1946). Similarly, Russian Formalism arose against a backdrop of biographical criticism, the dominant school of literary criticism at the time, in which the artwork was studied in terms of the life of its maker, using primary sources like diaries or letters (see Steiner 2014, 23). By focusing on the work independent of its creator, the formalists thus tried to differentiate their discipline from other paradigms and lay claims to an autonomous literary scholarship (Steiner 2014, 19). At the same time, as we will discuss below, Russian Formalism and also Neoformalist film criticism does not divorce the work from the context of its creation (Thompson 1981, 16–18). For example, in her analysis of *Ivan the Terrible* (Eisenstein 1944), Thompson, at times, makes reference to Eisenstein's notes about the use of vertical montage (Thompson 1981). However, for the formalists, the analysis always comes back to the work as the primary site of analysis.

Arguing against a focus on authorial intent, the Russian Formalists provide a specific metaphor for (and understanding of) the artwork which indeed characterizes it as relatively distinct from an author. Influenced by Italian futurism, Shklovsky compares literature to a "machine," a combination of different interrelating materials that are crafted in such a way as to cue certain poetic reader responses (Shklovsky 2012b, 46). This machine metaphor deromanticizes the role of the author because it focuses our attention on the work as the result of craftmanship, instead of the organic and almost sacred growth of creative ideas springing from the mind of an author genius. Here, the author is considered to have adopted the skills of working with literary techniques in a similar way to how a watchmaker is able to make a clock, or a car mechanic is able to build a car (Steiner 2014, 40). There is nothing particularly special about the creation of an artwork, at least not compared to other skilled crafts. Consequently, it makes little sense for the formalist critic to focus analytical attention on the external condition of the writing process like the author's thoughts and feelings leading to the work, which would equate to studying a car by studying the life of the car maker. Instead, the machine metaphor allows for a focus on the "internal laws of literature," a look "under the hood" of the literature machine (see Steiner 2014, 41–42).

However, the machine metaphor adds two other focus points in the formalist analysis of the work. Similar to how a car mechanic is interested in how the car works to make it drive, the Russian Formalists were interested in how the literary machine works to evoke an aesthetic experience in the reader. This means that Russian Formalists were specifically not interested in 1) (merely) asking what the machine consists of (its material properties), nor were they interested in 2) asking what the machine means (let alone what the author has meant with it). This leads to an understanding of form distinct from material and, at least at first glance, distinct from content or meaning. While we will delve into these distinctions more thoroughly below, we will briefly introduce them here and show how this already sets our videogame formalism apart from other formalisms in game studies.

Formal Analysis vs. Material Analysis

The Russian Formalist focus on the work's functioning of form over its material properties is justified by their sole focus on (and understanding of) literary texts vs. non-literary texts. Here, the Russian Formalists hone in on what they called the "literaturnost" or literariness of the work: "that which makes a given work a work of literature" (Jakobson 1921 quoted in Erlich 1980, 172). In doing so, they make a clear distinction between practical or informative use of language and poetic use of language. They argue that while ordinary speech-acts (and also scientific discourse) use the raw material of words as transparent media, a literary work "'lays bare' the phonic texture of the word" (Erlich 1980, 181–82). Hence, the focus of formalist scholarship is not on the material itself (which can be used for any type of writing) but lies squarely on the different ways in which literary techniques (which they call devices – see below) shape the material (the raw building blocks of literature) for a kind of aesthetic efficacy in which the material is "made strange" or unfamiliar (see below).

This focus on form over material clearly distinguishes a videogame formalism in the tradition of Russian Formalism and Neoformalism from formalist approaches in game studies that aim to describe, define, and categorize the material components of games. As Willumsen (2018) notes, methodologies like the one outlined by Lankoski and Björk (2015) but also, to a large extent, many of the game ontologies like Hunicke, LeBlanc and Zubeck's (2004) MDA-model or Zagal et al.'s (2007) game ontology project are better described as material analyses rather than formal analyses. Drawing from Aristotle's four causes, Willumsen (2018) explains that this is because these approaches focus their attention on the game's material cause (its matter or what it is made of) rather than on its formal cause (its essence, design or shape). This makes the end-result of these approaches very descriptive, only useful when coupled with a specific research question on design choices or the functioning or purpose of the game components (Lankoski and Björk 2015, 30), which, perhaps unsurprisingly, aligns with Aristotle's efficient cause (the source producing the thing) and final cause (what the thing is for).

The videogame formalism presented in this book indeed focuses more on the game's formal cause, with the added note that the formal cause overlaps with the game's final cause since, like all artefacts (see Ainsworth 2020), games are functionally defined. After all, Russian Formalists were not looking for the essence of literature in the machine but a priori assumed the essence in the literary experience ("ostranenie" or defamiliarization – see below) and looked under the hood to study how the material functioned to cue that experience. This means that, according to the Russian Formalists, the essence of literature does not reside in material but in formal function or purpose, making Russian Formalism more functionalism than essentialism. As Erlich (1980) puts it: "Shklovsky came to define poetry not in terms of what it is, but in terms of what it is for" (179).

Form and Meaning

In their focus on how the literary machine works, Russian Formalists offer an alternative to a "communications model of art" (1988, 8). Instead of assuming that the main activity involved in art is the sending of a message or meaning to the receiver via the medium of art, Russian Formalists assume that the role of an artwork (its essence or literariness) is to make things strange and thereby cue an aesthetic experience that is much broader than interpreting a work's meaning. This downplays the central role of meaning in the arts and instead puts meaning on equal footing with other formal devices (e.g., stylistic devices) capable of triggering the aesthetic experience.

At first glance, this downplaying of meaning to the benefit of a broader exploration of form seems to overlap with early ludologist approaches in game studies. After all, early ludologists tried to stake out their own academic terrain by arguing that games should not be considered as yet another medium capable of communicating meaning (e.g., narrative, fictional worlds) through their system of signs (representational elements) but instead should be studied for how they work to accommodate a configurative user function (rather than an interpretative one) (see Aarseth 1997; Eskelinen 2001). In this argument, ludologists similarly made use of the "machine" terminology. Aarseth (1997), for instance, famously saw a cybertext as a "machine," "a mechanical device for the production and consumption of verbal signs" (21). And Juul (2004; 2005), borrowing from computer science, terms the game a "state machine," a machine which changes states in response to user input. With this terminology, these scholars shift the focus away from the text or output (what they mean) towards the text producing machinery underneath (how they work) and claim that it is this underlying machinery that distinguishes a cybertext from a text, or a game from a non-game, which would in turn also justify an independent field of research, i.e., game studies (see Copier 2003). In other words, these scholars appear to be looking "under the hood" for the "heart of gameness" (Juul 2003), the empirically assessable components that make a given work a cybertext or a game.

However, from here on, the analogy grows less fitting. First of all, the literature machine that Russian Formalists speak of does not equal a hierarchically organized structure where one component is more central to its functioning than another and therefore more deserving of scholarly attention (i.e., because, according to ludologists, rules regulate output). Instead, Russian Formalists saw the machine as a set of interrelating devices, all of which are, at least in principle, equally important in cueing a reader's defamiliarizing experience and thereby all equally important for our analysis (see below under dominant). As we'll discuss below, later phases of the Russian Formalist movement in particular acknowledged that meaning can also be used as an important formal device in evoking the aesthetic experience. While, in this case, meaning is still subsumed under the broader category of form, it is certainly not trivialized and/or (largely) ignored.

Secondly, while Russian Formalism's focus on form over meaning aligned with their understanding of the essence or literariness of a work (defamiliar- izing rather than sending messages), this essence served methodological rather than ontological aims. Or, as Erlich puts it, the focus on form is a "matter of methodological expediency [...], a proposition about the critic's main sphere of interest rather than about the nature of literary art" (1980, 118). Ludologists like Eskelinen (2001) or Juul (2003), on the other hand, had more ontological ambitions. They argued that the nature and functioning of (video)games (that which sets them apart from other media) should be looked for in the underlying (and hierarchically organized) text producing machinery. In other words, where Russian Formalists jettisoned a communications model of art to focus their analyses on that which defamiliarizes (meaning and stylistic elements), ludologists steered away from this model to make claims about the gameness of games (Juul 2013) and their dominant (configurative) user function (Aarseth 1997; Eskelinen 2001).

Our videogame formalism based on Russian Formalism should thus focus on 1) methodology over ontology, and 2) the interrelation of devices (including but not favouring meaning) as they are manifested during the aesthetic play experience over the internal hierarchical organization of these devices in the machine. This focus on form through aesthetic experience immediately shows the important role of the player since form is always studied from within (and with a focus on) the resulting lived experience of play. This means that a videogame formalism in the Russian Formalist tradition has much in common with phenomenological works that look at videogame form through, and entangled with, the player's experience of embodiment (Keogh 2018), performativity (Jayemanne 2017), or affect (Anable 2018). However, unlike these works, the player experience has a clear focus on defamiliarization which functions as both the aesthetic result of, and the methodological departure point for, engaging with the game machine to discover through what combination of game devices and player backgrounds the experience comes about.

Form vs. Material: Poetic Gameplay Devices

As we noted above, Russian Formalists made a clear distinction between practical and poetic use of language (and techniques like hyperboles or parallelisms that manipulate language), with the interest of the literary scholar firmly focused on the latter. This means that for Russian Formalists like Shklovsky there is a distinction between language, or, at an even more fundamental level, "words" as material, and specific techniques that shape this material in such a way that it turns from daily communication method into art. These techniques or artistic "uses of material" is what Shklovsky (2012a) calls *techniques* or *devices* (priëm). Thompson translates this distinction to film studies and argues that a film's material of mise-en-scène, sound, camera/frame, editing, and optical effects, can be manipulated with a range of techniques such as a specific use of lighting in the mise-en-scène or specific continuity editing for aesthetic purposes (as opposed to, for instance, advertising purposes in a TV commercial) (Thompson 1981, 26).

For our videogame formalism it is important to uphold this material-device distinction since it shifts the focus away from listing the game's material components (material analysis) to studying their functioning in cueing our aesthetic play experience (formal analysis). However, to be able to study the specific ways in which game material is turned into aesthetic experience evoking devices, we do need a basic understanding of what a game's material consists of. Here we're on familiar ground in game studies where many attempts have been made to categorize the material components of games. Roughly speaking, these game component taxonomies can be found somewhere on the continuum between design-driven and analysis-driven approaches. At the design-driven end of the spectrum, we find approaches which aim to list and categorize game components in order to offer advice to future game designers. For example, Björk and Holopainen offer their famous game design patterns categorized into four groups: holistic, bounding, temporal, and objective (2003). And Fabricatore, Nussbaum and Rosas (2002) offer guidelines for the playability of action videogames divided into entities, scenarios and goals. A little further up the spectrum we find works which combine design and analytical aims. For example, Järvinen (2007) proposes applied ludology as a hands-on design and analysis methodology which identifies nine categories of game elements: components, environment, ruleset, game mechanics, theme, information, interface, players, and context. And also Hunicke, LeBlanc, and Zubek's (2004) famous MDA model (mechanics, dynamics, aesthetics) falls somewhere in between the design-driven and analysis-driven taxonomies. Finally, at the analysis end of the spectrum we find works like Lankoski and Björk's (2015) formal analysis method which identifies components, actions and goals or Zagal et al.'s (2007) game ontology project offering the categories of interface, rules, entity manipulation, and goals.

As you can see (and this is only a very small sample), there are a plethora of game component taxonomies out there, each one with its own focus and usefulness. It is important to realize that these taxonomies have specific purposes since their categories do not function as neutral labels but instead further research interests, foci, and agendas. While there are certainly ones that arrive at their categories more systematically and empirically (e.g., Fabricatore, Nussbaum and Rosas (2002) align their categories with player preferences drawn from interview data), many of these taxonomies are theory driven and are therefore simply proposed for analytical (or design) convenience. In the end, however, all taxonomies inevitably fall short in being able to cover the wide range of material components in games (e.g., Zagal et al. (2007) specifically focus their categories on the "design space" of the game, bracketing representational elements). They artificially cluster components which may only share minimal similarities (e.g., Hunicke, LeBlanc, and Zubek's (2004) category of mechanics covers the actions offered to a player, the control mechanisms, rewards and punishments, (the behaviour of) in-game entities, level design etc.). And they reduce components to a single category when they often fall in different categories (e.g., a player character can be considered an entity or a component that can be manipulated by the player to perform different actions from a specific point of action and point of view in the game's interface and whose backstory provides the game's scenario and goals).

So, in this tradition, we put forward our own categories of game materials. These categories do not reflect the broad range of different game components out there but merely align with our aim to advance a formalist analysis of games in the tradition of Russian Formalism and Neoformalism. Here, our videogame formalism only requires us to have a very basic grasp of what game material could be since the focus of the analysis lies elsewhere (on the functioning of game devices). At the same time, our categories should still provide equal attention to representational and rule-based components since, from a player perspective, all these components work equally in evoking an aesthetic player experience in spite of their internal hierarchical organization. We therefore follow Neoformalism's categorization of film material into stylistic and narrative elements making up the formal system (see Bordwell and Thompson 2010, 57) and add rule-based elements to these two categories. Stylistic elements include (but are not limited to) things like mise-en-scène, cinematography, editing and sound. Narrative elements include (but are not limited to) things like story-plot distinction, causality, and the use of time and space. And finally, rule-based elements include (but are not limited to) things like the different action affordances in the game (level of agency and point of action in the interface), rewards, and punishments. These purposefully broad categories merely function as a quick starting point, drawing our attention to a large set of different game components that can be considered when looking for those devices cueing our aesthetic responses. However, the bulk of the analytical attention should be directed at these devices.

Poetic Gameplay Devices

If our interest is not in the material as such, but in specific ways in which material is "made strange" to trigger an aesthetic effect, we need to start looking into the many devices that a game can employ to achieve this.

Here, Mitchell's work provides an excellent starting point. Over the years, Mitchell and his colleagues have generated a long list of examples of "poetic gameplay devices" which are capable of making elements of the game feel unfamiliar and thereby triggering the aesthetic experience of play. For example, taking *Thirty Flights of Loving* (Blendo Games 2012) as a case study, Mitchell (2016) distinguishes three categories of devices capable of triggering a defamiliarizing experience: undermining player expectations for control (such as when the game disrupts the player's action abilities within or in between scenes), disrupting the chronological flow of game time (such as when the game uses jump cuts to teleport the player into widely different and discontinuous spatial and temporal settings), and blurring the boundaries of form (such as when the game makes use of an unconventional amount of cinematographic conventions or when the game appears to comment on its own form in its level design). In a later publication, Mitchell, Sim and Kway (2017) report on an empirical player study into the experience of poetic gameplay devices in *Thirty Flights of Loving*, *The Stanley Parable* (Galactic Cafe 2013), and *The Graveyard* (Tale of Tales 2008). They code the player responses into similar categories of control (breaking expectations on interaction, movement, and agency), time (breaking expectations on chronology), and form (breaking expectations on form through metalepsis or self-referentiality). However, they also add another poetic gameplay device in terms of an unreliable narrator in *The Stanley Parable* which breaks expectations on the impartiality of a narrator.

These studies provide extensively illustrated examples of ways in which game devices can indeed be used to make things strange. However, they also show how the list of examples is highly dependent on the case material that they are drawn from. This also shows in Chew and Mitchell's (2020) more recent work where, drawing from different case material (nineteen "interactive life stories"), they now identify a total of thirteen ways in which expectations on player control can be subverted. Four of these devices affect the game's goal rules (what winning and losing mean and how to achieve those goals), such as when success in the drowning scene of *That Dragon, Cancer* (Numinous Games 2016) is achieved by pushing the father character underwater, effectively making an action usually associated with losing (drowning) into winning (continuing in the game). And nine other devices affect the game's manipulation rules (what the player can or cannot do at a local level), such as when the waiting room scene in that same game offers the player action opportunities (walking around) that, when executed, have no bearing on the outcome of the scene (which just transitions into the next after a set amount of time). This effectively leaves the agency irrelevant, thus disrupting expectations around player control.

Perhaps recognizing the case-dependent nature of their poetic gameplay devices, Mitchell et al. (2020) eventually draw on a much larger set of known games in an attempt to outline a more extensive list (see table 2.1). Here, they identify a total of twenty-six different devices in five different categories (interaction, gameplay, agency, time, and boundaries) across a total of twenty-seven different games. Instead of going through all of them, we'll add the overview of devices here and refer to the article for further clarification.

Table 2.1 Poetic gameplay categories and devices (taken from Mitchell et al. 2020).

Category	Device	Examples
Interaction	Unfamiliar interface controls	*Brothers, Bounden*
	Unexpected change of controls	*Akrasia, Brothers*
	Extreme granularity	*QWOP, ProgressQuest*
	Slowing down the interactive loop	*Shadow of the Colossus, Vesper.5, The Graveyard*
	Uncomfortable feedback	*Lim*
Gameplay	Game objective is not what it seems	*Akrasia, Shadow of the Colossus*
	Core mechanic is not what it seems	*Akrasia*
	Multiple, conflicting game objectives	*Gravitation*
	Multiple, conflicting core mechanics	*Gravitation*
	Unexpectedly high or low difficulty	*Getting Over It, Dear Esther*
Agency	Imperfect information	*Kentucky Route Zero*
	Inability to act	*That Dragon, Cancer, Shadow of the Colossus*
	Only provide the inevitable choice	*The Walking Dead, The Killer*
	Subverting the inevitable choice	*The Killer*
	Broken illusion of agency	*The Stanley Parable*
	Failure is success	*Dys4ia*
	Success is failure	*Gravitation, Shadow of the Colossus*
Time	Non-causal game sequences	*Firewatch, Tales from the Borderlands*
	Abrupt scene transition	*Thirty Flights of Loving*
	Repeat play within a session	*That Dragon, Cancer*
	Repeat play across sessions	*Save the Date, Undertale*
	Repeated refusal of closure	*Save the Date, Doki Doki Literature Club!, Nier: Automata*
Boundaries	Reference to player's world inside the game	*The Stanley Parable, Save the Date, Doki Doki Literature Club!, Undertale*
	Reference to game from the player's world	*Kentucky Route Zero, With Those We Love Alive*
	Import of other forms into the game	*Thirty Flights of Loving, The Stanley Parable, Kentucky Route Zero*
	Ludic Intertextuality (blurring the boundary between games)	*The Stanley Parable, The Beginner's Guide, Kentucky Route Zero*

In the end, of course, Mitchell et al. (2020) acknowledge that also this list is only provisional and the categories are only heuristic. As they put it, "there will always be examples that blur the boundaries of the categories, encourage the merging of two or more categories, or suggest the need for additional categories." Consequently, they also expect others to challenge and extend the list of categories and devices (Idem).

As said, these categories and examples of devices are highly useful in generating an understanding of the many ways in which games can defamiliarize things and thereby cue an aesthetic experience. However, we still steer clear of willy-nilly applying these categories and devices as a methodological framework to any other game for four specific reasons.

First of all, while Mitchell et al. (2020) appear to be aiming for what we have briefly described as "hollow categories" (Bordwell 1989, 381), categories that focus the analysis without determining how we should understand the functioning of the game in every case, the (very useful) detail of their categories and examples paradoxically risks them becoming too restrictive and inherently self-fulfilling, blinding us to other ways in which a game may be cueing our aesthetic experience. Or, put differently, if you assume that a game will defamiliarize in a highly specific way, you are only going to look into game elements that reinforce that assumption even if the game or game elements under investigation function very differently. This is why it is important to let the game (or, more accurately, our aesthetic experience of the game) determine the analytical focus and only provide broad assumptions and focus-points that can be used to construct a method that is able to tackle the interest raised by a specific game under investigation (see below under dominant, and also see chapter 4).

Secondly, as Mitchell et al. (2020) are well aware of, the functioning of these game devices is highly dependent upon the context of play. In other words, a player's background knowledge and skills impact the poetic efficacy of a device since they allow the player to detect deviations from the norms of prior experience. As they put it themselves in their concluding paragraph, it's important to acknowledge and further explore "at what point these poetic devices become assimilated into the set of conventions that players expect, possibly losing their effectiveness" (Mitchell et al. 2020). As we'll discuss more thoroughly below, this means that in the Russian Formalist tradition, the game machine is in no way divorced from its historical context and the player engaging with it since certain poetic gameplay devices which may effectively challenge specific norms during one moment in time, may in fact become highly conventional and therefore automatized during another moment.

Thirdly, Mitchell et al.'s devices are very much centred on a defamiliarization of the form of the videogame itself. However, as Pötzsch (2017) and also Mitchell et al. (2020) recognize, Shklovsky's (2012a) idea of defamiliarization can also be interpreted to include a renewal of habitualized perception of the world around us, which means that also the thing that is represented in the game (its content or meaning) should be recognized as something that can be made strange (see below). For example, while a game like *The Graveyard* (Tale of Tales 2008) is indeed defamiliarizing because it lacks the agency we've gotten used to in videogames, it is also defamiliarizing because it makes death, which is usually a mechanic for punishing players in games, the central drawn-out focus of the game thereby evoking a reflection on and potentially renewed understanding of the processes of growing old, losing loved ones, and dying.

Fourthly and finally, Mitchell et al.'s categories veer heavily towards a more ludically focused approach to games where our expectations are concerned with goals, agency, controls, and core mechanics, and less so with conventions around storytelling, graphics, sound, framing etc. Of course, videogames can also thwart those conventions, for example when *Passage*'s (Rohrer 2007) unconventional thin long screen encourages reflection on how venturing off the beaten path in games and in life may be risky and unclear (but also potentially more rewarding). It should be said that this appears to be mostly an issue with Mitchell et al.'s (2020) formulated categories since many of the devices that they discuss under these categories do in fact often defamiliarize in other categories beyond the ludic. Or, as Chew and Mitchell (2020) put it in earlier work, "altercations to expected control and feedback not only defamiliarize, by putting the player cognitively outside the anticipated schema [...], they subsequently also draw the player *back* into the narrative, with a renewed understanding of the game narrative" (6–7).

So, rather than using these categories of poetic gameplay devices as a cookie-cutter method for studying how game devices function to make things strange, we suggest taking these devices at face value: as good examples of how the games in these studies cue an aesthetic experience through defamiliarization. As such, these are good case studies that show us what our formalist analyses can focus on. However, to broaden our understanding of the various ways in which game devices can function to evoke defamiliarization, we instead look for analytical categories elsewhere. Here, we turn our attention back to the Russian Formalist and Neoformalist heritage and draw from Thomashevsky's (2012) and Thompson's (1988) categories of *motivation*.

Motivations

The Russian Formalists consider a work to be a form of craftmanship in which all devices will have a reason for being there. The reasons or justifications for being there are what Thomashevsky (2012) calls motivations. These motivations do not equate to authorial intent since Russian Formalists eschew a concentration on a romantic author figure. As Thompson explains it: "motivation is, in effect, a cue given by the work that prompts us to decide what could justify the inclusion of the device" (Thompson 1988, 16). In other words, to consider the motivation of a device, we only need the assumption of agency behind the presence of a device. Eventually, the motivations are drawn from the work itself by considering how a device functions in the overall structure of the work. This means that the motivation is not the justification given by the maker, but the justification given by the percipient on the grounds of the work's functioning.

Thomashevsky (2012) divides these motivations up into three basic categories: compositional motivation, realistic motivation, and artistic motivation. Thompson extends these categories with one more: transtextual motivation. In Thompson's (1988) words, these categories can be explained as follows:

> – *"compositional motivation* justifies the inclusion of the device that is necessary for the construction of narrative causality, space, or time" (Thompson 1988, 16).
> – *"realistic motivation* [...] is a type of cue in the work leading us to notions from the real world" (Thompson 1988, 16).
> – *"Transtextual motivation* [...] involves any appeal to conventions of other artworks" (Thompson 1988, 17) (e.g., genre conventions, previous work by the same actor, or the use of certain techniques such as the cliff-hanger).
> – *"Artistic motivation* [...] [concerns those devices that] contribute to the creation of the work's abstract, overall shape – its form" (Thompson 1988, 19). This is probably the most difficult type of motivation to define. The artistic motivation is often overshadowed by more prominent other motivations, and it only really becomes noticeable when the other ones are withheld. Generally speaking, abstract stylistic devices that trigger non-straightforward (symbolic) meanings can be considered to have an artistic motivation.

These motivations can help to expand the categories of game devices beyond the more ludically oriented categories identified by Mitchell et al. (2020).

In fact, as mentioned, many of the devices discussed by Mitchell and his co-authors (2016; 2017; 2020; 2020), can be considered for these motivations. The non-chronological presentation of time in *Thirty Flights of Loving* (Blendo Games 2012) or the unreliable narrator in *The Stanley Parable* (Galactic Cafe 2013) have clear compositional functions since they help structure and create unconventional narrative events in time and space. The narrator in *The Stanley Parable* also has a clear realistic function since his commentary on player choice in games has us appeal to our real-world play experiences, thereby breaking the fourth wall of the game. In fact, the narrator in *The Stanley Parable* also has a transtextual motivation because he explicitly plays with genre conventions that the player has learned from other games. Finally, the lack of a clear narrative or even game objectives in *The Graveyard* functions artistically since it leads to an artistic ambiguity in the game's meaning. This is further emphasized by other artistically motivated devices such as the use of black and white in the game or the overlay of a close-up of the elderly woman's face during the song.

Here, of course, these categories only take us so far. In line with Mitchell et al.'s (2020) categories of interaction, gameplay and agency, we should acknowledge that a game device may also be justified because it gives the player an opportunity to act, a goal to strive for, or an opponent to battle. Here we subsume Mitchell et al.'s (2020) categories focused on configurative user functions under the umbrella of *ludic motivation* (acknowledging that ludically motivated devices can still defamiliarize in a variety of ways as Mitchell et al. show):

– *Ludic motivation* justifies the inclusion of the device for facilitating players' rule-bound, goal-directed progress in a game. A device that is ludically motivated should facilitate a specific subset of play where players acknowledge the game's goals and strive for them actively while voluntarily subordinating themselves to a confining set of rules and challenges. A ludically motivated device facilitates play as a competitive process of winning and losing, it allows players to devise a strategy and execute it. This is not the broader play response we have with games, which may, for instance, also include the construction of a narrative out of the game's formal clues. Instead, ludically motivated devices should be seen to facilitate play behaviour in a narrower sense which is often understood as "gameplay" (e.g., Lindley 2002).

Ludic motivations can, of course, be found in a score counter that indicates success with some abstract units or points, or more generally in abstract casual games where devices are often only there to encourage strategic gameplay. However, many times, ludic motivations will overlap with other motivations. As Chew and Mitchell (2020) argue, typical ludically motivated devices such as a known time limit or a high difficulty level only become poetic gameplay devices once the ludic functionality connects to another functionality such as when the stress or difficult challenges faced by the player correspond with the stress and challenges faced by an in-game character.

These motivations are useful in drawing our attention to the different ways in which game devices can function and thereby offer a useful hand when doing a formalist analysis of games (see chapter 4). However, the mere functioning of a game component in a motivational category (or across different categories) does not make it of interest to a formalist critic. Or, put differently, while a game's rule-based, narrative, or stylistic material component can be functioning in or across any of these five categories, that does not make it into a device cueing our aesthetic experience. For material to turn into a device that is of interest to the formalist critic, it needs to function in a defamiliarizing way. That is what we'll get into next.

Form vs. Content: Defamiliarization

In their attempts to demonstrate how literature distinguishes itself from other uses of language in practical everyday life, Russian Formalists seemingly showed an interest in form over content. Their argument initially appears simple. Where everyday life is characterized by a practical use of language, literature is characterized by our difficult perception of it because its practical communicative function is moved to the background in favour of texture and sound, in other words, its form. According to this argument, we normally use language in an aesthetically neutral way to communicate information, which means its form has become habitualized or automatized to us, making us blind to what Shklovsky calls the "artfulness of an object" (2012a, 26). The purpose of art is then to make us see things again, not merely recognize them (Erlich 1980, 76). As Shklovsky has famously put it:

> art exists that one may recover the sensation of life; it exists to make one feel things, to make the stone stony. The purpose of art is to impart the sensation of things as they are perceived and not as they are known. The technique of art is to make objects "unfamiliar," to make forms difficult, to increase the difficulty and length of perception because the process

of perception is an aesthetic end in itself and must be prolonged. Art is a way of experiencing the artfulness of an object; the object is not important (2012a, 26).

Shklovsky's final disregard for the object seems problematic here. After all, a sole focus on form over content invites the very justifiable criticism that artforms like literature, films or games also have an artistic potential in what they express/communicate, not just in how they do so (see chapter 1). However, a closer look at Shklovsky's words and, by extension, the Russian Formalist distinction between poetic and practical language, makes what we initially held for a straightforward form-content split a much more ambiguous consideration of the interrelationship of the two.

As Pötzsch (2017) points out, Shklovsky's idea of the defamiliarizing purpose of art can be interpreted in two different ways (which Pötzsch makes especially apparent by comparing different translations of the closing sentence of this passage). On the one hand, Shklovsky suggests that the purpose of art is indeed to defamiliarize the formal material of a work (words), to "make forms difficult" and make artistic "perception an aesthetic end in itself." On the other hand, Shklovsky suggests that art's purpose is to "make objects 'unfamiliar'," i.e., to defamiliarize the outside world and eventually renew our habitualized day-to-day engagement with it (content). In this latter reading of Shklovsky, it is not practical language that has become habitualized or automatized, but our perception of the world around us since we perceive things economically, with a focus on practical day-to-day action (e.g., crossing the street, buying a sandwich). Pötzsch (2017), following Lachmann (1984 [1970]) also sees this ambiguity reflected in Shklovsky's own scholarly development in which the emphasis shifts "from an enstranging of form to a theory of a 'new seeing'." This means that in Shklovsky's own thinking, defamiliarization shifts from something internal to the artistic reading process (making form difficult) to something that encapsulates the value of literature and the arts for our society at large (making the portrayed difficult).

This dual or broadening understanding of defamiliarization also sets the stage for Brecht's related conceptualization of Verfremdung. After a trip to Moscow in 1935, Brecht appears to have been at least indirectly inspired by Shklovsky's idea of defamiliarization (Ungvári 1979, 217–25) and the two concepts clearly show similarities. However, while Shklovsky initially remains somewhat ambiguous about whether defamiliarization should be seen as directed towards the work's artistic form or the real world, Brecht's concept of Verfremdung is clearly directed at the latter. In fact, taking inspiration from Hegel and Marx, Brecht's Verfremdung has a more emancipatory purpose, aiming to install a more critical reflection in the audience and mobilize them towards political action. As Pötzsch puts it:

> Brecht's epic theatre [theatre that makes extensive use of Verfremdung's effects] facilitates a dialectical double-move where the naturalized and habitualized are first estranged and therefore made visible and explicit, before they become the object of critical analysis that leads to a better understanding of real conditions and relations thus enabling emancipa-tory practices and initiatives (Pötzsch 2017).

Shklovsky doesn't politicize defamiliarization in the way that Brecht uses Verfremdung (also see Pötzsch 2017), which consequently provides Marxist scholars with ammunition for critiquing Russian Formalism for being "reactionary" (see chapter 1). However, with Shklovsky's (and late Russian Formalism's) increasing attention for the value of defamiliarization for the reader's lived experience (i.e., a new way of seeing things), we can identify a similar "dialectical double-move." As we'll argue more thoroughly in the next chapter, this dialectic concerns the consecutive process of defamiliarization and refamiliarization whereby the latter involves the process of making sense of the initial defamiliarizing experience and placing it in the context of one's lived experience. It is through this process of refamiliarization that the unfamiliar becomes meaningful beyond the work.

With this broader understanding of the defamiliarizing purpose of art came a renewed appreciation of the artwork's meaning. Instead of focusing solely on the self-valuable word (its phonetic characteristics), late Russian Formalists could no longer uphold the separation between word and meaning and started to focus on the interrelation between the two. Here it is important to still distinguish the object which the artwork portrays, and *the object as portrayed*. As Erlich explains, late Russian Formalists followed Husserl's distinction between object and meaning, whereby "meaning [as opposed to object] is not an element of extra-linguistic reality, but a part and parcel of the verbal sign" (1980, 185). So, if meaning is no longer divorced from the word, and, by extension, the work's cumulative meaning, its content, is no longer separated from the work's form, then meaning and content simply become a part of the formal components of a work that artists have at their disposal to evoke an aesthetic effect. Consequently, Russian Formalists do away with the form-meaning or form-content split, or, as Erlich puts it, "Formalists [...] do away with the dualism of the 'object expressed' and the 'means of expression'" (1980, 186).

A videogame formalism in the tradition of this late Russian Formalism becomes a broadly focused analysis method in which the aesthetic play experience is not solely triggered by the single mechanism of making abstract videogame material unfamiliar but can now also be triggered by defamiliarization of meaning. In this formalism, as Steiner (2014) puts it, quoting Zirmunsky (1928): "The perception of the work is not limited to the pure enjoyment of self-centred devices but 'implicitly it includes cognitive, ethical, or religious elements'" (63). But while meaning is introduced back into the analytical equation, it is still subsumed under function (to defamiliarize). This also distinguishes our videogame formalism from formalisms that see "reading" or interpreting a game as its main critical activity (e.g., Bogost 2007; Treanor et al. 2011; Treanor 2013) (see below). Instead, both meaning and ludic components become a more inherent part of the formal devices and are studied in their dominating or subordinated relationship to other devices to defamiliarize things and evoke an aesthetic play experience. Here, the critic does not rely on an appreciation of the game's self-valuable material but looks for the struggle amongst narrative, stylistic, and rule-based devices in all their motivational categories (ludic, compositional, realist, transtextual, and artistic) to see where the aesthetic experience derives from. In this struggle, certain devices and motivations are pushed back and make way for other ones in a continuous alternating process. In the end, the aesthetic experience can concern ludic progress, narrative composition, realism judgements, transtextual references, as well as the artistic appreciation of self-centred devices.

For example, there is a specific moment in *Bioshock 2* (2K Marin 2010) where we are traversing the ocean floor until the music swells, and we come to the edge of a cliff with a view of the underwater city of Rapture. During the traversing of the underwater space, a wide range of devices and functions are at play. The action abilities, the diving suite and spatial architecture, function ludically, compositionally, realistically, and transtextually allowing for player progress to the next area, contributing to the identity of subject Delta (the player character) and the story of Rapture, and referencing old atmospheric diving suits and the story of Atlantis. These functions continuously alternate between dominant and subordinated until we get to the cliff edge when everything is pushed back to make way for the artistically motivated music and a view of the city. That particular moment cues us to appreciate the game as a crafted artefact. In this sequence, the game foregrounds different formal components that have us reflect on the notion of agency. Subject Delta's relative free will (compared to other Big Daddies), his diving suit the building music, the framing of the city, and the game's emphasis on choice (a near opposite focus compared to its predecessor) all have us expect a free exploration of the outsides of the city of Rapture. However, immediately after our view from the cliff's edge we have those expectations thwarted by the linear gameplay, almost reminding us of the "would you kindly" plot twist in the first *Bioshock* game (2K Boston 2007).

Form through aesthetic experience

As much as formalists are known to eschew a concentration on the author of a work, so too are they known to argue against a focus on the idiosyncratic experiences of it. Most famously, not long after arguing against "the intentional fallacy," the New Critics Wimsatt and Beardsley wrote their article "The Affective Fallacy" in which they argued against analysing and evaluating a work on the basis of its effects. Or, as they put it: "the affective fallacy is a confusion between the poem and its *results* (what it *is* and what it *does*)" (Wimsatt and Beardsley 1949, 31, emphasis in original). Similarly, Russian Formalists tried to push their approach as a "science" of literature or language by focusing solely on the work's devices as a series of facts, rather than on their effects or on their intention. Or, as Jakobson puts it: "if literary history wants to become a science, it must recognize the artistic device as its only concern" (Jakobson, quoted in Erlich 1980, 77).

Nevertheless, the Russian Formalists still ascribe an important role to the recipient of the work. As we have explained above, Russian Formalists have a specific interest in and focus on the aesthetic experience resulting from an engagement with the work. This aesthetic experience is the result of the cumulative functioning of defamiliarizing devices in their struggle for dominance in the work (also see below), and functions as the starting point of the analysis. Put differently, Russian Formalists take the aesthetic experience as a point of departure in their analysis and then ask what combination of (or struggle between) devices is at work in evoking that experience.

At first, this focus and reliance on the aesthetic experience appears at odds with formalism's sole interest in the work. After all, by taking the aesthetic experience as a methodological starting point, they appeared to shift their analytical focus from the work to the results of the work evoked in the reader (a kind of reader-response-criticism). However, a closer look shows us that the Russian Formalists simply used the aesthetic experience as the gateway through which to access the work's devices. This is a gateway which, in itself, provides focus on a specific defamiliarizing functioning of these devices. The aesthetic experience is thus a methodological means, rather than the focus of the analysis itself. As Erlich puts it:

> Works of literature are knowable objects, accessible only through individual experience. Consequently, the mechanism of the esthetic response

is a legitimate concern of an 'objectivist' art theoretician, provided that the emphasis is placed not on the individual reader's idiosyncratic associations, but on the qualities inherent in the work of art and capable of eliciting certain 'intersubjective' responses (1980, 178–79).

Here, formalists appear aware of the Kantian subject-object problem and are careful not to lay any claims to objective truths. Instead, as Erlich notes, the Russian Formalists (and more specifically the Moscow school) were highly influenced by Husserl's phenomenology, acknowledging that phenomena can only be studied from one's lived experience whereby knowledge of the phenomenon can never be considered objective but can be shared between different subjects who roughly share a system of intersubjective standards or (historical and cultural) backgrounds (Erlich 1980, 62). Acknowledging that the aesthetic experience arises in the interplay of the work, the analyst (reader, viewer, or player), and the context (see below) is important for our videogame formalism because it highlights how a formalist analysis of a single game can still lead to different results, depending on the (in-game choices of the) player (see, for instance, our *The Legend of Zelda: Breath of the Wild* (Nintendo 2017) case study in chapter 5) and the context against which the game's devices are analysed. It therefore becomes a methodological challenge for the player critic to establish this shared set of norms and make sure that the aesthetic experience comes from the characteristics inherent to the work (the cumulation of and struggle between defamiliarizing devices), rather than from their personal expectations, preferences, and background knowledge (what Husserl would call their "lifeworld").

As we will explain more elaborately in chapter 4, the player critic can do this in a number of ways. Firstly, the critic needs to be clear about what play strategy to adopt which informs what in-game choices they make. Secondly, the player critic needs to establish a shared set of norms by positioning the game in its historical context of genres and styles but also social, economic, and political conventions. Finally, the critic needs to acknowledge and be open about their own personal context of play or situatedness (play preferences, expectations, prior experiences) to assess personal biases and "bracket" these as much as possible.

Formalism as a Poetics

Following Culler's rough distinction between two types of literary criticisms, we can now categorize formalism as a poetics which "starts with attested meanings or effects and asks how they are achieved" (Culler 1997, 61). Culler distinguishes poetics from hermeneutics, arguing that where hermeneutics focuses on the work and then asks what it means, a poetics starts at the effects experienced by the recipient and then asks how a work works to cue those effects. As Bizzocchi and Tanenbaum put it, a poetics refers to "the design decisions instantiated within an artifact, and in a broader sense, the design channels or design principles commonly used within a medium," with a close reading serving to "uncover the design decisions manifest in representative artifact, and in the process to understand the effects of the design on the experience" (2012, 395). This draws directly from Bordwell, who argues that poetics encompasses "[a]ny inquiry into the fundamental principles by which artifacts in any representational medium are constructed, and the effects that flow from those principles" (2008, 12).

Recognizing our videogame formalism as a poetics rather than a hermeneutics reinforces our earlier claim that meaning should only be considered as part of the formal components of the game, rather than the sole purpose of the analytical (or, in this case, interpretative) process. While such a focus on interpretation makes sense for proceduralists like Bogost (2007) and Treanor (2011; 2013) who focus mostly on persuasive games, it becomes problematic when studying a broader range of games. From a Russian Formalist perspective, the problems here are twofold. First of all, as Thompson (1988, 14–15) also argues, an exclusive focus on interpretation suggests that even when a work has very explicit meanings, the analyst has to deal with them as if they were implicit. This problem, for instance, shines through in Murray's (1998) analysis of *Tetris* (Pajitnov 1988) which ignores the more obvious referential similarities with pentomino puzzles in favour of symptomatic meanings about the "overtasked lives of Americans in the 1990s" (144). Secondly, an exclusive focus on meaning ignores other functions that contribute to the aesthetic experience of a game. In this case, devices may, for instance, be motivated for artistic or ludic reasons without necessarily contributing to a game's message.[1]

As a poetics, videogame formalism thus steers away from solely looking for meaning in a work (without invalidating the importance of meaning which is still part of the work's form) and ascribes an important role to the player. However, starting the analytical process from the aesthetic experience of the player does not imply that the player experience (including the meanings that come with it) is a given. Oftentimes, our aesthetic experience will unfold and

---

1   While we do not explore this line of thinking further in this book, it is worth considering whether our videogame formalism can be applied to more abstract games. We return to this briefly in chapter 6 when discussing future directions for videogame formalism.

evolve during the analytical process when, for instance, certain meanings are found. This means that, while we may start from "whatever effects we can attest to" (Culler 1997, 62), the analytical process is eventually a very iterative one. In our search for how the videogame works to cue our initial aesthetic response, we 1) may identify certain devices in their struggle for dominance, which in turn 2) may make us aware of another set of devices, which 3) may change or refine our initial aesthetic experience, which 4) has us focus on yet another set of devices, and so on and so forth.

The question that remains here is, of course, how to recognize specific devices at work in the game and how to determine which ones (or better yet, the struggle between which ones) to eventually focus on as the most interesting ones in evoking our aesthetic response. This is where the idea of the dominant comes in. As we will explain below, the dominant functions as a heuristic methodological strategy to look at a specific subset of interrelating devices which become foregrounded by considering them within the context of (social, technological, aesthetic, cultural) conventions in other works of its time. But let us first consider the Russian Formalist heritage that this idea of the dominant comes from.

Foregrounding Form: The Dominant as a Methodological Strategy

What makes the Russian Formalist and Neoformalist consideration of devices specifically interesting for a study of games is that, at least in principle, these devices are all equally important in cueing our responses (Bordwell 1985, 33). By considering game devices this way, we escape an emphasis on rules over narrative or stylistic devices, or a focus on ludic functionality to the detriment of, for instance, narrative construction or transtextual references. As such, the approach gives us a balanced consideration of the plethora of different devices and their oftentimes multiple motivations for their inclusion in the work and tackles one of the prominent anti-formalist sentiments identified in chapter 1, that of formalism as focusing on rules to the detriment of story or representation.

However, if we start from the basic premise that all devices are equally important in cueing our play responses, how do we determine which devices and motivations to focus on? Here, the idea of the dominant comes in handy. Thompson defines the *dominant* as "a formal principle that controls the work at every level, from the local to the global, foregrounding some devices and subordinating others" (1988, 89). On a global level, the dominant helps to focus on certain moments or elements that are important for the overall characteristics of the work (due to their salient relationship with genres or styles in other works). At a local level, where we single out a specific moment in the work, the dominant helps to focus on the more significant motivations during that moment (due to their role in the overall aesthetic effect of the work).

This idea of the dominant comes from a late phase in Russian Formalism in which the approach moved away from a purposive explanation of literature (triggering defamiliarization of abstract form) to a more functional explanation in which all devices work together to shape the material towards an overall form (Steiner 2014, 63–66). According to Zirmunsky, it is not the critic's task to individually study all devices for their defamiliarizing effects (as Shklovsky initially claimed), but instead to study devices in their harmonious relationship in support of this overall form which Zirmunsky called *style* (Steiner 2014, 58). In this harmonious relationship, certain devices emerge as more important than others, which means the critic then focuses on those devices.

While this idea of style sets us on course for the dominant, the dominant still differs in two distinct ways from Zirmunsky's style. Firstly, the dominant is not characterized by harmony but by a struggle between foregrounded and subordinated devices (Steiner 2014, 89–90). Secondly, the dominant is determined by a work's distinguishing relationship to a larger literary system of genres, schools and styles rather than by the internal characteristics of the work (Steiner 2014, 91–93). This means that it is the critic's task to establish the work's dominant on the basis of its difference from or resemblance with other works in its historical context to see which devices become foregrounded. The critic then focuses on those foregrounded devices in their relationship to the subordinated ones which in turn help to heuristically draw out other important devices.

For example, when playing *Thirty Flights of Loving* we may at first be thrown when we learn that certain expectations we have from playing other games are thwarted. The game, for instance, starts off as a relatively straightforward shooter, signalling the WASD-controls, allowing for the traversal of space, opening of doors, jumping, and picking up items like drinks and guns. However, we soon learn that drinks and guns cannot be stored and therefore never be used, thus breaking with those shooter conventions we have learned from other games. Similarly, prior experience of games has us expect a rather chronological and continuous presentation of events, especially during moments of interaction (Juul 2004). However, these conventions are also quickly frustrated when the game presents us with jump-cuts during gameplay and a non-chronological editing of scenes. This gets us thinking that the game's dominant may lie in raising specific expectations we have learned from playing other games only to then break those expectations. However, that is not the full story yet. Upon continued play, we may also become aware of other odd or confusing moments. For example, interacting with the side characters Anita and Borges in the opening scenes triggers a fast-paced montage introducing the characters' expertise (demolition expert, sharp-shooter etc.) for an upcoming heist. While this does not necessarily reference other games we may have played, we are certainly familiar with the device from heist film conventions. Here also, however, we never participate in, see, or hear anything about the actual heist, thus also frustrating these conventions. This slowly but surely has us realize that the game distinguishes itself by its mixture of media and genre conventions. This "mixture" functions as a dominant that raises expectations on the basis of one set of conventions only to thwart those expectations by adhering to another set. Or, put differently, the game's dominant lies exactly in those moments of subordinated film/game conventions which force players to step back from their expectations and see game elements in a new light.

In the end, the dominant gives us three important take-ways for game studies. First of all, it provides us with a heuristic but systematic way of focusing the analysis beyond the intuition of the critic. This allows us to methodically draw out dominant user functions without having to individually study all devices and still helps to better understand a game and even hypothesize about dominant play experiences. Secondly, the dominant puts our analytical focus squarely on a struggle between game devices rather than a presupposed or sought-after harmony. This focus is important because it acknowledges that dissonances in games (where devices may have different conflicting motivations) should not be ignored as faulty game design but rather explored and exploited as interesting ways in which players are confronted with preconceived ideas about how games frame ludic action, tell stories, reference other works etc.[2] Finally, Zirmunsky helps to move the formalist approach away from an aesthetic purism in which the work is torn from its social context and is interesting solely for its defamiliarizing effect, to a broader relational methodology in which the linkage to a social context is acknowledged and the aesthetic effect cannot

---

2   See Roth, van Nuenen, and Koenitz (2018) for an interesting discussion of the use of this perspective to explain the possible productive use of the underlying tension between games and stories that often surfaces in discussions of storytelling and games.

be reduced to a single mechanism. This importance of context is what we will get into hereafter.

The Importance of Context

This idea of the dominant also shows how Russian Formalism (with the exception of the polemics of early Russian Formalists who were mostly busy with disciplinary flag-planting),[3] does in no way tear the artwork from its social context. In later Russian Formalism, the artwork's "form is always seen against the background of other works rather than by itself!" (Eikhenbaum 2012, 90–91). This means that, as Steiner (2014) puts it, "the identity of every literary fact is determined by sets of norms we call genres, schools, or historical styles" (88). Only because a formal component shows similarities or in fact dissimilarities with a larger literary system, does it acquire its literary character and does it become foregrounded. The task of the literary critic is then to understand this literary system *in time* and *over time*. Or, put differently, it is only by looking into the work both synchronically and diachronically can Russian Formalists establish the literariness of a work and its devices.[4]

Synchronically, historical context functions as a methodological tool to gain shared access to a work by perceiving the work "according to the norms prevailing at the given period" (Erlich 1980, 48). For early formalists this means that a critic should invest effort into familiarizing him/herself with norms drawn from other artefacts making up the literary system because only then can s/he understand the tradition in which the work should reasonably be understood and recognize conventional or norm-challenging

---

3   Similar to Aarseth's (2004) early claims that games are somehow "self-contained" (48), the early Shklovsky was keen to tear art from its social context. However, just like Aarseth's claims, these early formalist polemics are best seen as disciplinary flag planting. As Eichenbaum (2012) himself puts it: "many of the principles advanced by the Formalists in the years of tense struggle were significant not only as scientific principles, but also as slogans, as paradoxes sharpened for propaganda and controversy" (91). Early formalism was thus characterized by its disassociation from other schools of literary criticism (focused on symbolism or authors). As such, the polemics fit the revolutionary times in Russia in which there was a general tendency to do away with the old (Erlich 1980, 78–79).

4   We should add that the terms synchrony and diachrony are used here only for methodological expedience, i.e., to help direct attention of the critic to the game during a specific moment in time (drawing on shared context) as well as over time (acknowledging the changing position of the work in different contexts). This is different from, for instance, Jayemanne (2017; 2020) who employs the terms for the characterization and segmentation of play performances (2017) and temporal frames (2020).

devices. For later formalists, domains outside of the literary system also had to be taken into account, such as the technological, social, economic, and cultural circumstances of its creation (Bordwell 1989, 382–83). Only then can a formalist also recognize how a work may be breaking with technological constraints of its time, or – with meaning now being considered a part of a work's formal components – how a work may be challenging certain dominant social values.[5]

Positioning a game within its historical context in order to pinpoint its innovative or otherwise significant qualities is very common in videogame criticism. A book like *100 Greatest Video Game Franchises* (Mejia, Banks, and Adams 2017) is filled to the brim with arguments that characterize a game in relationship to other games of its time (e.g., in terms of mechanics or storytelling conventions), but also other media or socio-political issues. However, aside from helping to foreground the more obvious norm-challenging characteristics, exploring a game's historical context can also help to gain an understanding of a game that is more appropriate for its time. For example, according to Bradford (2009), we should not understand *Bully* (Rockstar Vancouver 2006) in the context of Rockstar's controversial predecessors, but instead in a tradition of works that parody traditional school settings such as *Tom Brown's Schooldays* (T. Hughes 1857) or films like *Ferris Bueller's Day Off* (J. Hughes 1986) and *The Breakfast Club* (J. Hughes 1985). Situating the game in this context shows that the "bullying" in the game actually functions to revolt against a representation of a stuffy conservative boarding school establishment and even how it helps to challenge class divides between the privileged rich "preppies" and the less fortunate lower-class students.

Diachronically, the interest of the Russian Formalist focuses on the movement of the literary system rather than on a specific historical period. This focus is important for several reasons. First of all, it helps to put the author genius back into her/his place by subordinating her/him to the larger literary system of prevailing norms. In this understanding, the author functions merely as a subconscious generator of devices adhering to and/ or challenging norms of its time to eventually help rejuvenate the system (Steiner 2014, 110). Secondly, this diachronic focus helps to distinguish mistakes from literary innovation. By testing the literary deviation against the system, Russian Formalists can see whether it becomes implemented

5   This clash of preconceived social values with the values built into the videogame system, comes close to Bogost's (2006) understanding of simulation fever. However, where Bogost (2006) sees assumptions about social values as personal (99), Russian Formalists consider them as shared in time and changing over time.

in more than a single accident thereby signalling literary change (Steiner 2014, 103). And finally, and most importantly, diachrony ties into the idea of defamiliarization because Russian Formalists show how a linguistic fact can turn into a literary fact when it challenges the norms of a given period which itself eventually withers back into an automatized linguistic fact, and so on and so forth[6] (Steiner 2014, 103–5). As Shklovsky puts it: "each art form travels down the inevitable road from birth to death; from seeing and sensory perception [...], to mere recognition" (in Erlich 1980, 252).

Following from this last point, diachrony also helps to account for changes in perception over different periods of time in the sense that a device will become automatized after a while but can also regain relevance in a new context. For instance, the controversies around the first *Mortal Kombat* (Midway Games 1992) can be understood in light of the breaking of real-ism conventions (drawn from experiences with other games and other cultural artefacts) and technological constraints of its time (e.g., by using photographic sprites). Nowadays, however, we are not likely to be shocked by the pixelated representations of deaths in the game because our situatedness has changed and thereby our frame of reference.

In line with Russian Formalism, the formalist game critic thus takes form in the knowledge of aesthetic as well as social, cultural, economic and technical conventions in time and over time that s/he would reasonably draw upon to come to her/his understanding of the work (Thompson 1981, 15). This comes close to the idea of an *implied* player; an adaptation of Iser's (1980) *implied reader*, by Aarseth (2014) and others (e.g, Vella 2015; van Vught and Glas 2018). This player consists of "a set of expectations that the player must fulfil for the game to 'exercise its effect'" (Aarseth 2014, 184). This is not an ideal player who always performs the same activities in service of the game since that would deny the possibility of different readings in different historical contexts. However, neither is the player an actual person whose personal background leads to an idiosyncratic understanding of the game

---

6   Amongst Russian Formalists there was some disagreement on what caused literary change and therefore also on what counts as historical context. According to the more orthodox Russian Formalists, literary change was self-propelled in the sense that "new form arises [...] because old form has exhausted its potentialities" (Shklovsky in Erlich 1980, 254). This means that the formalist critic has no business outside of the literary system of norms. According to later Russian Formalists, however, literary change was as much self-propelled as it was caused by external factors. Zirmunsky and Engelhardt, for instance, argued that while automatization of literary devices can provide the spark that ignites literary rejuvenation, the direction of change must be sought in the larger cultural atmosphere of the time period (Erlich 1980, 255). For these scholars, historical context concerns domains both inside and outside of the literary system.

since that would detach the player from his/her historical context where certain established norms are shared. The player is thus a "hypothetical entity" that does not exist wholly in the work but as a historically shared point outside of it that is referred to by the work (Thompson 1988, 29).

Conclusion

In this chapter we have elaborated on the concept of videogame form by historicizing our approach in relation to Russian Formalism and Neoformalism. In line with these traditions, form differs from material and aligns more with the functioning of a videogame in the context of the aesthetic player experience. A videogame formalist therefore does not ask what the materials are that constitute a game, but instead asks how a game works to evoke an aesthetic effect. This draws our attention to a game's poetic gameplay devices: devices making elements of the game feel strange. These devices can function in a myriad of ways but to structure our analysis we can ask what the reasons are for a game's devices being here. These reasons, or motivations, serve as categories for the purpose of devices and can be divided up into ludic, compositional, realistic, transtextual, and artistic. Many devices will be situated in a combination of these categories and will be struggling with one another for dominance in eliciting the player's aesthetic response.

In our videogame formalism, the aesthetic game experience of the player is intertwined with game form and serves as the methodological starting point for doing the analysis. It becomes the task of the formalist videogame critic to establish which combination or clash of devices is functioning in which way to evoke our aesthetic game experience. In the context of (evoking) this aesthetic experience, form also includes meaning. This implies that we do away with a form-content split and simply see content (the cumulative meaning of a work) as part of the set of formal devices that can be used to make things unfamiliar.

Finally, we discussed how form becomes foregrounded in relation to the game's historical context. By understanding the game in relation to conventions in other works, the formalist critic tries to iteratively establish what struggle of devices distinguish this game from those other works, making that the game's dominant. Here, addressing the game in its synchronic historical perspective helps us see conventional and norm-challenging devices and gain intersubjective access to the game by drawing on a limited, shared and game-invoked reference point. Furthermore, addressing the game in a diachronic perspective helps to distinguish aesthetic innovation from mistakes, but also account for different play experiences of the same game over time.

After establishing form in relation to the contextual and aesthetic experience of play, we further elaborate on that experience and the role of the player in the next chapter. This eventually allows us to establish how the main assumptions of our formalist approach work, which provides the groundwork for the more practical methodological considerations in chapter 4. In the next chapter we slowly move away from the heavy historicizing we have done in this chapter and turn our attention to the medium specific qualities of games with the use of multiple examples. We'll continue this trajectory in the remainder of this book to end up with two extended case studies in chapter 5.

References

2K Boston. 2007. "BioShock [Xbox360 Game]." 2K Games.

2K Marin. 2010. "Bioshock 2 [Xbox360 Game]." 2K Games.

Aarseth, Espen. 1997. *Cybertext: Perspectives on Ergodic Literature*. London: The Johns Hopkins University Press.

Aarseth, Espen. 2004. "Genre Trouble: Narrativism and the Art of Simulation." In *First Person: New Media as Story, Performance, and Game*, edited by Noah Wardrip-Fruin and Pat Harrigan, 45–55. Cambridge, MA: MIT Press.

Aarseth, Espen. 2014. "I Fought the Law: Transgressive Play and the Implied Player." In *From Literature to Cultural Literacy*, edited by Naomi Segal and Daniela Koleva, 180–88. London: Springer.

Ainsworth, Thomas. 2020. "Form vs. Matter." In *Stanford Encyclopedia of Philosophy*. https://plato.stanford.edu/entries/form-matter/.

Anable, Aubrey. 2018. *Playing with Feelings: Video Games and Affect*. Minneapolis: University of Minnesota Press.

Bizzocchi, Jim, and Theresa Jean Tanenbaum. 2012. "Mass Effect 2: A Case Study in the Design of Game Narrative." *Bulletin of Science, Technology & Society* 32 (5): 393–404.

Björk, Staffan, and Jussi Holopainen. 2003. "Describing Games: An Interaction-Centric Structural Framework." In *Proceedings of the 2003 DiGRA International Conference: Level Up*, edited by Marinka Copier and Joost Raessens. Utrecht: Utrecht University.

Blendo Games. 2012. "Thirty Flights of Loving [MacOS Game]." Blendo Games.

Bogost, Ian. 2006. *Unit Operations: An Approach to Videogame Criticism*. Cambridge, MA: The MIT Press.

Bogost, Ian. 2007. *Persuasive Games*. Cambridge, MA: The MIT Press.

Bordwell, David. 1985. *Narration in the Fiction Film*. Madison, Wisconsin: University of Wisconsin Press.

Bordwell, David. 1989. "Historical Poetics of Cinema." In *The Cinematic Text: Methods and Approaches*, edited by R. Barton Palmer, 369–98. Cambridge, MA: Harvard University Press.

Bordwell, David. 2008. *Poetics of Cinema*. New York: Routledge.

Bordwell, David, and Kristin Thompson. 2010. *Film Art: An Introduction*. 9th ed. New York: McGraw-Hill.

Bradford, Clare. 2009. "Playing at Bullying: The Postmodern Ethic of Bully (Canis Canem Edit)." *Digital Culture and Education* 1 (1): 67–82.

Chew, Evelyn C., and Alex Mitchell. 2020. "Bringing Art to Life: Examining Poetic Gameplay Devices in Interactive Life Stories." *Games and Culture* 15 (8): 874–901.

Copier, Marinka. 2003. "The Other Game Researcher. Participating in and Watching the Construction of Boundaries in Game Studies." In *Proceedings of the 2003 DiGRA International Conference: Level Up*, edited by Marinka Copier and Joost Raessens, 404–19. Utrecht: Utrecht University.

Culler, Jonathan. 1997. *Literary Theory: A Very Short Introduction*. New York: Oxford University Press.

Eikhenbaum, Boris. 2012. "The Theory of the 'Formal Method'." In *Russian Formalist Criticism: Four Essays*, edited by Lee T. Lemon and Marion J. Reis, 2nd ed., 78–104. Lincoln: University of Nebraska Press.

Eisenstein, Sergei, dir. 1944. *Ivan the Terrible*. Mosfilm.

Erlich, Victor. 1980. *Russian Formalism: History, Doctrine*. 4th ed. The Hague: Mouton & Co.

Eskelinen, Markku. 2001. "The Gaming Situation." *Game Studies* 1 (1).

Fabricatore, Carlo, Miguel Nussbaum, and Ricardo Rosas. 2002. "Playability in Action Videogames: A Qualitative Design Model." *Human-Computer Interaction* 17 (4): 311–68.

Galactic Cafe. 2013. "The Stanley Parable [MacOS Game]." Galactic Cafe.

Hughes, John, dir. 1985. *The Breakfast Club*. Universal Pictures.

Hughes, John, dir. 1986. *Ferris Bueller's Day Off*. Paramount Pictures.

Hughes, Thomas. 1857. *Tom Brown's Schooldays*. London: MacMillan.

Hunicke, Robin, Marc LeBlanc, and Robert Zubek. 2004. "MDA: A Formal Approach to Game Design and Game Research." In *Proceedings of the Challenges in Game AI Workshop, Nineteenth National Conference on Artificial Intelligence*. San Jose, CA.

Iser, Wolfgang. 1980. *The Act of Reading: A Theory of Aesthetic Response*. London: The Johns Hopkins University Press.

Jakobson, Roman. 1921. *Noveĭshaia Russkaia Poeziia*. Tip. "Politika."

Järvinen, Aki. 2007. "Introducing Applied Ludology: Hands-on Methods for Game Studies." In *Proceedings of the 2007 DiGRA International Conference: Situated Play*, 134–44. Tokyo: The University of Tokyo.

Jayemanne, Darshana. 2017. *Performativity in Art, Literature, and Videogames*. Cham: Palgrave MacMillan.

Jayemanne, Darshana. 2020. "Chronotypology: A Comparative Method for Analyzing Game Time." *Games and Culture* 15 (7): 809–24.

Juul, Jesper. 2003. "The Game, the Player, the World: Looking for a Heart of Gameness." In *Level Up: Digital Games Research Conference Proceedings*, 30–45. Utrecht: Utrecht University.

Juul, Jesper. 2004. "Introduction to Game Time/Time to Play: An Examination of Game Temporality." In *First Person: New Media as Story, Performance, and Game*, edited by Noah Wardrip-Fruin and Pat Harrigan, 131–42. Cambridge, MA: MIT Press.

Juul, Jesper. 2005. *Half-Real: Video Games between Real Rules and Fictional Worlds*. Cambridge, MA: MIT press.

Juul, Jesper. 2013. *The Art of Failure: An Essay on the Pain of Playing Video Games*. Cambridge, MA: The MIT Press.

Keogh, Brendan. 2018. *A Play of Bodies: How We Perceive Videogames*. Cambridge, MA: MIT Press.

Lachmann, Renate. 1984. "Die 'Verfremdung' Und Das 'Neue Sehen' Bei Viktor Sklovskij." In *Verfremdung in Der Literatur*, edited by H. Helmers, 321–51. Darmstadt: Wissenschaftliche Buchgesellschaft.

Lankoski, Petri, and Staffan Björk. 2015. "Formal Analysis of Gameplay." In *Game Research Methods: An Overview*, edited by Petri Lankoski and Staffan Björk, 23–36. Pittsburgh: ETC Press.

Lindley, Craig A. 2002. "The Gameplay Gestalt, Narrative, and Interactive Storytelling." In *Proceedings of the Computer Games and Digital Cultures Conference*, edited by Frans Mäyrä, 203–15. Tampere: Tampere University Press.

Mejia, Robert, Jaime Banks, and Aubrie Adams. 2017. *100 Greatest Video Game Franchises*. Lanham: Rowman & Littlefield.

Midway Games. 1992. "Mortal Kombat [Arcade Game]." Midway Games.

Mitchell, Alex. 2016. "Making the Familiar Unfamiliar: Techniques for Creating Poetic Gameplay." In *Proceedings of the First International Joint Conference of DiGRA and FDG 2016*. Dundee: Digital Games Research Association.

Mitchell, Alex, Liting Kway, Tiffany Neo, and Yuin Theng Sim. 2020. "A Preliminary Categorization of Techniques for Creating Poetic Gameplay." *Game Studies* 20 (2).

Mitchell, Alex, Yuin Theng Sim, and Liting Kway. 2017. "Making It Unfamiliar in the 'Right' Way: An Empirical Study of Poetic Gameplay." In *Proceedings of* the 2017 *DiGRA International Conference*. Melbourne, Australia: Digital Games Research Association.

Murray, Janet H. 1998. *Hamlet on the Holodeck: The Future of Narrative in Cyberspace*. Cambridge, MA: MIT Press.

Nintendo. 2017. "The Legend of Zelda: Breath of the Wild [Nintendo Switch Game]." Nintendo.

Numinous Games. 2016. "That Dragon, Cancer [MacOS Game]." Numinous Games.

Pajitnov, Alexey. 1988. "Tetris [MS DOS Game]." Spectrum Holobyte.

Pötzsch, Holger. 2017. "Playing Games with Shklovsky, Brecht, and Boal: Ostranenie, V-Effect, and Spect-Actors as Analytical Tools for Game Studies." *Game Studies* 17 (2).

Rockstar Vancouver. 2006. "Bully [Playstation 2 Game]." Rockstar Games.

Rohrer, Jason. 2007. "Passage [Microsoft Windows Game]." Jason Rohrer.

Roth, Christian, Tom van Nuenen, and Hartmut Koenitz. 2018. "Ludonarrative Hermeneutics: A Way Out and the Narrative Paradox." In *International Conference on Interactive Digital Storytelling*, 93–106. Cham: Springer.

Shklovsky, Victor. 2012a. "Art as Technique." In *Russian Formalist Criticism: Four Essays*, edited by Lee T. Lemon and Marion J. Reis, 2nd ed., 21–34. Lincoln: University of Nebraska Press.

Shklovsky, Victor. 2012b. "Sterne's *Tristam Shandy:* Stylistic Commentary." In *Russian Formalist Criticism: Four Essays*, edited by Lee T. Lemon and Marion J. Reis, 2nd ed., 35–54. Lincoln: University of Nebraska Press.

Steiner, Peter. 2014. *Russian Formalism: A Metapoetics*. Geneva: Sdvig Press.

Tale of Tales. 2008. "The Graveyard [MacOS Game]." Tale of Tales.

Thomashevsky, Boris. 2012. "Thematics." In *Russian Formalist Criticism: Four Essays*, edited by Lee T. Lemon and Marion J. Reis, 2nd ed., 55–77. Lincoln: University of Nebraska Press.

Thompson, Kristin. 1981. *Eisenstein's "Ivan the Terrible": A Neoformalist Analysis*. Princeton, New Jersey: Princeton University Press.

Thompson, Kristin. 1988. *Breaking the Glass Armor: Neoformalist Film Analysis*. Princeton, New Jersey: Princeton University Press.

Treanor, Mike. 2013. "Investigating Procedural Expression and Interpretation in Videogames." PhD Thesis, UC Santa Cruz.

Treanor, Mike, Bobby Schweizer, Ian Bogost, and Michael Mateas. 2011. "Proceduralist Readings: How to Find Meaning in Games with Graphical Logics." In *Proceedings of Foundations of Digital Games (FDG 2011)*, 115–22. New York: ACM.

Ungvári, Tamás. 1979. "The Origins of the Theory of Verfremdung." *Neohelicon* 7 (1): 171–232.

Vella, Daniel. 2015. "The Ludic Subject and the Ludic Self: Analyzing the 'I-in-the-Gameworld'." PhD Thesis, IT University of Copenhagen.

Vught, Jasper van, and René Glas. 2018. "Considering Play: From Method to Analysis." *Transactions of the Digital Games Research Association* 4 (2).

Willumsen, Ea Christina. 2018. "The Form of Game Formalism." *Media and Communication* 6 (2): 137–44.

Wimsatt, William K., and Monroe C. Beardsley. 1946. "The Intentional Fallacy." *The Sewanee Review* 54 (3): 468–88.

Wimsatt, William K., and Monroe C. Beardsley. 1949. "The Affective Fallacy." *The Sewanee Review* 57 (1): 31–55.

Zagal, José P., Michael Mateas, Clara Fernández-Vara, Brian Hochhalter, and Nolan Lichti. 2007. "Towards an Ontological Language for Game Analysis." In *Worlds in Play: International Perspectives on Digital Games Research*, edited by Suzanne de Castell and Jennifer Jenson, 25–36. New York: Peter Lang.

Zirmunsky (Zhirmunskij), Viktor. 1928. "K Voprosu o Formal'nom Metode." In *Voprosy Teorii Literatury* [*Literature Theory Questions*]. Leningrad.

3.   On Aesthetic Experience

Abstract: In this chapter, we explore the relationship between defamiliarization and the player's aesthetic experience, which we see as the starting
point for our formalist videogame analysis. We begin by clarifying what
we mean by "player experience," and then discuss how, from a formalist
perspective, this experience relates to automatization and defamiliarization
(or foregrounding). From this, we draw on empirical studies of literature to
consider how players exert effort to refamiliarize and thereby make sense of
these foregrounded elements of a work by making connections both within
and beyond the work. This process of sense-making is grounded in the form
of the work, within a particular play context. It is this aesthetic experience
that provides the starting point for our formalist videogame analysis.

Keywords: aesthetic experience, defamiliarization, refamiliarization,
sense-making

Videogame formalism is not so much interested in *what* a videogame means
but rather in *how* a videogame works to trigger an aesthetic experience
(which includes, but is not limited to, meaning making). In the previous
chapter we drew extensively from the heritage of Russian Formalism to
reflect on form as distinct from material and in relationship with meaning
or content. We also positioned videogame formalism as a poetics to explain
how form is always foregrounded and understood through the aesthetic
experience of the player whereby the historical context of the videogame
and the player are taken into account. In this chapter, we step away from the
Russian Formalist heritage a bit to make the approach our own and delve
more extensively into the *experience* of videogames. We begin by exploring
how defamiliarization can be used as a starting point for an understanding
and a study of aesthetic experience. We then discuss how the struggle
between various devices within a work creates a tension that leads to an
aesthetic effect, a tension that also includes broader sense-making processes.
This is followed by a detailed discussion of a set of poetic gameplay devices

Mitchell, A. and J. van Vught, *Videogame Formalism: On Form, Aesthetic Experience, and Methodology.* Amsterdam: Amsterdam UniversityPress, 2024
DOI 10.5117/9789463720663_CH03

which are introduced, not as a definitive set of devices, but as a starting point for exploration of *how videogames evoke experience*. This will provide a foundation for our discussion of the methodological considerations and procedures of our videogame formalism in the following chapter.

The "Play Experience"

Our formalist approach to videogame analysis starts from the *experience* of videogames. As a multimodal one, the experience of videogames is necessarily complex, involving the emotional, cognitive, and physical processing of narrative, (audio-visual) stylistic, and rule-based components, functioning in a range of different ways from the ludic to the artistic. All of this together creates a very particular experience. To begin our discussion of the experience of videogames, we need to have some clarity of what we mean by "experience."

We follow Wright et al. in taking a pragmatic perspective on experience as "an orientation toward life as lived and felt in all its particulars" (2008, 3). Here Wright et al. take a holistic approach, which "focuses on the interplay of [the] constituents of the totality of a person acting, sensing, thinking, feeling and meaning-making in a setting, including his/her perception and sensation of his/her own actions" (2008, 4). Wright et al. conceptualize experience as "a braid made up of four intertwining threads: the sensual, the emotional, the compositional, and the spatio-temporal" (2008, 4). Although they are discussing experience in the context of human-computer interaction more broadly, we argue that Wright et al.'s perspective can be productively applied to videogames. Thus, the player's *experience* of a videogame can be seen as the combination of cognitive and emotional/affective responses to external stimuli and the player's own person in a specific, lived context. These responses can be seen as the result of the influence of the player themselves, the play context and the game system, and include a temporal dimension that brings in previous experiences and (potential) consequences (Nacke and Drachen 2011).[1]

In particular, we focus on the *aesthetic* experience of play. As argued by Bopp, player experience is often equated with positive affect, or "fun," and research into player experience often "lacks both an empirical and conceptual understanding of players' aesthetic experiences, such as the appeal of traditionally negatively valenced emotional experiences" (2020, 17). We take heed of

---

1   See also (Calleja 2007; Ermi and Mäyrä 2005; Folkerts 2010; Holbrook et al. 1984; Hu and Xi 2019; Jayemanne 2017; Keogh 2015; Sekhavat et al. 2020; Anable 2018; Isbister 2016; Swink 2008).

Bopp's warning here and, with our focus on the aesthetic experience of play, we aim to address a broad range of experiences, not just "fun." Furthermore, as explained by Wright et al., "pragmatism sees aesthetics as a particular kind of experience that emerges in the interplay between user, context, culture, and history, and should not be seen exclusively as a feature of either the artifact or viewer" (2008, 2). This aligns with our focus on starting from the player experience and incorporating awareness of the context of play.

Approached from a formalist perspective, the *aesthetic* experience of a work can be seen as engaging the player's emotional, cognition, and physical responses in a process of *defamiliarization* and *refamiliarization*. Defamiliarization is the process of making the familiar strange to enable us to see things anew, whereas refamiliarization is the process of working to find connections between the unfamiliar foregrounded elements and the larger context, so as to make sense out of the process of defamiliarization and find a way for this to be meaningful to the player beyond the game. Hereafter we first focus on the process of defamiliarization. In the following section, we move on to focus on refamiliarization and sense-making.

Automatization, Foregrounding and Defamiliarization

To begin to understand the aesthetic experience of a work, and the role of foregrounding and defamiliarization in that experience, we first need to introduce the concept of *automatization*. According to Shklovsky:

> as perception becomes habitual, it becomes automatic [...]. By this 'algebraic' method of thought we apprehend objects only as shapes with imprecise extensions; we do not see them in their entirety but rather recognize them by their main characteristics. We see the object as though it were enveloped in a sack. We know what it is by its configuration, but we see only its silhouette [...] The process of 'algebrization,' the over-automatization of an object, permits the greatest economy of perceptive effort [...] And so life is reckoned as nothing (2012a, 25-26).

Mukařovský (2014) argues that this automatization of perception can be disrupted by means of deviations from expectations in the form of *foregrounding*:

> Foregrounding is the opposite of automatization, that is, the deautomatization of an act; the more an act is automatized, the less it is consciously

executed; the more it is foregrounded, the more completely conscious does it become. Objectively speaking: automatization schematizes an event; foregrounding means the violation of the scheme (2014, 44).

In addition, Balint et al. (2016) suggest that foregrounding can be viewed from three different perspectives: in terms of specific textual *features* or deviations; as *perception*: "when recipients' perceive an element in the text as a deviation" (2016, 177); and as *experience*: "how recipients sense or undergo the perceived deviation" (2016, 177). In this chapter we are interested in all three of these perspectives: what are the *features* in a videogame that possibly lead to foregrounding, why does the player *perceive* these as deviations, and what is the resulting player *experience*. The *features* of a videogame are what formalism refers to as the materials (rule-based, stylistic and narrative – see chapter 2). When these materials deviate from the norms or conventions prevailing during a specific moment in time (i.e., the *context*), the player has an experience of *defamiliarization*, as both an experience related to the work's abstract form, and an experience related to the context that the work refers to.

Shklovsky introduced the concept of defamiliarization as a way to explain the undermining of expectations to slow down perception and "impart the sensation of things as they are perceived and not as they are known" (2012a, 26). This delay in perception is the result of the "[s]ystematic disturbance of the categorization process [which] makes low-categorized information, as well as rich pre-categorial sensory information, available to consciousness" (Tsur 2008, 4), something that Shklovsky argued serves to draw attention to and encourage reflection on the form of a work. This process of slowing down perception to encourage reflection has been explored in the context of film. According to Thompson, "[t]he aesthetic film seeks to prolong and roughen our experience – to induce us to concentrate on the processes of perception and cognition in and of themselves, rather than for some practical purpose [...]" (1988, 36). This slowing down is the result of what Thompson calls "roughened form," which consists of "all types of devices and relations among devices that would tend to make perception and understanding less easy" (1988, 37). Note that while in his earlier work Shklovsky saw defamiliarization as drawing attention to the form of the work (see chapter 2), here Thompson is suggesting that roughened form draws attention to the experience. This may seem incompatible, but as we argued in chapter 2, form and experience are inextricably linked – form is only perceived through experience, and experience emerges from the encounter with form.

Discussing the impact of the slowing down of perception on the experience of art, Bordwell suggests that "[In the reception of art] what is nonconscious in everyday mental life becomes consciously attended to. Our schemata get shaped, stretched, and transgressed [...] like all psychological activities, aesthetic activity has long-range effects. Art may reinforce, or modify, or even assault our normal perceptual-cognitive repertoire" (2013, 32). Here, Bordwell seems to be touching on the impact of defamiliarization not just on the process of perception and how this draws attention to form, but also the impact this has on how we make sense of the work, and even perhaps on how we see the world around us, echoing our discussion in chapter 2 of Pötzsch's argument that Shklovsky's concepts apply not just to form (which we consider as including content), but also to context.

Let us now investigate how a similar process can take place in videogames. Here we'll discuss a few different points of entry, from the broad perspective (voiced by Myers (2009)) that games are inherently defamiliarizing due to their controller-confined and rule-based resistance against (or slowing down of) a more effortless conventional experience (or progression through the game), to the more specific perspectives that games can include unnatural narratives (Ensslin 2015) or a variety of poetic gameplay devices (Mitchell 2016) to defamiliarize more conventional ludo-narrative experiences.

Considering how games slow down the player's progress towards the conclusion of the game directs us to the notion of difficulty, which consists of a set of deliberate ways of hindering the player's achievement of the game's goals as a means of creating pleasure. However, in games, difficulty is the norm, whereas foregrounding and defamiliarization often involves the violation of expectations and deviation from the norm. As Juul (2009) argues, players expect games to be difficult. This suggests that difficulty can have a defamiliarizing function when either the difficulty level clearly deviates from the norm (i.e., becomes foregrounded), such as when the difficulty is much higher, or much lower (or even non-existent), than expected; or the ludic functionality of the difficulty level (i.e., providing a challenge for the player) overlaps with other motivations, such as narrative delay, character stress, or clearly referencing other games or forms of media. We will return to this in our discussion of poetic gameplay devices below.

In fact, there have been arguments to suggest that videogames are inherently defamiliarizing. For example, Myers (2009; 2010) suggests that

[b]y confining the video game play experience within the mechanics of the video game controller and habituated response, video game rules and relationships undermine and deny conventional experience in much the

same manner that poetic language undermines and denies conventional language (Myers 2010, 46).

In contrast, in his comments on Myers' (2009; 2010) application of formalist approaches to videogames, Pötzsch argues that while "certain devices deployed at the level of game mechanics can prolong and complicate reception to enable poetic experiences of enstrangement" (2017, 11), this in not always the case for all videogames. In line with Pötzsch, we argue that taking the position that all game mechanics are defamiliarizing, as Myers does, would render the concept of defamiliarization meaningless for the analysis of videogames.

Ensslin (2015), approaching the question of whether all videogames are defamiliarizing from the perspective of unnatural narratology (Alber et al. 2010), similarly makes a distinction between videogames that represent some degree of either physical or logical impossibilities, following Alber's (2014) notion of the "unnatural," and those that are what Richardson (2011) considers "anti-mimetic." Alber sees the "unnatural" as including anything within the storyworld that is physically or logically impossible but very familiar to use in fictions, such as flying pigs or invisible people. Richardson, on the other hand, sees the unnatural more akin to defamiliarization, namely as anti-mimetic narratives that

> conspicuously violate [...] conventions of standard narrative forms, in particular the conventions of nonfictional narratives, oral or written, and fictional modes like realism that model themselves on nonfictional narratives. Unnatural narratives furthermore follow fluid, changing conventions and create new narratological patterns in each work. In a phrase, unnatural narratives produce a defamiliarization of the basic elements of narrative (Richardson 2011, 34 quoted in Ensslin, 47–48).

Richardson's definition of unnatural narrative is clearly referring to similar processes of violation of conventions and the making strange of elements of the narrative as can be seen in the concept of defamiliarization. As Ensslin highlights, what is important to Richardson is "the degree of unexpectedness that the text produces, whether surprise, shock, or the wry smile that acknowledges that a different, playful kind of representation is at work" (Richardson 2015, 5). Ensslin argues that rather than seeing all videogames as unnatural narratives, as would be suggested by Alber's version of unnatural narrative, what is more productive is to follow Richardson's perspective, and focus our analysis on "games that seek to defamiliarize and innovate the gaming experience through highly idiosyncratic ludo-narrative mechanics" and that "deliberately violate the ludo-narrative conventions of their genre and the medium itself in order to evoke meta-ludic and meta-fictional reflections in the player – as well as other types of philosophical and critical processes" (Ensslin 2015, 22).

As we have discussed in chapter 2, Mitchell (2014; 2016) similarly sees defamiliarization in the context of videogames as a process of slowing down perception and drawing the player's attention to the form of the work. Mitchell coined the term "poetic gameplay," which he sees as

> the structuring of the actions the player takes within a game, and the responses the game provides to those actions, in a way that draws attention to the form of the game, and by doing so encourages the player to reflect upon and see that structure in a new way (2016, 2).

Going beyond Mitchell, we argue that foregrounding and defamiliarization can lead to sense-making. We will now explore the ways in which different devices, and combinations of devices, work together to create an aesthetic experience and how the player, in context, engages with and reflects upon how their expectations are disrupted as part of this experience, and how they gradually make sense of and refamiliarize these disruptions so that they are meaningful to the player.

Refamiliarization and Sense-Making

We will now discuss how foregrounding and defamiliarization can go beyond simply drawing the player's attention to the form of the work, and in addition lead to a process of sense-making. We argue that the player's response to foregrounded, defamiliarized aspects of the work, which taken together form the dominant, can trigger reflection and encourage the player to begin to make sense of or integrate these strange aspects of the work into their experience, through a process of foregrounding, defamiliarization and refamiliarization. This process involves the player dealing with cognitive dissonance and revising their mental model of what is happening as they experience the work. Here we are examining how, through their encounter with the work, players are able to reconcile the defamiliarizing aspects of the work as they begin to form an understanding of the dominant, and from that understanding, actively find a connection to their own lived experience.

Returning to our earlier consideration of pragmatic aesthetics, Wright et al. see experience as

> constituted by continuous engagement with the world through acts of sense-making at many levels [...] Meaning is constructed out of dynamic interplay between the compositional, sensual, emotional, and spatio-temporal threads. It is constituted by experiences with particular qualities, be they satisfying, enchanting, disappointing, or frustrating (2008, 6).

Wright et al. consider sense-making to consist of six processes: anticipating, connecting, interpreting, reflecting, recounting, and appropriating. What is interesting here from a formalist perspective is what it is that constitutes the "particular qualities" of an experience such that sense-making can take place and allow the player to find the experience meaningful and make connections with their broader experience of the world. This aligns with our argument in chapter 2 that the player's experience of foregrounding and defamiliarization, and the resulting aesthetic experience, within a particular context, emerges from their encounter with the work. To better understand how this happens, we turn to empirical studies of literature.

According to Leech and Short (2007), the process of de-automatization or defamiliarization can lead to new awareness and new insights. In literature, several studies (Fialho 2007; Miall and Kuiken 1994) have explored the role of defamiliarization in sense-making, suggesting that foregrounding in the form of stylistic variations can induce defamiliarization, which in turn "strikes readers as interesting and captures their attention" (Miall and Kuiken 1994, 392). They go on to cite earlier studies (Miall 1992) that suggest a connection between defamiliarization and the emergence of feeling. In fact, the resulting feelings are an important part of the sense-making process:

> Defamiliarization evokes feelings in a way that makes it not merely incidental but actually a constructive part of the reading process. When perception has been deautomatized, a reader employs the feelings that have been evoked to find or to create a context in which the defamiliarized aspects of the story can be located. This is a central part of the constructive work of the reader of a literary text (Miall and Kuiken 1994, 392).

Following on from this, they propose that "during an encounter with foregrounded text, the reader may engage in what we have called 'refamiliarization': the reader may review the textual context in order to discern, delimit, or develop the novel meanings suggested by the foregrounded passage" (1994, 394). Refamiliarization is the process of finding connections between the defamiliarized and automatized materials in the work, going beyond comprehension and engaging in interpretation.

This can be seen as similar to Aarseth and Moring's (2020) description of Heidegger's (1962) notion of a movement during tool use from an initial "understanding as coping" to a second type of understanding, which they label "understanding as interpreting." This involves a process in which a tool (for example, a hammer or a software interface) that was originally "ready-to-hand" and transparent, changes to being "present-at-hand" through what Winograd and Flores (1986) term "breakdown," the disruption of the "habitual, standard, [and] comfortable" (Winograd and Flores 1986 quoted in Koschmann, Kuutti, and Hickman). This disruption "may make visible aspects of the situation that might otherwise elude awareness" (Koschmann, Kuutti, and Hickman 1998). This is very similar to the process of defamiliarization we have been discussing so far.

An important issue that often arises regarding defamiliarization or foregrounding is whether this slowing down of perception is disruptive to the experience of the work. However, Kuijpers (2014) sees foregrounding and absorption as able to co-occur within a single text, with the reader potentially able to "weave in and out" of absorption as they either become lost in the text, or their experience is slowed down by foregrounding, and they work to engage in refamiliarization. Further, Balint et al. explain that foregrounding

> does not diminish recipients' focus but rather shifts their attention from content to form, that is, from story-world events to some aspect of the artifact ... this shift of attention from *what* is told to *how* it is told may result in readers' increased awareness of the artifact. As a consequence, recipients may involve themselves in a different kind of interpretation: Why is this story told in an unusual way? Does the deviation have an additional communicative purpose? (2016, 180)

Note that here Balint et al. are starting from the assumption that there is a separation between form and content, something we have argued against in chapter 2. Despite this, the idea that the process of defamiliarization and refamiliarization encourages reflection on how the elements of the work come together to create the experience and what broader connections that experience may have aligns with our formalist approach.

Here, it is worth considering how the reader or player approaches this process of refamiliarization. Balint et al. (2016) empirically identified a number of strategies employed in response to foregrounding, including: striking/novelty, uncertainty/disambiguation, symbol/insight, blank/imagination, obstruction/adjustment, forceful absorption, and forceful character engagement. In the context of videogames, Mitchell, Sim and Kway (2017) have explored player responses to defamiliarization, in the form of poetic gameplay devices. Their results suggest that, beyond the initial drawing of attention to the form of the game, players do start to "reflect upon issues beyond the immediate game experience." However, they caution that "this tended to happen when the gameplay was made unfamiliar in ways that directly supported the emerging meaning of the game."

A similar process has been discussed in the context of unnatural narratology. As Ensslin says, "when we encounter anything unfamiliar, or strange ... we try to make sense of it in some way, by applying a range of reading strategies" (2015, 18). She draws on Alber, who says that we are "ultimately bound by [our] cognitive architecture, even when trying to make sense of the unnatural. Hence, the only way to respond to narratives of all sorts (including unnatural ones) is through cognitive frames and scripts" (2013, 451 quoted in Ensslin). Alber (2013) proposes nine reading strategies that readers can use to "come to terms with the unnatural": frame blending, generification, subjectification, thematic foregrounding, allegorical reading, satirization and parody, positing a transcendental realm, "do it yourself," and "the zen way of reading."

What is important in all of these descriptions of the process of defamiliarization and refamiliarization is that there is some disruption of the processing of the experience of the work through a violation of expectations, thereby drawing attention to the site of disruption, followed by an effort to make sense of that disruption, and a resulting connection to the reader/viewer/player's own experiences and context so that it becomes meaningful to the player.

The Role of Poetic Gameplay Devices

Having explored first the notion of defamiliarization, or the slowing down of perception through foregrounding, and then the process of refamiliarization and sense-making that potentially results from this as the player tries to accommodate the foregrounded materials into their understanding of the work, we now look specifically at some of the ways in which the videogame can be made strange so as to trigger this process. Building from Mitchell (2016), Chew and Mitchell (2019) and Mitchell et al. (2020), we will now discuss how videogames undermine player expectations through a number of techniques, categorizing these techniques in terms of the *motivations* of these devices within the work – what purpose they serve within the overall structure of the work.

Mitchell et al. (2020), in defining a series of "poetic gameplay devices," focus largely on what could be seen as devices with ludic motivations (see chapter 2). However, many of Mitchell et al.'s devices also fall within other motivational categories. In chapter 2 we looked briefly at Mitchell's analysis of *Thirty Flights of Loving* (2016) and *The Graveyard* (2020), suggesting how a range of devices with both ludic and non-ludic motivations work together to create the player experience in these games. This is an important point, as for our videogame formalism we explicitly want to avoid reducing videogames purely to their ludic components, and instead focus on the entirety of the work, with motivations from across the set of categories being of equal importance both to the player experience, and to the critic's analysis of the work.

Before we do this, we will clarify some of our terminology. Mitchell et al. (2020), when identifying poetic gameplay devices, did not specifically define what is meant by a "device," instead suggesting that these are "the various elements within a game (the poetic devices) that are creating poetic gameplay," which are "analogous to the 'literary devices' used in literature." So, what are "literary devices"? According to Thompson:

> [t]he word *device* indicates any single element or structure that plays a role in the artwork – a camera movement, a frame story, a repeated word, a costume, a theme, and so on. For the neoformalist, all devices of the medium and of formal organisation are equal in their potential for defamiliarization ... The structure of devices is seen as organised but not solely in order to express meaning, but to create defamiliarization (1988, 15).

This seems to suggest that everything that makes up a work (a film, a poem, a game) can be considered devices. However, it is important, as van Vught (2016) notes, to recognize that while Thompson is not particularly clear about the distinction between material and the use of the material in the form of devices, the neoformalist perspective focuses on the use of elements of a work to create defamiliarization so as to cue the aesthetic experience. This suggests a need to make the distinction between *material* and *device* clearer.

Discussing the use of these terms by Russian formalists, Thomson-Jones explains that

> words are the common material for both "practical" and poetic discourse, and this is the case even if particular ways of using words – say figuratively

or literally, are more commonly associated with one form of discourse than the other. What distinguishes the work of literature, therefore, is not that it contains certain words with certain connotations but that those words are used in a certain way to serve a particular purpose [...] Insofar as a device is any medium-specific technique for manipulating, transforming, and structuring materials, the neo- and Russian formalists understand the work of art simply as a set of devices (2008, 133).

Thinking about this from the perspective of the dominant is useful. As discussed in chapter 2, the dominant is the organizing principle that foregrounds some devices and subordinates others, suggesting that those elements that contribute to foregrounding are worth studying, and those that don't contribute can be ignored, or at least downplayed. The formalist perspective assumes that a work is created with some intention, and that every device is there for a reason (Thomson-Jones 2008, 133). This is the *function* of the device, "the purpose served by the presence of any given device" (Thompson 1988, 15 after (Tynianov 2019)) within a work. A device may have different functions in different works, according to the context of the work, and the other devices present within the work. The interplay between devices, and the resulting tension, is what leads to foregrounding and the presence of the dominant. Note that devices can become automatized (thus turning back into material) and be replaced by other devices to create defamiliarization, but that functions are more stable. In addition, a device's *motivation* "operates as an intersection between the work's structures and the spectator's activity" (Thompson 1988, 16), and is the reason the work suggests for the device being present.

According to Thompson, "[a]nalysis of function and motivation will always remain the analyst's central goal, and it will subsume interpretation" (1988, 21). Devices can have different functions in the different motivational categories that are also outlined by Thompson and by Thomashevsky (2012). However, in many cases, this functioning will not be defamiliarizing. For example, if something has a compositional function, that does not necessarily mean that it is a device cueing an aesthetic effect. In many cases it will be automatized, and in that case, we should really be talking about *material* rather than device. Only when it evokes defamiliarization does it become a device.

To summarize, for our purposes we will be using the following terminology:

1. Elements of a work (the *material*) perform a certain *function* (put there deliberately);

2. When the material is *foregrounded*, it becomes a *device*;

3. When a device is *automatized*, it returns to just being material; and

4. A device's *motivation* is its role within the work, which is seen in relation to other devices, unlike its function which is more individual.

To help us to further explore the role of materials and devices, how they fit within the different motivational categories, and their impact on the player's aesthetic experience, we now selectively expand on several more of the games analysed by Mitchell et al. (2020), broadening the focus of the analysis to include a range of motivations, and examining additional devices that may be manifest beyond those that demonstrate ludic motivations. In particular, we focus on how the devices within a game are potentially working together or in tension with each other, and how this relates to the player's experience of the game. From this, we raise questions as to how a critic should go about examining these devices, issues we explore in detail in chapter 4.

Lim

We will begin with the game *Lim* (k 2012), as this is a game that initially appears to be an abstract videogame, and a videogame in which it is easy, as Mitchell et al. (2020) did, to focus almost exclusively on the devices with ludic motivations. In the discussion below, we aim to show how the full range of devices contribute to the player's aesthetic experience.

Lim is described in its entry on the "Games for Change" website as "a game about violence. About the violence of standing out, and even more about the violence of blending in" (Games for Change 2013). The gameplay consists of navigating a coloured block through a maze containing other coloured blocks which react with extreme violence to the presence of blocks of a colour different from themselves. As described by Mitchell et al.:

> These squares react to squares of differing colours by blocking the way and possibly attacking, resulting in violent shaking of the viewport. The only way to pass is to press "z" to imitate the colours of other squares. If the player "blends" for too long, the viewport shrinks and shakes violently, accompanied by loud audio feedback. This is very uncomfortable, mimicking the discomfort felt by someone who must pretend to be something they are not (2020).

In their categorization of poetic gameplay devices, Mitchell et al. focus on what they describe as "uncomfortable feedback," which they place under their "interaction" category of devices. While this device is clearly present and could perhaps be considered the most prominent device within the game, from which the player's experience of the game emerges, it also works together with and is supported by a number of other devices, some of which are implicit in Mitchell et al.'s (2020) description of the videogame.

To help understand what these other devices are, and how they impact the player's experience, we'll first consider the various materials used within the game, then consider which of those materials are foregrounded, thereby taking on the role of devices. This will help us to identify the dominant.

The world of *Lim* consists of a set of grey blocks forming a maze, placed on a solid pink background (see figure 3.1). The player controls a block, the same shape and size as the "wall" blocks. The maze consists of a number of corridors, each exactly the width of the player's block, connecting a number of larger open spaces. Each of these spaces may contain several other blocks, all of a single colour, whereas the player's block initially flickers between colours. The player moves the player's block past the challenges of the other blocks and eventually to the end of the maze, where the player's block meets another block, and both flicker between colours in synchronization, suggesting a "happy" ending. It is also possible for the player's block to end up "outside" the walls, but still reach the end of the maze (but outside). In this case, the player's block and the other block flicker in synchronization, but are separated, suggesting a "sad" ending.

While some of the blocks clearly represent "walls," it becomes clear once the player engages with the game that certain blocks represent the player and other "characters" within the gameworld, characters that are antagonistic to the player's character. The player can press the up, down, left, and right arrow keys to move their block around the gameworld. The player's block cannot deliberately move through the walls, although as we will discuss below, the player's block can be "shoved" through a wall when repeatedly attacked by another block. The player will also discover that when they encounter other blocks, those blocks will move towards the player's block and begin to collide with the player's block, forcing the player's block backwards and causing the player's viewport to shake violently. If, however, the player presses the "z," the player's block will change colour to match that of the other blocks. The longer the "blend" is activated, the more the viewport shakes and shrinks, accompanied by uncomfortable audio feedback.

At first glance, many of these materials – the controls, the inability to move through walls unless "shoved," the response of the other blocks to the player's block, and the ability to "blend" – can be seen as functioning

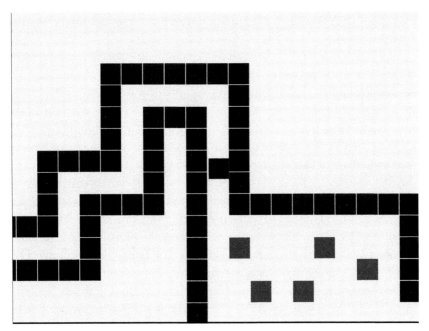

Figure 3.1: *Lim* (screenshot by the first author).

within the ludic motivational category, as they set out the rules and actions
governing gameplay. However, once the player starts reading a story of social
acceptance into the movement and collision mechanics of the abstract
shapes, many of the materials can also be seen to function within other
categories as well. For example, the visual elements on the screen that
represent the walls, the player's block, and the other blocks, can now be
seen as functioning within the *compositional* motivational category, as they
serve to create a sense of the spatial structure of the game's "story world" and
the characters in it. Similarly, the behaviour of the antagonist blocks, the
"blend" mechanic and the representation and visual indication of a happy
and a sad ending all serve to provide some narrative structure. Here, the fact
that the player's block can be "shoved" outside the walls of the maze, unable
to get back in, can be seen as representative of exclusion of those who are
different, and the "blending" mechanic can be seen as representative of the
difficulty of fitting in when you are different from others. The fact that this
references our social reality beyond the game means these materials could
also be considered functioning within the *realistic* motivational category.
And finally, the choice of an abstract representation for the gameworld and
the connection of the "blend" function to a change of colour can be seen
as functioning within the *artistic* motivational category, as they help to

encourage the player to engage in a certain degree of non-straightforward interpretation.

Having identified the materials and the motivational categories within which they function, we will now consider whether any of these materials are foregrounded, thereby taking on the role of *devices* within the game. An obvious starting point is the uncomfortable feedback that occurs when the player's block is attacked and during the use of the "blending" function, as identified by Mitchell et al. (2020). This is clearly beyond the type of feedback players usually expect from a game, qualifying it as a device. Beyond this device, there are several other materials which can be seen as foregrounded. When the player is repeatedly attacked, it is possible for the player's block to be "shoved" out through the wall, unable to get back into the maze. This ejection from the game world is also somewhat beyond what players usually expect – in fact, when this first happens it could be seen as a glitch. However, this works together with the uncomfortable feedback to encourage the player to think about the implications of the difficulties of fitting in when you are different from the majority. Finally, the use of minimal visuals, including the stark pink background, a flickering block to represent the player, and the solid-coloured blocks for the aggressors, while not completely unfamiliar, is in contrast to the complexity of the ideas being explored in the game, and as such also creates somewhat of a defamiliarizing effect.

The main point here is that there are a number of materials that make up *Lim*, covering a number of motivational categories: compositional, artistic, realistic, and ludic. Of these materials, several are foregrounded, serving as devices and working together to create a defamiliarizing effect on the player. This foregrounding focuses on the uncomfortable feedback identified by Mitchell et al. (2020), something that can be considered the dominant within this game. As the player experiences these devices, they will be working to make sense of the various foregrounded materials, undertaking "reading" strategies to try to connect these to some context. The resulting understanding will be based on their experience of the game as an object, within a particular context of play, but at the same time influenced by the original context of production, and any awareness the player may have of that context.

For example, *Lim* was originally released in 2012, a time that marked the beginning of an "ongoing rise of independent video games made by queer creators that either represent or are inspired by the experiences of queer people" (Ruberg 2020, 59). The game "has frequently been cited as an example of a queer game" (Clark 2017, 8). The game has been unavailable for play for some time, a deliberate move on the part of the developer. In an interview in 2017, the developer explained their reasons for making their older games unavailable online:

> In terms of killing a lot of the archive, a lot of it felt personal in a way that I was uncomfortable with. I used to be freer with the things I shared with the internet [until] around 2014, when organized hate campaigns – stuff like Gamergate – got taken to a new level. Not that those kinds of things didn't happen before, but being personal online was a much more dangerous proposition after that for a lot of people (Spiegel 2017).

It is only more recently that k has re-released the game on itch.io, citing "popular demand," but including the disclaimer that "I think it isn't very good mechanically and is pretty confused thematically" (k 2023). All of this is likely to figure into the player's process of sense-making, as the discomfort and mechanics surrounding the difficulty of trying to fit in are associated to the contexts both of production and reception. How we, as critics, should go about carrying out an analysis of this sense-making process is something we will discuss in detail in chapter 4.

Getting Over It with Bennett Foddy

In *Lim*, there were a set of devices working together to create a specific effect, enabling the player to experience to some extent a representation of the violence involved in having to "fit in." These devices worked together to create this specific effect. To further explore the ways in which devices work together within a game to create an aesthetic experience, we will now look at another game that makes focused use of several devices within a range of motivations.

Getting Over It with Bennett Foddy (Foddy 2017) explores frustration and extreme, almost unreasonable difficulty. The player controls Diogenes, a man who stands inside a large jar or cauldron and carries a long hammer (see figure 3.2). The gameplay consists of using the "hammer" to attempt to catapult Diogenes and his cauldron across the terrain and eventually reach the top of the mountain. As explained by Mitchell et al. (2020), "the combination of extremely fine granularity of controls, a very steep difficulty curve, and lack of checkpoints makes it very difficult to progress." This analysis focuses exclusively on the difficulty, which is indeed something that violates players' usual expectations for a game with a reasonable level of difficulty. However, there are a number of other aspects of the game that

Figure 3.2: *Getting Over It with Bennett Foddy* (screenshot by the first author).

work together with the unexpectedly high difficulty to create the player's experience.

Here, the gameworld takes the form of a side-scrolling "platformer" that is represented in semi-realistic fashion as mountainous terrain. The player's character is represented by a similarly semi-realistic human figure, as is the "hammer" that is controlled by the player and used as a means of locomotion. All of these materials can be seen as having a compositionally motivated function, as they create a sense of a consistent, if limited, storyworld. This works together with the materials that function within the ludic motivational category. The gameworld itself provides a clear set of challenges, in the form of obstacles to be climbed over, and an overall objective, the top of the mountain. The level design forms a significant part of the difficulty in the game. The game interface and controls are also materials that have ludically motivated functions, as they provide the means by which the player can attempt to overcome the challenges. There is also a degree of transtexutal motivation at work here, as the player's character is fashioned to resemble the ancient Greek philosopher Diogenes, who "famously took a tub, or a pithos, for an abode" (Piering n.d.). There is also a degree of ludic intertexuality in the relationship between this game and an earlier game, *Sexy Hiking* (Jazzuo 2002), which Foddy cites as the inspiration for *Getting Over It with Bennett Foddy* (Macgregor 2018).

Of these various materials, the extreme difficulty, fine grained controls, and lack of checkpoints have been identified by Mitchell et al. (2020) as poetic gameplay devices. The game also includes a voice-over by Bennett Foddy, the game's developer. This voice-over includes philosophical comments, and discussion of disappointment and frustration. The latter comments are triggered when the player fails. This "designer commentary" is something that appears in other games, but usually as a particular mode that can be enabled by the player, much like a director's commentary in a DVD. Here, however, the commentary is always present as part of the experience. In addition, the commentary makes direct reference to the player's failure. This is somewhat unusual, serving to defamiliarize the experience of the voice-over, and transforming it from material to a device. Further, once the player reaches the top of the mountain (a very unlikely occurrence), they are potentially granted access to a chat room, but only if they claim not to be streaming or recording their gameplay. As Soderman argues, this "foregrounds individual resolve as a prerequisite for social connection" (2021, 71), making the chat room "a club for elite, successful climbers" (2021, 72).

Finally, consider the name of the game, *Getting Over It with Bennett Foddy*. The fact that Foddy included his name in the title, which he claims is a reaction to the fact that "[c]ulturally we just don't recognize the individuals who make games" (Macgregor 2018), is something not often seen in the game industry (although there are rare exceptions, such as *American McGee's Alice* (McGee 2000)). While not necessarily defamiliarizing, there is clearly a deliberate effort here to catch the player's attention, even before the game is played. This, together with the voice-over narration, and the highly personal description of the game on Steam – "A game I made for a certain kind of person. To hurt them" (Foddy n.d.) – serve to create a feeling that this game is targeting you as a player. The difficulty isn't simply there to create a challenge, but to challenge *you*.

In *Getting Over It with Bennett Foddy*, we see a number of materials, such as the level design and visual representation of the world, working together with devices such as the almost abusive commentary from the game developer. The extreme difficulty, however, stands out as the distinguishing feature that ties a lot of these different elements together. The extreme difficulty sets up the challenge, the voice-over mocks the player and at the same time encourages them to continue playing, and the inclusion of the developer's name in the title makes it all seem personal. It is this combination of devices in the game that create the game's particular aesthetic experience, acting as the dominant. And it is this combination that also makes the game's difficulty different from the extreme difficulty that players have come to expect from some other games such as the *Dark Souls* (Miyazaki 2011) series, *Super Meat Boy* (McMillan and Refenes 2010) and *Celeste* (Thorson 2018).

Here much of the impact of the defamiliarization is to encourage re-flection on game difficulty and the resulting frustration, whereas in *Lim*, attention is drawn to the difficulty of blending in when you don't fit. This suggests that here the foregrounding is focused more inward, on the form of the game itself, although perhaps also towards the game community (both industry and players), whereas *Lim* points outwards to issues within society more broadly.

Akrasia

Akrasia (Team Aha! 2008) explores the problem of addiction. The player controls a small, blob-like character that initially moves through a colour-ful maze (see figure 3.3), collecting "pills" that, when eaten, increase the player's score (shown in the top right of the screen), and cause a red bar to gradually spread from the right to the left in a tree-like display (shown at the top left of the screen). As the red bar passes a number of objects hanging from the tree, these objects drop from the branch. The objects appear to be iconic representations of a house, a cat, a family, and a heart. The maze also contains a white "dragon" character that moves around the maze. A green arrow floating in front of the player's character points towards the dragon. When the "life" bar reaches the left of the screen, the character collapses, foaming at the mouth, and the game is over, the player character having overdosed. If, instead, the player either avoids eating the "pills," or touches the white "dragon," the world changes from a colourful maze to a grayscale maze, and the "dragon" becomes large and menacing. The word "exit" appears above the player character, and the arrow now points towards a yellow door. At this point, the player's controls are inverted, making movement challenging. If the player is able to avoid eating any pills and enters the door, the game ends with the player character experiencing a positive outcome. Depending on how many of the objects were still hanging on the branch, the ending may include a home, a pet cat, friends and family, and love.

We can see a number of materials and devices at work here. Mitchell et al. (2020) identified several devices with ludic motivations, including the unexpected change of controls when the world changes to the grey "sober" state, and the change in the player's understanding both of the game objective and the core mechanic. As they describe, "the player initially thinks the goal is to collect all the 'pills', but these pills, while keeping the player in the 'high' state, actually negatively impact the character's life. The 'true' objective is to stay 'sober' by avoiding the pills." This works together

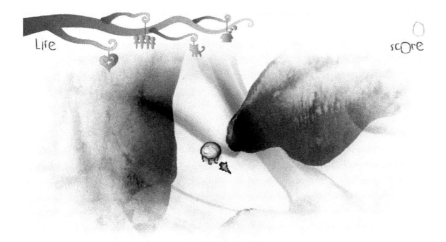

Life   score

Figure 3.3: Screenshot of *Akrasia* from http://gambit.mit.edu/images/loadgame_akrasia_03.jpg, Copyright © 2012 the Massachusetts Institute of Technology ("MIT"), used by permission of the Massachusetts Institute of Technology ("MIT").

with the player's realization that, in addition to the game objective, the core mechanic is also not what it first appeared, as "the core mechanic first appears to be 'collect pills', whereas in fact the core mechanic is 'avoid pills' so as to achieve the objective 'stay sober'." As with their discussion of *Lim* and *Getting Over It with Bennett Foddy*, Mitchell et al. (2020) focus primarily on the ludic functioning of the poetic gameplay devices (although they do mention a number of other materials in their analysis).

In contrast, in Chew and Mitchell's (2016) earlier analysis of *Akrasia*, attention was drawn to the ways in which the work "employs a coordinated audiovisual and interactive strategy" (219), whereby the changes in the game mechanics impact the control the player has over the avatar, in coordination with the change to the audiovisual elements, creating "an integrated and synesthetically consistent sense of 'how the subject feels' when in the state of addiction, sobriety or withdrawal" (219). This is connected to the ways in which the point system, game objectives, controls, and overall game experience is made strange. This is also tied to the game's narrative and multiple endings, which are unlocked based on the "life" remaining when the game ends. As Chew and Mitchell (2016) comment, the "score" that the player achieves has no impact on the outcome of the game. All of this works together to create an aesthetic experience that can lead to sense-making for some players. Chew and Mitchell have argued elsewhere that, in *Akrasia* as in other works, "interactivity produces widely different effects based on its interrelation with the other semiotic modes of the work" (2019, 350). This underscores the importance of attending to a range of devices and their motivations when considering *how* a game works.

In *Akrasia*, there are a number of materials that function within the compositional, transtextual, and artistic motivational categories. The game is depicted from a "side scroller" perspective, with the player's character depicted as a small grey blob with arms and legs eating pills, transtextually referencing the pill eating character Pac-Man (Iwatani 1980). The world is depicted as initially colourful, and changes to a sinister grey when in the "sober" state. There is a change in music related to changes in state, with sinister-sounding music played when the dragon appears, and upbeat music played when the player transitions back to the "addicted" state, and positive "juicy" feedback (Juul 2010) is shown when a pill is eaten. All of these materials work together to create a sense of the experiential world of someone struggling with substance abuse, including the temptations and accompanying hardships, showing them to be compositionally motivated. At first, most of these materials work as expected, with the ludic functioning of colour scheme and music for the "addicted" versus the "sober" states, and the "juicy" feedback when eating a pill, and the transtextual similarities to *Pac-Man* (Namco 1980), reinforcing the player's initial (mis)understanding of the game's goals and core mechanic. However, once the player learns that these materials also function compositionally to represent the temptations and effects of substance use, the visual style and music also come to seem somewhat dissonant, foregrounding them as devices.

The overall combination of the materials and devices creates a sense of *akrasia*, or loss of control, which the player works to overcome once they "get it." This loss of control can be seen as forming the dominant. Note that here we are focusing on the player's experience of the game. We will discuss identifying the dominant as a critic in more detail in the next chapter.

Even beyond the gameplay and the construction of the game world, there are a number of elements around the game that serve to set up how we make sense of the game. We can examine how these relate to the in-game materials and devices, and whether they also form part of the dominant. One of these materials is the use of a quotation from *Alice's Adventures in Wonderland* (Carroll 1865), "if you drink too much from a bottle labelled 'poison' it is certain to disagree with you," in the main screen before the game starts. This has functionality that is both transtextually (a reference to *Alice's Adventures in Wonderland*) and artistically (creating a sense of mystery and foreshadowing the upcoming trip "down the rabbit hole") motivated. Following from this, to actually start the game the player must move the character towards, and then collect, the first of many "pills," setting the character up as an addict from the start. When first encountered, both the quote and the need to collect a "pill" seem a bit unusual but may not be so unexpected as to create defamiliarization. However, despite their continued status as materials, the quote and the collection of the pill work effectively with the player's in-game experience to point towards the game's overall evoked experience around addiction and loss of self-control, thereby enabling the player to gain a renewed perception of the struggles involved with addiction.

Shadow of the Colossus

From our discussion of *Lim*, *Getting Over It with Bennett Foddy*, and *Akrasia*, we have seen how a number of materials and devices, with a range of motivations, work together to create a set of tensions within a work, leading to the player's aesthetic experience. In the examples we have seen so far, the devices have been very prominent, arguably setting the overall tone (dominant) of the work. We conclude this chapter by focusing on a more "mainstream" game, *Shadow of the Colossus* (Team Ico 2005), and show how in this work there is a similar combination of materials and devices with a range of motivations, which come together to create a dominant.

In *Shadow of the Colossus*, even more so than in the games we have discussed above, there are a range of materials used to create the player's experience of the game. *Shadow of the Colossus* makes more extensive use of cinematic techniques to create a sense of the storyworld and to move both the gameplay and the story forward. This includes cutscenes, deliberate movements of the camera, ambient music, and detailed rendering of a 3D world. This makes the game a good example of a work with a number of non-ludically functioning materials and (potential) devices that contribute to the overall player experience. We will begin by describing the game, and then discuss the various materials and devices, their motivations, and how they work together to create the dominant.

The player's character, Wander, is a young man on a quest to revive Mono. Mono is a young woman who was "sacrificed for she had a cursed fate," as Wander explains to Dormin, the entity he hopes will bring Mono back to life. The game begins with Wander carrying Mono on horseback across the wilderness to a massive, ruined temple, where Dormin resides. Dormin agrees to revive Mono, but only if Wander will destroy the sixteen idols lining the walls of the temple, something that can only be done by defeating the sixteen colossi that embody the idols. Dormin warns Wander that by doing so, "the price you pay will be heavy indeed."

Following this introduction, the player is tasked to find and then defeat each of these sixteen colossi. To do this, Wander has a horse, Agro, who can help him to journey across the vast, largely empty world to each of the locations where the colossi are waiting. Wander also has a sword, which when held aloft shines a light in the direction of the currently targeted colossus, and a bow with unlimited arrows. The bow and arrows can be used against the colossi, but also to hunt small lizards that occasionally appear in the wilderness. Killing certain lizards increases Wander's maximum stamina, which is indicated on a circular gauge at the lower right of the screen. Stamina determines how long Wander may hang from a colossus when climbing it. There are also fruits that can be shot with the bow and arrow to increase the maximum value of Wander's health metre, also shown at the lower right of the screen. Wander's health decreases when attacked by a colossus or when he falls from a great height.

The main game loop involves locating a colossus, travelling to its location, and defeating it. The colossi are much larger and more powerful than Wander, although each has one or more weak spots. Holding the sword overhead when facing the colossus will shine light on these weak spots. The player's task is to figure out how to make use of the environment and the body of the colossus to climb to these weak spots and stab them, causing the colossus damage. Once the colossus's health metre, shown at the top of the screen during combat (see figure 3.4), is depleted, the colossus is defeated.

What is interesting about *Shadow of the Colossus* is the extent to which the various materials and devices within the game work together to create a sense of uncertainty in the player. From the start, there is a feeling that something is not quite right about the quests being undertaken by Wander. The long introductory sequence, showing the beauty of the game world but also highlighting its emptiness, accompanied by the haunting soundtrack, work together to create this feeling of mystery. These materials can be seen as having both compositional and artistic motivations – they sketch out the spatial details of the storyworld while also establishing the tone of the experience. Camera movement is also used to good effect here, with the camera often panning to focus on the direction that Wander is to travel. This has both a compositionally and a ludically motivated function – creating a sense of space while also guiding the player's movement through that space. The game world consists of large open spaces to be travelled to reach each colossus. While the game has an orchestral soundtrack, during travel the world is quiet except for environmental sounds representing Wander, Agro, and the world around them. This increases the feeling of a large, empty world. The richly simulated and rendered 3D world also helps to create the

Figure 3.4: *Shadow of the Colossus* (screenshot by the first author).

sense of a real place. In the original PS2 version of the game, the graphics and physics pushed the limits of the console (Nishikawa 2005). Later re-releases on PS3 and PS4 also emphasized the unique visual style of the game. All of these materials are clearly functioning within the compositional and artistic motivational categories, and work together to create a sense of mystery and foreboding.

So far, we have focused on materials that are not foregrounded. While working to create a specific feeling of mystery and uncertainty in the game, these materials do not in any way undermine expectations or defamiliarize the experience. Still, Mitchell et al. (2020) identified a number of poetic game-play devices in *Shadow of the Colossus*. Here, we expand on their analysis, arguing that, in addition to the ludic motivations highlighted by Mitchell et al. there are a number of devices with compositional and artistic motivations at work here. Together, these devices create the dominant within the game.

As identified by Mitchell et al., and also discussed by Sicart (2008), the process of stabbing the colossus, which represents the core game mechanic in the game, is slowed down and in the process made unfamiliar. To carry out an attack with the sword, the player must first press a control to raise the sword, and then press it again to stab. The longer the delay between raising the sword and stabbing, the more damage is inflicted. Mitchell et al. call this "slowing down the interactive loop." As they suggest, "[b]y undermining expectations of how a sword-wielding hero will behave, the game draws out this simple action, and encourages the player to reflect on whether this is the right thing to do" (2020).

This device does not, however, work in isolation. The player has already been primed by Dormin's warning of the price to be paid for defeating the colossi. The sense of doubt the player has about Wander's quest is also reinforced by several other ludically and compositionally motivated devices. A number of the colossi are initially passive until attacked, and the depiction of the death of each colossi works to create sympathy for the creatures. Once the final blow is dealt, the game switches to a slow-motion cutscene (making use of the convention of "letterbox format"), during which the colossus majestically collapses, accompanied by sombre music. This sequence is very much the opposite of what one would expect when defeating an enemy. The death scene ends with a shift back to interactivity. However, the return of control to the player is momentary. Almost immediately, black tendrils explode from the dying colossus and penetrate Wander. Before the player can escape, control is removed and the "letterbox" format returns, and Wander collapses, with black energy emitting from his mouth and chest. The game then transitions back to Dormin's temple, where Wander is shown lying unconscious on the ground, with a shadowy black figure standing over him. Wander stirs, stumbles over to Mono's body, and the idol representing the recently defeated colossus cracks and explodes into rubble. This sequence is repeated for each colossus. In addition, as more colossi are defeated, Wander's appearance gradually changes, with his clothing becoming increasingly ragged, his face becoming pale and ghastly, and a set of horns growing on his head.

This set of events makes use of several poetic gameplay devices. The depiction of the death of the colossus begins to suggest that the "game objective is not what it seems," something that becomes clearer later in the game. It also is an example of what Mitchell et al. (2020) call "inability to act" – control is removed from the player just as the tendrils move towards Wander, making it impossible for the player to escape. While the entire sequence could have been a cutscene, by momentarily returning control to the player, there is the illusion of control, but this is immediately removed. Finally, there is an element of "success is failure" here – the player has successfully defeated the colossus, but the way in which this is depicted creates a sense of uncertainty, suggesting to the player that killing the colossus may not have been the right thing to do. There is, however, no other course of action to be taken. While not used as an example by Mitchell et al. (2020) this could be seen as an instance of their device "only provide the inevitable choice": even if the player realizes that defeating the colossi may be the wrong thing to do, there is nothing else the player can do other than stop playing the game.

These devices build towards the final twist in the game, where it is revealed that Dormin has been making use of Wander to free itself from imprisonment. A cutscene after the twelfth colossus is defeated shows a band of warriors who are in pursuit of Wander. After the defeat of the final colossus, these warriors arrive at Dormin's temple, where they confront Wander and accuse him of "steal[ing] the sword and trespass[ing] upon this cursed land," and finally using "the forbidden spell," presumably referring to the summoning of Dormin to bring Mono back to life. At this point, Wander stumbles to his feet, extremely pale, and is first shot with a crossbow bolt, and then stabbed by one of the warriors. Wander then staggers up, pulls the sword out of his chest, and is rapidly engulfed in shadow, growing to an enormous size. The shadowy beast speaks with Dormin's voice, explaining that although the warriors had split it into sixteen fragments, it has now been reformed (with the help of Wander, and the player). This is definitely not the sort of ending most players would expect from a game. Here, the content of the story is defamiliarized, making the player realize that they have essentially been playing the villain, at least from the perspective of the band of warriors. This reinforces the sense that the game objective is not what it seems, and that success is, from Wander's perspective, most likely failure.

Interestingly, here the letterbox format fades, and the player is given control of Wander-as-colossus. As the warriors run towards the shrine at the back of the temple, the player takes on the role of the colossus, moving sluggishly and able to deal powerful blows to the warriors. Here there is again a slowing down of the interactive loop, as both movement and attack controls are very slow. There is also a role reversal, with the player able to experience what it would have been like for the colossi that they have just defeated to fight against a human opponent. This interactive sequence is brief, with the game shifting back to a cutscene to show the warriors ascending to the top of the temple and throwing the sword into a well, which creates a vortex and sucks Wander-as-colossus towards it, gradually stripping away all of its bulk and just leaving a Wander-sized shadow figure. At this point, the letterbox format fades, and the player is once again given control of the character, who is still being sucked inevitably towards the well. Once the character reaches the edge of the well, this final interactive sequence ends, and a cutscene shows the warriors galloping away from the temple and sealing the entrance to the lands surrounding the temple.

This sequence has made complex use of a combination of cutscenes, narrative reversals, and brief interactive sequences that again embody the "inability to act" and "success is failure." The non-interactive materials here, with their compositional and artistic motivations, are largely familiar.

Even the twist ending, something that has been foreshadowed throughout the game, while not necessarily expected, is not in any way unfamiliar. What stands out is the careful manipulation of gameplay to reinforce the narrative and thematic elements of the game. The mysterious, empty world, the absence of any opponents other than the sixteen colossi, the alteration of the core game mechanic, the selective removal and provision of control, and the twist to the game objective and eventual sense of failure despite what seems to have been a successful defeat of the sixteen colossi, work together to create an overall, dominant sense of loss of control. The player, much like Wander, has been used, in this case by the game designers, to create a particular aesthetic experience.

Beyond this, there is a final sequence in the game, shown during the credits, in which Mono wakes, just as Argo, who was presumed dead in the lead-up to the battle with the final colossus, limps into the temple. Together they walk to the well at the back of the temple, and find a newborn baby, with horns on its forehead. The warriors are shown leaving the lands of the temple, wondering whether Wander is alive and whether he will atone for his crimes. Mono carries the baby and, together with Argo, ascends to an idyllic garden on the top of the temple. This sequence seems to provide what could be seen as a successful ending, as Mono has been saved. There is also a possible transtextual element here, as it has been suggested by Fumito Ueda, the director of *Shadow of the Colossus*, that the baby is actually Ico, the main character from *Ico* (Team Ico 2001), an earlier game from the same developers (WIRED Staff 2006). However, these elements are not foregrounded. What most strongly characterizes the game is the way in which the player has been led to believe that they are in control, whereas in fact they have been manipulated by Dormin (and the game designers) throughout the game. This illusion of control forms the dominant and is the focus of the player's aesthetic experience. As the player works to make sense of this experience, they are likely to connect this to other experiences they have had of illusory control in other games that they have played (*Bioshock* (2K Boston 2007), for example), but also potentially in society more broadly, helping to give them a renewed perception of questions of agency and freedom in their lives.

The Dominant and the Aesthetic Experience

Stepping back from the discussion of specific games, we can consider what the range of devices showing a number of different motivations that we have seen in *Lim, Akrasia, Getting Over It with Bennett Foddy,* and *Shadow of the Colossus* can tell us about the formalist perspective on games, and about the aesthetic experience of games.

As we have seen, in all of these games, to varying degrees, there are a number of materials that work together to create the experience of the game. These materials can be seen as contributing to the composition, realism, transtextuality, artistic and ludic aspects of the game. In addition, certain materials tend to be foregrounded, often by undermining the player's expectations and creating a sense of strangeness. These materials can then be considered devices. These devices work both with and against the materials and each other. The resulting set of tensions creates the dominant, the overall characteristics of the work. In *Lim*, the visuals and suggestions of meaning behind these visuals (materials), together with the uncomfortable feedback associated with using the "blend" mechanic (a device) work together to convey what it feels like to blend in when you are not the same as the majority of a population. This description of the game, while touching on a possible interpretation, is more concerned with the formal structure of the game and *how* these materials and devices set up the potential for interpretation through the process of defamiliarization and refamiliarization. Similarly, we have seen how *Getting Over It with Bennett Foddy*, *Akrasia* and *Shadow of the Colossus* use specific compositional and ludic devices, together with a range of non-foregrounded materials, to evoke our aesthetic experience. It is from the player's encounter with the dominant that the aesthetic experience emerges. And part of this aesthetic experience involves the work required to grapple with and refamiliarize the defamiliarized elements of the game, in the context of play.

As we have discussed, defamiliarizing is what the work does to evoke our aesthetic experience. The aesthetic experience of a work is basically its "literaturnost," or its "literariness" (Jakobson 1921, in Erlich 1980). In line with Russian Formalism, this is essentially the same as the player's experience of the dominant, i.e., many devices may be defamiliarizing things (expectations/conventions around how games do things or what/how things mean), but it is in the overall experience of (the struggle between) these devices, i.e., the dominant, that our aesthetic experience lies. This is where and how the work can become meaningful for the player. Sense-making is the process and effort involved on the part of the player to connect the aesthetic experience of the dominant with the broader context of play so that this experience comes to act as a referent to something external to the work. It is important to emphasize that what makes the work meaningful is the result of the connections that the player has found between their aesthetic experience of the work and their lived experience outside of the work. This emerges from the aesthetic experience of the work by a particular player in a particular context, and the effort of the player to connect the aesthetic experience to their context through the process of defamiliarization and refamiliarization.

Conclusion

In this chapter, we have explored the ways in which the formalist perspective can be used to discuss the *aesthetic experience* that emerges from playing a game, focusing on the materials and devices, their motivations, and the ways in which they work to create the dominant. We have also discussed how the player's effort to make sense of the dominant in a particular context allows the player to make a meaningful connection between the work and their own lived experience, grounded in the formal elements of the game as object and the process of player's experience of that object, in a particular play context. In the next chapter, we will focus on ways in which to apply the formalist perspective as a *methodology* for analysing videogames.

References

2K Boston. 2007. "BioShock [Xbox360 Game]." 2K Games.

Aarseth, Espen, and Sebastian Möring. 2020. "The Game Itself? Towards a Hermeneutics of Computer Games." In *Proceedings of the 15th International Conference on the Foundations of Digital Games*, 1–8. New York: ACM.

Alber, Jan. 2013. "Unnatural Narratology: The Systematic Study of Anti-Mimeticism." *Literature Compass* 10 (5): 449–60.

Alber, Jan. 2014. "Unnatural Narrative." In *Handbook of Narratology*, edited by Peter Hühn, Jan Christoph Meister, John Pier, and Wolf Schmid, 887–95. New York: de Gruyter.

Alber, Jan, Stefan Iversen, Henrik Skov Nielsen, and Brian Richardson. 2010. "Unnatural Narratives, Unnatural Narratology: Beyond Mimetic Models." *Narrative* 18 (2): 113–36.

Anable, Aubrey. 2018. *Playing with Feelings: Video Games and Affect*. Minneapolis: University of Minnesota Press.

Bálint, Katalin, Frank Hakemulder, Moniek M. Kuijpers, Miruna M. Doicaru, and Ed S. Tan. 2016. "Reconceptualizing Foregrounding." *Scientific Study of Literature* 6 (2): 176–207.

Bopp, Julia Ayumi. 2020. "Aesthetic Emotions in Digital Games: The Appeal of Moving, Challenging, and Thought-Provoking Player Experiences." PhD Thesis, Aalto University.

Bordwell, David. 2013. *Narration in the Fiction Film*. New York: Routledge.

Calleja, Gordon. 2007. "Digital Games as Designed Experience: Reframing the Concept of Immersion." PhD Thesis, Victoria University of Wellington.

Carroll, Lewis. 1865. *Alice's Adventures in Wonderland*. London: MacMillan.

Chew, Evelyn, and Alex Mitchell. 2016. "'As Only a Game Can': Re-Creating Subjective Lived Experiences through Interactivity in Non-Fictional Video Games." In *Subjectivity across Media: Interdisciplinary and Transmedial Perspectives*, edited by Maike Sarah Reinerth and Jan Noël Thon, 214–32. New York: Routledge.

Chew, Evelyn, and Alex Mitchell. 2019. "Multimodality and Interactivity in 'Natively' Digital Life Stories." *POETICS TODAY* 40 (2): 319–53.

Clark, Naomi. 2017. "What Is Queerness in Games, Anyway?' In *Queer Game Studies*, edited by Bonnie Ruberg and Adrienne Shaw, 3–14. Minneapolis: University of Minnesota Press.

Ensslin, Astrid. 2015. "Video Games as Unnatural Narratives." *Diversity of Play*, 41–72.

Ermi, Laura, and Frans Mäyrä. 2005. "Fundamental Components of the Gameplay Experience: Analysing Immersion." In *Proceedings of the 2005 DiGRA International Conference: Changing Views – Worlds in Play*. Vancouver, BC, Canada: Digital Games Research Association.

Fialho, Olivia da Costa. 2007. "Foregrounding and Refamiliarization: Understanding Readers' Response to Literary Texts." *Language and Literature* 16 (2): 105–23.

Foddy, Bennett. 2017. "Getting Over It with Bennett Foddy [Microsoft Windows Game]." Bennet Foddy.

Foddy, Bennett. n.d. "Getting Over It with Bennett Foddy." Steam. Accessed June 24, 2021. https://store.steampowered.com/app/240720/Getting_Over_It_with_Bennett_Foddy/.

Folkerts, Jef. 2010. "Playing Games as an Art Experience: How Videogames Produce Meaning through Narrative and Play." *At the Interface / Probing the Boundaries* 69 (October): 99–117.

Games for Change. 2013. "Play | Lim." Games for Change. June 5, 2013. http://legacy.gamesforchange.org/play/lim/.

Heidegger, Martin. 1962. *Being and Time*. Translated by John Macquarrie and Edward Robinson. 1st English ed. Malden, MA: Blackwell.

Holbrook, Morris B., Robert W. Chestnut, Terence A. Oliva, and Eric A. Greenleaf. 1984. "Play as a Consumption Experience: The Roles of Emotions, Performance, and Personality in the Enjoyment of Games." *The Journal of Consumer Research* 11 (2): 728–39.

Hu, Junyao, and Tao Xi. 2019. "The Relationship between Game Elements and Player Emotions by Comparing Game Frameworks." In *HCI International 2019 – Late Breaking Papers*, edited by Constantine Stephanidis, 320–29. Cham: Springer International Publishing.

Isbister, Katherine. 2016. *How Games Move Us: Emotion by Design*. Cambridge, MA: MIT Press.

Iwatani, Toru. 1980. "Pac-Man [Arcade Game]." Bandai Namco Entertainment.

Jakobson, Roman. 1921. *Noveĭshaia Russkaia Poeziia*. Tip. "Politika."

Jayemanne, Darshana. 2017. *Performativity in Art, Literature, and Videogames*. Cham: Palgrave MacMillan.

Jazzuo. 2002. "Sexy Hiking [Microsoft Windows Game]." Jazzuo.

Juul, Jesper. 2009. "Fear of Failing? The Many Meanings of Difficulty in Video Games." In *The Video Game Theory Reader 2*, edited by Bernard Perron and Mark J. P. Wolf, 237–52. New York: Routledge.

Juul, Jesper. 2010. *A Casual Revolution: Reinventing Video Games and Their Players*. Cambridge, MA: MIT Press.

k, merritt. 2012. "Lim [Browser Game]." merritt k.

k, merritt. 2023. "LIM by Merritt k." Itch.Io. January 7, 2023. https://merrittk.itch.io/lim.

Keogh, Brendan. 2015. "A Play of Bodies: A Phenomenology of Videogame Experience." PhD Thesis, RMIT University.

Koschmann, Timothy, Kari Kuutti, and Larry Hickman. 1998. "The Concept of Breakdown in Heidegger, Leont'ev, and Dewey and Its Implications for Education." *Mind, Culture, and Activity* 5 (1): 25–41.

Kuijpers, Moniek. 2014. "Absorbing Stories: The Effects of Textual Devices on Absorption and Evaluative Responses." PhD Thesis, University Utrecht.

Leech, Geoffrey N., and Mick Short. 2007. *Style in Fiction: A Linguistic Introduction to English Fictional Prose*. 2nd ed. Harlow: Pearson Education.

Macgregor, Jody. 2018. "The Creators of Spelunky and Getting Over It Talk about Sexy Hiking and 'B-Games'." *PC Gamer*, April 11, 2018. https://www.pcgamer.com/the-creators-of-spelunky-and-getting-over-it-with-bennett-foddy-on-sexy-hiking-and-b-games/.

McGee, American. 2000. "American McGee's Alice [MacOS Game]." Electronic Arts.

McMillan, Edmund, and Tommy Refenes. 2010. "Super Meat Boy [MacOS Game]." Team Meat.

Miall, David S. 1992. "Response to Poetry: Studies of Language and Structure." In *Reader Response to Literature: The Empirical Dimension*, edited by Elaine F. Nardocchio, 153–70. The Hague: Mouton de Gruyter.

Miall, David S., and Don Kuiken. 1994. "Foregrounding, Defamiliarization, and Affect: Response to Literary Stories." *Poetics* 22 (5): 389–407.

Mitchell, Alex. 2014. "Defamiliarization and Poetic Interaction in Kentucky Route Zero." *Well Played: A Journal on Video Games, Value and Meaning* 3 (2): 161–78.

Mitchell, Alex. 2016. "Making the Familiar Unfamiliar: Techniques for Creating Poetic Gameplay." In *Proceedings of the First International Joint Conference of DiGRA and FDG 2016*. Dundee: Digital Games Research Association.

Mitchell, Alex, Liting Kway, Tiffany Neo, and Yuin Theng Sim. 2020. "A Preliminary Categorization of Techniques for Creating Poetic Gameplay." *Game Studies* 20 (2).

Mitchell, Alex, Yuin Theng Sim, and Liting Kway. 2017. "Making It Unfamiliar in the 'Right' Way: An Empirical Study of Poetic Gameplay." In *Proceedings of the 2017 DiGRA International Conference*. Melbourne, Australia: Digital Games Research Association.

Miyazaki, Hidetaka. 2011. "Dark Souls [Microsoft Windows Game]." Namco Bandai Games.

Mukařovskỳ, Jan, and Jan Chovanec. 2014. "Standard Language and Poetic Language." In *Chapters from the History of Czech Functional Linguistics*. Brno: Masarykova univerzita.

Myers, David. 2009. "The Video Game Aesthetic: Play as Form." In *The Video Game Theory Reader 2*, edited by Bernard Perron and Mark J. P. Wolf, 45–64. New York: Routledge.

Myers, David. 2010. *Play Redux: The Form of Computer Games*. Ann Arbor: University of Michigan Press.

Nacke, Lennart, and Anders Drachen. 2011. "Towards a Framework of Player Experience Research." In *Proceedings of the Second International Workshop on Evaluating Player Experience in Games at FDG*. Bordeaux.

Nishikawa, Trizette Zenji. 2005. "3Dゲームファンのための「ワンダと巨像」グラフィックス講座." *GAME Watch Impress*, December 7, 2005. https://game.watch.impress.co.jp/docs/20051207/3dwa.htm.

Piering, Julie. n.d. "Diogenes of Sinope." In *Internet Encyclopedia of Philosophy*. Accessed November 15, 2022. https://iep.utm.edu/diogenes-of-sinope/.

Pötzsch, Holger. 2017. "Playing Games with Shklovsky, Brecht, and Boal: Ostranenie, V-Effect, and Spect-Actors as Analytical Tools for Game Studies." *Game Studies* 17 (2).

Richardson, Brian. 2011. "What Is Unnatural Narrative Theory?" In *Unnatural Narratives, Unnatural Narratology*, edited by Jan Alber and Rüdiger Heinze, 23–40. Berlin: Walter de Gruyter.

Richardson, Brian. 2015. *Unnatural Narrative: Theory, History, and Practice*. Columbus, Ohio: The Ohio State University Press.

Ruberg, Bonnie. 2020. "Empathy and Its Alternatives: Deconstructing the Rhetoric of 'Empathy' in Video Games." *Communication, Culture & Critique* 13 (1): 54–71.

Sekhavat, Yoones A., Samad Roohi, Hesam Sakian Mohammadi, and Georgios N. Yannakakis. 2020. "Play with One's Feelings: A Study on Emotion Awareness for Player Experience." *IEEE Transactions on Games*, 1–10.

Shklovsky, Victor. 2012a. "Art as Technique." In *Russian Formalist Criticism: Four Essays*, edited by Lee T. Lemon and Marion J. Reis, 2nd ed., 21–34. Lincoln: University of Nebraska Press.

Sicart, Miguel. 2008. "Defining Game Mechanics." *Game Studies* 8 (2).

Soderman, Braxton. 2021. *Against Flow: Video Games and the Flowing Subject.* Cambridge, MA: MIT Press.

Spiegel, Amy Rose. 2017. "Merritt k on Changing Your Path." *The Creative Independent*, March 28, 2017. https://thecreativeindependent.com/people/merritt-k-on-changing-your-path/.

Swink, Steve. 2008. *Game Feel: A Game Designer's Guide to Virtual Sensation.* London: CRC Press.

Team Aha! 2008. "Akrasia [Microsoft Windows Game]." Singapore-MIT GAMBIT Game Lab.

Team Ico. 2001. "Ico [Playstation 2 Game]." Sony Computer Entertainment.

Team Ico. 2005. "Shadow of the Colossus [Playstation 2 Game]." Sony Computer Entertainment.

Thomashevsky, Boris. 2012. "Thematics." In *Russian Formalist Criticism: Four Essays*, edited by Lee T. Lemon and Marion J. Reis, 2nd ed., 55–77. Lincoln: University of Nebraska Press.

Thompson, Kristin. 1988. *Breaking the Glass Armor: Neoformalist Film Analysis.* Princeton, New Jersey: Princeton University Press.

Thomson-Jones, Katherine. 2008. "Formalism." In *The Routledge Companion to Philosophy and Film*, edited by Paisley Livingston and Carl Plantinga, 131–41. New York: Routledge.

Thorson, Maddy. 2018. "Celeste [MacOS Game]." Maddy Makes Games.

Tsur, Reuven. 2008. *Towards a Theory of Cognitive Poetics.* 2nd ed. Eastbourne: Sussex Academic Press.

Tynianov, Yuri. 2019. "On Literary Evolution (1927)." In *Permanent Evolution: Selected Essays on Literature, Theory and Film*, edited by Morse Ainsley and Philip Redko, 267–82. Boston, MA: Academic Studies Press.

Vught, Jasper van. 2016. "Neoformalist Game Analysis: A Methodological Exploration of Single-Player Game Violence." PhD Thesis, University of Waikato.

Winograd, Terry, and Fernando Flores. 1986. *Understanding Computers and Cognition: A New Foundation for Design.* Norwood, New Jersey: Alex Publishing.WIRED Staff. 2006. "Behind the Shadow: Fumito Ueda." *Wired*, 2006. https://www.wired.com/2006/03/behind-the-shadow-fumito-ueda/.

Wright, Peter C., Jayne Wallace, and Jack C. McCarthy. 2008. "Aesthetics and Experience-Centered Design." *ACM Transactions on Computer-Human Interaction (TOCHI)* 15 (4): 1–21.

4.   On Methodology

Abstract: In this chapter, we build on the concepts developed in chapters 2 and 3 and lay out a set of considerations for a formalist critic to keep in mind as they undertake a formalist analysis of a videogame. This involves first considering what intrigues the critic about the work, and then identifying the various materials and devices, to begin to understand the tensions within the work. This leads to an understanding of the dominant, or the central set of devices that organize the work. We also discuss the importance of the critic considering their own position as a player, and the need to account for the context of play. We end with practical suggestions for undertaking a formalist analysis.

Keywords: methodology, strategies for reading, context, formalist analysis

Videogame formalism is best considered as a flexible approach as opposed to a clear-cut method which explains a game according to the same set of procedures every time (see also (Thompson 1988, 3)). Nevertheless, this chapter delves into a set of considerations a formalist critic should have at different steps of the way to make any claims attributable to a systematic, rigorous and well documented analytical process. This includes examining the tensions within the work; identifying the "dominant," the central set of devices that organize the work; and considering how the dominant works against and foregrounds or defamiliarizes the automatized elements of the work. We discuss how the formalist game critic needs to carefully consider their position as a "player critic," and how to account for the context of play, both in terms of when the game was originally played and when it is being played by the critic. We then provide some practical suggestions for actually carrying out a textual analysis of a game from a formalist perspective. Finally, we briefly consider ways in which the textual analysis commonly used in formalist criticism can be complemented by qualitative observational studies of play grounded in a formalist approach to analysis. This chapter provides a bridge between the theoretical foundations laid out in chapters

Mitchell, A. and J. van Vught, *Videogame Formalism: On Form, Aesthetic Experience, and Methodology.* Amsterdam: Amsterdam University Press, 2024
DOI 10.5117/9789463720663_CH04

2 and 3, and the extended examples of the use of the formalist methodology in two case studies which will be provided in chapter 5.

Identifying the "Dominant"

First of all, we further develop the idea of the "dominant" as a way to heuristically but systematically focus the analysis on a set of devices due to their distinguishing relationship to a larger gaming landscape made up of genres and styles as well as the social, economic, political and technical circumstances of its creation. As mentioned in chapters 2 and 3, the dominant represents the idea that the various devices within a work come together to create the form of the work, and that certain devices will be foregrounded over others. As stated by Jakobson, Pomorska and Rudy, "[t]he dominant may be defined as the focusing component of a work of art: it rules, determines, and transforms the remaining components. It is the dominant which guarantees the integrity of the structure" (1987, 41).

Identifying the dominant provides the critic with a way to focus their analysis of a work. As Thompson (1988, 89) suggests, the critic asks what it is about the work that intrigues us, that sets it apart. The (Neo)formalist critic then uses this as a starting point, and proceeds to examine the tensions within the work, and how the dominant works with and against the automatized elements of the work. In the context of Neoformalist film criticism, van Vught explains:

> The neoformalist sets himself the task of analysing the devices that manipulate the film's material and focuses on those devices that the film foregrounds as the more important ones in cueing our responses. To understand how the film's devices function to cue responses, neoformalists assume the existence of an intelligent filmmaker and then consider the 'reasons' (motivations) that this filmmaker may have had to add these devices. However, neoformalists only need the suggestion of authorial intent because the presence of the different devices is eventually based on the work itself and the way the devices function in cueing our viewing responses (van Vught 2016, 32).

There are a number of interesting points that can be unpacked from this discussion of Neoformalist film criticism, to help us build an approach to formalist game criticism. The Neoformalist critic sees the work as a "constructed machine" put together by an intelligent artist/designer, with specific intentions (see chapter 2). The work is situated against a background or context, and the viewer brings this context and the related assumptions and expectations to the work (see below). The job of the critic is to look for the interconnected set of devices that potentially cue a player's defamiliarizing experience. This can be a daunting task, as Bizzocchi and Tanenbaum describe:

> Interactive digital media in general, and digital games in particular, are challenging to read due to their indeterminate and shifting natures, their size, and the inherent difficulties of engaging with the medium which are built into them (2011, 11).

Making the examination of the dominant the focus of investigation and using the critic's own initial sense of intrigue about the work based on their own aesthetic experience as a starting point, provides the critic with a means of grappling with this indeterminacy, scale, and challenge and making it tractable.

What Is It about the Work That Intrigues Us (as Players)?

Often, the problem faced by a critic is where to start when conducting a formalist analysis of a game. As we discussed in chapter 2, we view formalism as a poetics, and as such, argue that formalist game analysis starts from the player experience: what is it about the work that intrigues us as players? From there, the critic can start looking at the game, both as an object and as a process, and consider the following questions: what tensions are at work within the game? What is automatized and what is defamiliarized? While doing this, it is important to keep in mind the context of the game – where and when was it played or is it now being played? Who are the players? Who created it? And how might all of this impact the play experience?

Building from our initial intrigue with the experience of playing a game, we can then start to explore what it is about the game(play) that caught our attention. One point to make here is that we are starting from our interest in the game *as a player*, not as a critic. Of course, as a player critic it is hard not to be influenced by our academic and critical interests in a work, but it is important, if we want to eventually analyse a game not just from the perspective of what makes it stand out to an academic, to stay focused to some extent on our original reaction as a *player* (see below).

Example: What Is Intriguing about Paratopic?

We can see how to start our analysis from that initial intrigue by examining a specific example. *Paratopic* (Arbitrary Metric 2018b) is "an atmospheric retro-3D horror adventure through a cursed fever dream" (Arbitrary Metric 2018a). The review on game journalism website "RockPaperShotgun" begins by describing the game as "a short first-person horror game which draws ideas from *Thirty Flights of Loving* but takes them somewhere terrible, leading them down an alley and through an unmarked door into a world which looks a bit like ours but just isn't right." (O'Connor 2018) This description in itself is intriguing, highlighting as it does the potentially strange and unusual nature of the game, and was enough to convince me[1] (Alex) to pay US$5.49 to try it.

On starting the game, I was presented with a simple menu screen, listing "begin," "settings" and "exit" in a pixelated, jittery font, accompanied by a line-art graphic vaguely resembling an electricity pylon. After I chose "begin," the loading screen presented the message "Paratopic has no save feature, and must be completed in a single sitting." This is followed by the first scene, in which I appeared to be in a long, run-down corridor confronted by a slightly menacing-looking individual, and what appears to be dialogue: "You have an enemy, friendo," with a single option as a response: "1. What?" (see figure 4.1). As with the menu screen, the visuals are distorted and low-fidelity, the rendering is blocky, and the colour scheme is drab. The background music is menacing, and the dialogue is accompanied by a garbled "voice-over" that sounds like spoken dialogue run backwards. This combination of materials begins to set up certain expectations: the dark visuals and equally dark background music, the retro graphics and on-screen text, the distorted voice-over, all begin to suggest that this is a horror game. This, combined with the seemingly *in media res* nature of the start of the game, and the suggestion that "You have an enemy," piqued my interest as a player, and at the same time aroused my curiosity as a researcher.

As I began playing the game, I encountered a number of unexpected jump cuts, long scenes with apparently little or nothing to do (including several long driving sequences), and what appeared to be multiple changes in who the playable character was that were not clearly signalled to the player but only hinted at. After completing my first playthrough, it was unclear to me what exactly had happened, but I was curious both to try to

---

1   Note that when discussing specific play experiences, we will use the first person to acknowledge that this is the experience of one or the other of the authors.

Figure 4.1: The first encounter with an NPC in *Paratopic* (all screenshots of *Paratopic* are by the first author).

piece together the fragmented narrative, and to figure out what the game was doing and how it was doing it. My first impression was that the game seems to be a potentially interesting twist on the walking simulator genre, as the review mentioned above had said. In this sense, it was indeed a bit like *Thirty Flights of Loving* (Blendo Games 2012) but darker, both visually and in terms of the subject matter. My experience suggested that there was something interesting happening here, something which may be worth examining in more detail. At this point I had several questions in mind: how does the game create its unsettling atmosphere and ambiguity in terms of the narrative and character point of view? And how does this compare with, for example, *Thirty Flights of Loving*?

Here, much as in our extension of Mitchell's (2016) analysis of *Thirty Flights of Loving* in chapter 2, there is an intriguing mixture of conventions being suggested and then thwarted. Recall from chapter 2 that the dominant is the "formal principle that controls the work at every level, from the local to the global, foregrounding some devices and subordinating others" (Thompson 1988, 89). As with *Thirty Flights of Loving*, in *Paratopic* there is the initial suggestion that this is a first-person shooter, or perhaps more accurately a first-person horror game. As a horror game, there is less of an expectation of being able to take action than in a first-person shooter, as many horror games deliberately limit the player's ability to fight, as part of the process of creating a sense of powerlessness and horror in the face of the unknown (Perron 2018; Szabó 2022). However, at the same time, the long sequences of inaction with no apparent threat appearing, combined with the seemingly irrelevant and often interminable dialogue, gives the game more of the feeling of an episode of *Twin Peaks* (Lynch 1990) than a horror game.

All of these elements of the game are present throughout and seem to be guiding the ways in which the player's expectations are raised and then thwarted. There are in fact moments that can be seen as jump scares, and there is at least one scene where the player is, indeed, required to use the gun they are given early in the game, but this is overshadowed by the otherwise unfulfillment of the expectations a player would have for either a first-person shooter or a horror game. These observations, made initially in my role as a player and then considered in more detail as I switch to my role as a neoformalist critic, can be seen as the beginning of an identification of the materials and devices that will form the dominant, and provides me with a solid starting point for further analysis. In particular, as we will discuss below, the next step is not simply to list the materials and devices being used, and their accompanying motivations, but instead to begin to consider how those materials and devices are in tension, and how this tension creates the overall aesthetic experience of the game.

Example: What Is Intriguing about A Short Hike?
As a contrast to *Paratopic*, we will now provide a similar discussion of the game *A Short Hike* (Robinson-Yu 2019). The game is described by the developer as "a little exploration game about hiking up a mountain," in which you will

> hike, climb and soar through the peaceful mountainside landscapes of Hawk Peak Provincial Park. Follow the marked trails or explore the backcountry as you make your way to the summit. Along the way, meet other hikers, discover hidden treasures, and take in the world around you (Robinson-yu n.d.).

As with *Paratopic*, the game's visual design consists of interestingly compelling graphics (see figure 4.2), once again with a "retro" style but this time very colourful and inviting instead of dark and menacing. There seems to be an unusual combination of dialogue and a goal to be reached (get mobile phone reception) with what seems to be a walking (or more accurately a flying) simulator, suggesting there may be something worth exploring in terms of the game experience. All of this made me (Alex) curious as to how the game works, how it feels, and what/how it means.

The initial screen was deliberately low-resolution, with the title, "new game," "options" and "quit" text all rendered in a blocky font, framing an animated, low-resolution image of a car driving through a mountainous

Figure 4.2: *A Short Hike* (all screenshots of *A Short Hike* are by the first author).

forest at night. The menu controls consisted of up/down arrows and pressing "space" to select. After selecting "new game," I was shown a series of dialogue boxes, also rendered in a blocky font, accompanied by a chirpy pseudo-voiceover. Based on the names presented in the dialogue, this seemed to be a conversation between Claire, the main character, and someone who was driving her to a ferry terminal, from where she would be conveyed to the location of the game. This scene then faded out, and the main game screen faded in (see figure 4.2).

Upon starting to play, I quickly discovered simple movement controls (arrow keys), the ability to jump, fly (space bar), and interact with objects (the first scene contains a small beach with a "shell" which you can pick up), and some dialogue interaction. During the first scene, I tried to walk up to the top left of the screen, but the figure seated by the fire asked me where I was heading and whether I was "going to just wander off without saying hi to old Aunt May." This conversation introduces the central motivation for the player – the main character, Claire, is waiting for a call, but there is no cellphone reception. "Aunt May" suggests that there may be a signal at Hawk Peak, and provides directions: "just take White Coast Trail and head north at the fork." On further conversation you realize that the call Claire is waiting for is "the thing," which Aunt May tells you, "don't worry about it dear, I'm sure it will all work out fine. I think." Starting to walk towards "White Coast Trail," I encountered another bird, who reminded me that I can "hold space while running" to fly. This immediate and casual breaking of the fourth wall somehow didn't seem intrusive, which made me even more curious to investigate this game. On further exploration, I encountered a number of different characters, engaged in quirky dialogue, and got some additional hints as to how to play the game.

In *A Short Hike*, there seems to be an intriguing combination of a core game mechanic of walking/flying which can be augmented by object collection (golden feathers increase your ability to fly), spatial exploration of the island, and an overarching narrative related to Claire's goal. Each character that I encountered started to provide some background about the main character, Claire, and why they were concerned about getting a phone call. All of this was done against the background of a colourful visual design and soothing music. Much like *Paratopic*, but to very different effect, the many different elements of the game were working together to create an intriguing but much more welcoming experience. Unlike *Paratopic*, it was not so clear what was in tension here, as the various elements of the game seemed to be working well together. This itself encouraged me to further explore the game, although I wasn't immediately able to identify the dominant at this point in my analysis. To tease out the dominant in *A Short Hike* will require careful consideration of various play strategies, something we will address below. For now, we will focus on using *Paratopic* as an example of how to identify the tensions at work within a game, and to eventually identify the dominant. This is what we turn to next.

What Tensions Are at Work within the Game?

Having made an initial observation as to what is intriguing about a game, the next step is to explore the tensions at work within the game, and how certain tensions come together to form the dominant. As part of this process, the critic considers the player's expectations, and what is being foregrounded and used to create or cue an (aesthetic) response. The dominant often works against conventions to do this. It is important to remember, however, that "[a] list of devices does not equal the dominant, but if we can find a common structure of functions running through them all, we can assume that this structure forms or relates closely to the dominant" (Thompson 1988, 44). So, as a critic, what we will be doing is first looking for the materials in the work under consideration, together with their functions and the motivational categories for those functions. As we do this, we will be looking out for those materials that seem to be foregrounded, so as to become devices, and in the process consider the role that each of these devices is playing in the work, which will form their motivations. However, it is not enough to simply enumerate the various devices, functions and motivations we encounter, but how they work together to create the dominant.

Example: Identifying the Materials in Paratopic

To show how this can be done, we will begin by listing the various materials in *Paratopic* and their functions. Once we have this list, we can examine how these materials play off against each other, and which are foregrounded so as to become devices. But first, let's consider the materials.

The game's *visual style*[2] is created with low polygon models, a limited visual palette, and deliberately glitchy textures, particularly when it comes to the faces of the non-player characters. This is coupled with *atmospheric music* that changes as the scene changes. These materials can be seen as having largely compositional motivations, as they help to construct the storyworld, but they also have artistic motivations, as the unusual glitchy visuals and the atmospheric music emphasize the game's abstract form and help to create a certain unease in the player. This also raises expectations that this is a mysterious narrative, and possibly a horror game.

There are several materials that can be considered part of the game's narrative structure. This includes the starting of the game *in media res*, with no indication of who the playable character is or what is happening. This creates a sense of mystery and confusion in the player, supported by the frequent use of *jump cuts* with no transitions between scenes, and the accompanying *non-chronological sequencing* of scenes. The game's *pacing* is generally very slow, with long sequences where nothing happens followed by sudden jump cuts with no apparent triggers. This is particularly evident in three scenes where the player is driving a car for several minutes with nothing else to do, followed by seemingly unrelated scenes. These materials all help to build up the narrative, so can be considered to have a compositional motivation. However, similar to *Thirty Flights of Loving*, the use of non-chronological sequencing and unexpected jump cuts can also be considered to have artistic motivations, as they help to create the overall artistic shape of the game. Also, like *Thirty Flights of Loving*, the jump cuts are sometimes accompanied by an unsignalled change in the playable character, suggesting there may also be a ludic motivation at work here. It is worth noting that these materials both set up the narrative structure and serve to make it difficult for the player to actually make sense of the narrative. This tension foregrounds these materials, suggesting that they are possible candidates for devices.

---

2   For clarity, we will indicate the materials in *italics*.

Figure 4.3: Seemingly meaningless dialogue in *Paratopic*.

The game incorporates a tree-based branching *dialogue system*, where the player is shown some dialogue spoken by a non-player character, and then is given between 1 and 3 options for responses. These dialogue sequences are often very long, and it is frequently unclear whether the player has sufficient information to make a choice (see figure 4.3). It is also not clear how much impact the dialogue has on the subsequent story events. For example, there is one scene early in the game where the player is approached by the playable character's neighbour, who repeatedly asks the player to give her a video tape. At this point the player can choose to do so or not. While there is a local impact of this choice – either the neighbour goes away in frustration, or you give her a tape, which she goes to watch, with dire consequences for her – but there is no apparent impact on the overall game narrative. The dialogue system can be seen as having a compositional motivation, as it helps to structure the narrative. However, it may also be considered to have a (possible) ludic motivation, as it may or may not impact the player's movement through the game. This doubt as to whether the choices the player makes actually have an impact, coupled with the odd nature of some of the conversation, and the lack of knowledge on the player's part as to how to make some of these choices, also suggests an artistic motivation. The tension between the player's expectations that the dialogue choices will impact the game, and the uncertainty as to whether they actually do have an impact, foregrounds this material, suggesting it is a possible device.

The various *settings* in the game, such as the diner, apartment, and forest, clearly reference the real world (although in a somewhat distorted fashion), clearly indicating that these materials have a realistic motivation.

In addition, there are a number of *very detailed interactions* that the player is required to perform at several points in the game. For example, in the second scene in the game, the player needs to load bullets, one-by-one, into a gun, which is not used until much later in the game. Similar sequences include waiting for the lift, driving the car, and walking through the forest and taking photos. Each of these tend to take up a long time, and do not seem to serve any gameplay purpose, suggesting there are also artistic motivations at work. As these materials are all related to what the player is doing to make their way through the game, there is a ludic motivation.

Finally, there may be a transtextual motivation at work here. *Thirty Flights of Loving* similarly requires the player to pick up a gun and ammunition, which is only used much later in the game, for example. There are also a number of other games that include "tedious" realistic sequences, such as *Heavy Rain* (Quantic Dream 2010), *Red Dead Redemption 2* (Rockstar Studios 2019), and as an extreme case, the infamous Desert Bus sequence in the unreleased game *Penn & Teller's Smoke and Mirrors* (Imagineering unreleased), later remade as *Desert Bus VR* (Dinosaur Games 2017), which may or may not be referenced by these sequences in *Paratopic*. It is worth noting that these long gameplay sequences contribute to the slow pacing mentioned above. In addition, there are also similarities between the use of the term "friendo" and the strange conversations in the gas station in *Paratopic*, and the gas station scene in the film *No Country for Old Men* (Cohen 2008), where the character Anton Chigurh refers to the gas station attendant as "friendo" and the ensuing conversation is similarly surreal.

Finally, there are a number of elements of the game that are external to the game's storyworld, but have an impact on the play experience, and therefore should be considered materials. These include the *lack of a save function* and the *inability to pause* the game, which force the player to complete the game in a single session, as the game explicitly communicates to the player when the game is started (see figure 4.4). These can be seen as having both a ludic motivation, as they impact how the player plays the game, and an artistic motivation, as they contribute to the overall form of the game and the feeling of playing it.

In the above paragraphs, we have gone through the elements in the game, and identified those that can be considered the materials that make up the game, by virtue of their specific motivations within the game. In the process, we have also indicated where some of these can possibly be considered *devices*, meaning they are foregrounded and stand out from the other materials in some way. However, as the Thompson quote above mentions, a list of devices on its own is not the dominant. What needs to

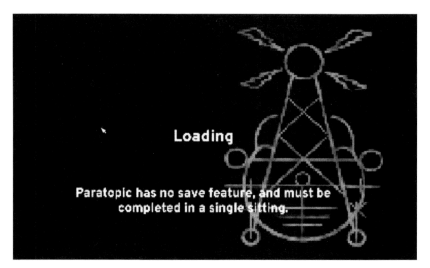

Figure 4.4: *Paratopic* telling the player that there is no save feature, so the game must be completed in one sitting.

be identified is the answers to the following questions: How do the various materials/devices relate to each other? How do they relate to the expectations and conventions that the player brings to the game? Where do they work against each other? How do they trigger a response in the player? And what purpose does that response serve? As can be seen in the above discussion, even in the process of identifying materials and their motivations it is difficult not to already begin to notice how they are working together, and against, each other.

Example: Examining the Tensions at Work in Paratopic
A number of the materials listed above can be seen as devices, meaning (as we will discuss further below) they are no longer automatized, and instead the player's attention is drawn to them through a process of defamiliarization. Key among these are the *dialogue*, the *pacing*, and the *non-chronological sequencing* of the scenes. The dialogue serves to continually suggest some underlying narrative, and provides some indication of what the player's objective might be: to deliver the tapes? To clean up any trace of an unspecified incident? This creates both a sense of purpose and one of confusion, as the player is constantly trying to adjust their understanding of what is happening in the game, where they are, when they are, and even who they are. Are there conflicting objectives? Is the player playing one or several different characters? The non-chronological sequencing of the scenes works together with the dialogue, making it difficult for the player to

piece together the narrative. The lack of indications as to when a jump cut is going to happen, and lack of cues to help the player orient themselves after a jump cut, make it difficult at times to figure out which of several possible characters the player is controlling at a given moment. This creates a sense of expectation that something will happen sometime soon, increased by the atmospheric music and sound effects. This is in tension with the pacing, which can be very slow and even frustrating at times. The overall feeling is one of anticipation, but there is rarely any follow-through.

There is a specific point at which something *does* happen, late in the game, with the last few scenes seeming to follow directly from certain earlier scenes: after a final driving sequence and a conversation with the gas station attendant, in which the attendant implies that someone is travelling with you (you are alone), the game cuts back to what is possibly a continuation of the earlier scene in the diner where one character (the assassin) has been tasked to clean things up. In this scene you finally get to shoot the gun, killing a man in the back room of the diner and then watching a video tape. Interestingly, this scene then repeats until you choose a specific tape, after which it cuts back to (presumably) a continuation of the first scene, where the border guard who watched one of your tapes stumbles out of the back room, with his head replaced with a television. This then cuts (forward?) to the final sequence, where the assassin comes across the body of the photographer in the forest, and calls emergency services. The game ends with the assassin hanging up, and the final scene shown underneath the closing credits.

All of this builds up and further highlights the tension between the player's expectation of something happening and nothing happening, and between uncovering what is happening in the game when something finally does happen and yet remaining confused as to how the various scenes fit together even when the game has come to an end.

What Is Automatized and What Is Defamiliarized?

Following on from the above, once you have identified the materials in the game, and examined the tensions between those materials, it is important to begin to look for what is automatized (not noticed, conventionalized, or familiar) and what it is that is working against that (foregrounded or defamiliarized) and leading to the player's aesthetic response, or the intriguing reaction that initially suggested that the game was worth examining critically. An important point to keep in mind here, which we will return to in the next section, is that what is automatized is largely dependent on the context of play, as those materials that follow conventions are likely to go unnoticed. What is conventionalized can change over time, suggesting that in the moment when the critic is playing the game, conventions may not be the same as when the game was first developed and released. This can impact how the game is analysed. We will first discuss the process of identifying what is automatized and what is defamiliarized, and then return to and complicate this process in the next section, when we talk about the importance of context.

As you will have noticed, we have already started to suggest which of the materials in our example might be considered devices. This is hard to avoid, as the process of noticing what is intriguing about a game, and then looking for tensions, is likely to make it increasingly clear which of those materials does not seem to be acting in line with our expectations as a player. To distinguish between material and device, the critic should carefully think about how a given material fits into the overall structure of the game, how it relates with other materials in the web of interactions that form the player's experience, and whether the material stands out, or is foregrounded, in a manner that seems to be running counter to their expectations as a player. This makes the material a strong candidate for being a device.

Once the critic has a good sense for the devices at work in the game, how those devices and the various materials work together and are in tension, and which devices seem to dominate and relate to the overall aesthetic experience, it should start to become clear what the nature of that aesthetic experience is. This is what forms the dominant.

Example: What Is Automatized and What Is Foregrounded in Paratopic?
Returning to the example of *Paratopic*, we can start to identify which of the various materials discussed above can be considered automatized, and which are foregrounded or defamiliarized. As a "walking simulator," materials such as the movement controls, spatial navigation (to a certain extent), and the player's expectations for the type of story that is being told, based on the visuals and atmospheric audio, seem to be following conventions. It is where these conventions are undermined, such as the player's expectation for some progression in the narrative, and the ability to explore the game space and dialogue trees so as to start to form a coherent narrative in which something "happens," that the game becomes interestingly defamiliarizing. Instead of allowing the player to make sense of the ways in which the various incidents fit together into an overall narrative, the game (particularly the dialogue and repetitive interactions such as driving) provides lots of interesting but seemingly incidental details which

serve to build up the atmosphere, but that may or may not actually come together to create a coherent narrative.

What is interesting here is that the automatized, unnoticed materials such as navigation, the "horror" theme, and the overall atmosphere are working together with those materials that are foregrounded to create the overall experience. Without the deliberate use of low-resolution, retro visuals, a strongly atmospheric audio track, the horror theme, and the framing of the experience as a first-person walking simulator, the player would not be primed to try to find out what is happening, and to determine what the overall narrative is. It is against this backdrop that the abrupt cuts, meandering and seemingly irrelevant dialogue, and long, tedious stretches of inaction while driving and while exploring the forest break the player's expectations and give the game an additional "strangeness."

All of this creates the feeling that the game is a combination of a walking simulator and a horror game, but one in which the sequence of events is scrambled, and there seems to be almost, but not quite, enough information to piece the narrative together. The dialogue system, non-chronological sequencing, change in playable character, and slow pacing replaced by a sudden flurry of events and a sudden ending lacking in resolution, all work together and are in tension with each other, suggesting that this is where the analysis of the game should focus. This is the *dominant*.

Taking on the Role of the "Player Critic"

A key point to consider here is the notion of the *player critic*, and what stance you should take as a critic when carrying out an analysis of a game, in particular the importance of being aware of what you bring to the analysis and how a player, as opposed to an academic, would play the game. In line with our argument in chapter 2 that formalism can be seen as a poetics, the focus should be on playing. Play, play, and play again, looking at first at your overall reaction to the game, and then starting to consider what you are drawn to, what stands out, what it is about the work that intrigues you (as a player). However, you are not simply playing the game, you are playing it to analyse it, so you need to actively consider your role as a critic, in this case a player critic. In this section, we outline various considerations about the role of the player critic in terms of instantiating a set of gameplay devices and "reading" or analysing these devices within a specific context.

Our approach, which involves a close reading or close playing of a videogame, is essentially a form of textual analysis. According to Carr, textual analysis "depends on fragmentation" and involves "improvisation, iteration and adaptation" (2019, 717). While Carr is very much looking at the *meaning* of a game as a text, particularly in terms of representation, their reflections on the challenges of a close playing approach to analysis are very relevant to our discussion. Much of Carr's (2019) approach focuses on what they refer to as "fragmentation," or the identification through play of particular "fragments" of the game, those subsets of the overall experience that can be focused on for analysis. An important point here is the need to be aware of the fact that "[g]ames offer play, replay, and repetition with degrees of variation" (2019, 714), meaning it is impossible to ever capture for analysis the entirety of a game (unless it is a very short "game of progression" (Juul 2005) that only affords limited options for playthroughs). As mentioned in chapter 1, Carr suggests that one way to deal with this complexity and to give the critic a means of focusing their attention is to consider the game through three different "lenses": structural, textual, and intertextual.

Bizzocchi and Tanenbaum (2011) raise a similar issue, that of games' "indeterminate and shifting natures, their size, and the inherent difficulties of engaging with the medium which are built into them" (2011, 272). Here we encounter the problem of a game potentially being encountered differently on different playthroughs, and the need to potentially play a game many times to even begin to encounter "all" of the game. One suggestion they provide for dealing with the complexity of the game experience is to choose specific "analytical lenses" that can focus the critic's attention on aspects of the game experience that are relevant to the current analysis. They see Carr's three lenses as examples of this type of an approach, but further suggest that these lenses can be selected specifically for the purposes of the analysis being undertaken. It could be argued that our formalist approach to game analysis represents one specific set of lenses, that of the dominant and the materials that make up the videogame. By choosing to take on a formalist perspective, the critic is looking specifically at the materials within the game, which of those materials are automatized and which are foregrounded, what tensions are at work, and what seems to be standing out as the dominant. This allows the critic to deal more manageably with what might otherwise be an overwhelming amount of information. It also provides a flexible focus, one that is both rigorous and grounded in a particular methodological stance, but at the same time is iterative, and can be adapted to the critic's developing understanding of the videogame under investigation.

In addition, Bizzocchi and Tanenbaum raise the problem of the mechanical difficulty involved in actually playing the game successfully. There is the initial problem that a critic may not be able to successfully play the game. Beyond that, as the player critic repeatedly plays a game as part of the process of analysis, they will inevitably become better at playing the game. As result, as Bizzocchi and Tanenbaum argue, "[r]eadings of games must contend with the changing skill level of a player over time" (2011, 275). There is also the problem that repeated play of the type involved in game analysis "has an inherent danger of distancing the player from the pleasures of the game" (2011, 275). To address this, they suggest that the player critic adopt a dual role, that of the critic and that of the naive player. They also acknowledge that this "imagined naive player" may not capture all possible play experiences, suggesting that it can be complemented with deliberate formation of specific player types. This is very similar to van Vught and Glas's (2018) notion of taking on specific strategies for play, which we will discuss in more detail below.

Another point to raise here is that you also need to be careful not to focus too exclusively on what only a critic might find interesting. Aarseth (2014) describes a tension between the "real, historical player" and the "implied player," roughly analogous to a social sciences versus a humanities approach to studying games. Aarseth further describes implied play as encompassing three levels: the implied player (as suggested by what the game allows or expects in terms of behaviour), the interface addressee (the concrete mechanisms that allow input and output to the game), and the avatar/vehicle (the representation of the player in the game, if any). This model provides a structure whereby the critic can "understand the expectations laid down by the game for the player" (2014, 132). It does not, however, provide access to "actual" players, as players "do unexpected things, often just because these actions are not explicitly forbidden" (2014, 132). These types of play, which Aarseth calls "transgressive play," are part of the potential experience of the game, and are likely to be of relevance, if not central importance, to the analysis of a game.

At the same time, it is important to avoid being too focused on these outlying behaviours. As Tyack and Mekler highlight, there is a tendency for researchers to emphasize "extra-ordinary experiences" (2021), possibly to the exclusion of the ordinary player experience. As they argue, much of the research on games, both in game studies and related areas such as human-computer interaction, begins from the notion of games leading to an "optimal experience," or "flow" (Csikszentmihályi 1990). Even work that critiques this strong focus on flow and optimal experience, such as Bopp et al., still begins from a focus on experiences that involve "both strong emotion and memorability" (Bopp, Mekler, and Opwis 2016). While much of this critique is focused on quantitative approaches to studying the player experience, it is worth keeping this in mind as this mirrors the possible tension between the implied player and transgressive play. This is particularly important as we are arguing that the formalist critic both starts from their own aesthetic experience and is looking for elements of the game that are foregrounded, which are, by definition, those elements that break with expectations, and thus are not "ordinary." What this suggests is that, as we have discussed earlier in this chapter, it is even more important that the player critic not limit themselves to the game as an object or a process, but also attends to the context, part of which will involve being aware of what the "ordinary" player experience might entail. We will return to this later in this chapter.

Strategies for "Reading"

The above discussion highlights the complexity of forming a strategy for reading a game. As such, we follow van Vught and Glas (2018) and argue for an instrumental or implied playing strategy which allows the critic to stay within the material architecture of the game while still taking into account the assemblage of socio-cultural contexts the game and the player exist in. According to van Vught and Glas, there are several ways to approach playing a game as a critic. An important point they highlight is that play is an iterative process, one in which each action the player takes is informed by the understanding they have developed of the game as the result of previous actions. As Wardrip-Fruin describes, this can be seen as a process of improvisation (2009) in which the player combines their goals and plans with their context and personal experience when determining what action to take next.

This suggests that, as the player critic plays a game, they need to attend to their moment-by-moment decisions and consider "what would the player do?" Van Vught and Glas suggest two ways of framing this choice. The first, much like Aarseth's implied player, follows "what the game's formal components are encouraging us to do, so that we may progress through the game and achieve its goals" (2018). They refer to this as "instrumental play" and consider it to be aligned with the perspective of *games as object*. The idea of an instrumental play approach is drawn from Iser (1980), who introduced the notion of the "implied reader" that has formed the basis for Aarseth's use of the term "implied player" as discussed above. Here, the idea is that the player will follow the goals and strategies suggested by the structure of the game. As van Vught and Glas highlight, this can be seen as a way to avoid the intractableness of trying to play every possible variation of a game. van Vught and Glas describe three heuristics that the player critic can use to determine what actions to take so as to enact instrumental play: the gameplay condition, rational play, and cooperative play. We argue that this is the most appropriate way to at least begin a close reading of a game.

In contrast, they suggest that it is also possible to more fully embrace play in the broader sense, embracing what Salen and Zimmerman describe as "free movement within a more rigid structure" (2004, 305). Here, the critic is exploring the range of possibilities enabled by the game, much like what Aarseth describes as transgressive play. Van Vught and Glas call this "free play." Taking a free play approach to playing a game involves a focus more on *games as process*, as it allows the player critic to go beyond the ways that the game is suggesting to the player that it *should* be played, and instead play the game in the many ways that it *can possibly* be played. As van Vught and Glas suggest, here the player critic is "not just following but exploring, pushing, bending, deviating from and transgressing the intended playing paths – not just 'playing' but 'gaming' a game" (2018). The idea is to adopt what Aarseth (2014) calls transgressive play, exploring the boundaries of what the game allows, not just what it encourages or suggests as being appropriate for play. Van Vught and Glas provide three suggested ways of approaching free play: exploration, transgressive play, and "going native." As we will discuss below, care needs to be taken not to lose sight of the game as object when engaging in free play – for a formalist analysis, the game as process is still grounded in the game's formal elements and pushing beyond those formal elements opens up the possibility of defamiliarizing the play experience based on the critic's own choices, rather than on the basis of the game's inherent qualities. We will argue that some forms of free play, such as van Vught and Glas's transgressive play, may not be appropriate for a formalist analysis. Their other two forms of free play, exploration and "going native," however, do help to complement the more instrumental approaches to play.

We will now examine each of these approaches in detail, providing examples of how the critic might go about making use of each of these types of play during the process of undertaking a formalist analysis of a videogame, and pointing out possible shortcomings for the use of transgressive play.

Playing for *Continuation* and Playing to *Win*

The gameplay condition, a term coined by Leino (2010), is the idea that there are certain successful actions that a game requires for play to continue. By using this as a way to decide what to do next, the player critic is basically playing to keep playing. We can consider this to be *playing for continuation*. Interestingly, this can lead to a very broad set of possible play experiences, depending on the type of game being analysed. For a very linear game, the critic may be able to narrow down their path through the game by using this strategy, but for a more open game it may be insufficient to enable the critic to determine what to do next.

To go beyond this, van Vught and Glas turn to Smith's (2006) notion of rational play. Smith argues that success, for a rational player, is not just continuing to play, but rather making progress towards the game's goals. This shifts the focus from the moment-to-moment choices to a view of how those choices impact the overall state of the game and the player's ability to move towards a winning condition. Here, play is informed by a desire to optimize your chance of achieving the game goals. This can be seen as *playing to win*. In a game that involves a number of possible paths for continuation, taking a rational play perspective helps the critic to consider how the game's formal elements work together to suggest ways that the player should play the game.

As an example of taking a rational play approach to instrumental play, consider Sharp's (2010) analysis of *Drop7* (Lantz 2009). *Drop7* is an abstract videogame, played on a mobile phone, in which the play space consists of a 7x7 grid. Players drop number discs into columns, with the immediate goal of avoiding filling up a column (at which point the game is over), and the longer-term game objective of getting a high score by surviving as long as possible and clearing as many discs as possible. Sharp conducts a close reading of this game, describing in detail how the various game elements work together to create a particular aesthetic experience, that of "sustaining the focus necessary to keep the advancing rows of gray discs at bay" (2010, 55). Sharp describes himself as a "practitioner," someone who is "able to find more in the game than one might suspect an iPhone game could provide" (2010, 51). The way that Sharp describes his gameplay, and the strategies he uses to play the game, clearly go beyond what could be considered play informed by the gameplay condition. Instead, he is (at least) taking the approach of rational play. This can be seen in the following passage, where he describes a specific situation in the game and the possible choices he is facing as a player:

> I have a 3 disc to place and a number of possibilities to consider: the rightmost column would convert the broken gray disc to a number while breaking the 3; atop the second column from the right would clear the three 6 discs, and then trigger a chain by having the 3 disc land as the

third in that row and column; on the third column from the right would clear the two 5 discs, and then create a threedisc row chain; dropping it on the fourth column from the right would simply create a three in a row; placing it on the second column from the left would create a break when the next row is added; or finally, dropping it on the leftmost column would prepare the two 6 discs to break when the next row advances. Each of these choices has a consequence in that moment, but also for the disc drops to come (Sharp 2010, 55).

For a player making decisions based purely on the ability to continue to play, all of these actions would be valid. The critic who limits themselves to this stance will get some insight into how the game works but is not likely to go beyond that. Although Sharp argues that *Drop7* is very much about playing in-the-moment, the type of thinking shown in the above passage is not simply about continuation, but about playing well, about moving forwards, about achieving the game's goals. He is playing to win. It is also worth considering the type of highly experienced play that is involved here – as Sharp says, he considers himself a "practitioner." We will return to this below when we discuss playing as an expert.

Similarly, if we consider our earlier example of *A Short Hike*, we can compare adopting a play strategy based on the gameplay condition with one based on rational play. In *A Short Hike*, the player's moment-to-moment decisions involve movement around the island, choices such as whether to interact with objects and non-player characters, and choices such as how to move – walk, run, jump, climb, or fly. The larger gameplay loop involves deciding whether and how to collect "golden feathers," which in turn increases the length of time that the player's character can climb or fly. While there is an overall goal, that of reaching the "peak" to receive a call on the player character's mobile phone, there is no time limit for achieving this, and no "losing" condition. Approached purely from the perspective of the gameplay condition, there is no possible move that would lead to the game *not* continuing. Given this, it becomes meaningless for the critic to use this strategy to determine how to play, as every next action is a valid action. Initially playing for continuation does, however, help the critic to become aware of this – there is no losing condition, suggesting that any expectation the player might have that they can fail at the overall game is undermined.

To go beyond this, though, the critic is likely to have to adopt a play strategy based on rational play. This enables the critic to start to consider whether each action they take will lead them to be more likely to reach the peak, most likely through optimization of the collection of golden feathers.

Playing this way, I (Alex) was able to discover a number of different ways to collect golden feathers – they are scattered around the island, often in locations that are not immediately accessible until you already have a certain number of feathers, but they can also, for example, be bought from the student who is hanging around at the entrance to the "peak" area of the island. The student apparently had collected a large number of feathers and was trying to make money to pay for his tuition by selling the feathers at a high price. Having failed a few times to scale the peak with a smaller number of feathers, and not being able to find any more "in the wild," I eventually gave in and bought several feathers from the student. By taking this *playing to win* approach, I was able to see beyond the basic gameplay loop and begin to understand how other elements of the game, such as the currency system and the non-player characters, also factored into the gameplay experience.

However, I was still focused on taking actions to *win*, whereas there were many other actions I could take, such as fishing or exploring the outlying islands, which didn't seem to contribute to my ability to achieve the game objective, but would likely provide further insight into how the game creates meaning. To explore these, I would need to take on a slightly different play strategy, as will be discussed below.

Playing the *Right Way*

In addition to the two forms of instrumental play described above, van Vught and Glas also draw from van Vught's (2016) idea of the cooperative player as a way to go beyond the purely ludic aspects of a game, and include other forms of "success" such as "constructing a narrative, or being able to see connections to other artworks or the world beyond the game" (2018, 215–16). They call this cooperative play, in which play is based on what seems most appropriate based on the functioning of the game's formal components. This can be seen as *playing the right way*, in which the player critic attends to the cues provided by the game's formal elements and uses this to make decisions as to what to do next based on an overall sense of how the game is intended to be played. This approach can be thought of as a way to include not only those materials with ludic motivations, but also those with non-ludic motivations, namely the compositional, realistic, transtextual, and artistic motivations.

As van Vught and Glas argue, this also connects the player critic's analysis to the broader context, as any decisions the critic makes in terms of the next action to take in the game must necessarily be done with some awareness

Figure 4.5: The framing story and revelation of the reason for Claire's trip to the island in *A Short Hike*.

of the context of play. This includes play *in time*, so considering how the implied cooperative player would be informed by other games they could have played (or known about) when the game was released, and *over time*, including an awareness of ever-shifting game conventions both of which might influence the implied player's decisions as they move through the game and encounter the various materials in the game. (We return to the issue of context in more detail below). In addition to informing the player critic's choices as to what actions to take, this strategy will also help the critic to think about and make decisions regarding which materials to see as automatized and which as foregrounded, and how to make sense of the various tensions at work within the game.

Returning again to our example *A Short Hike*, approaching this from the perspective of cooperative play allowed me (Alex) to broaden my perspective when playing the game. Rather than focusing exclusively on attaining the overall goal of reaching the peak, I considered the other elements of the game, and how they work together with the core gameplay loop and ludic motivations to create the overall experience of the game. In particular, while it is not the main focus of the experience, there is a narrative framing to the game, one that involves the call that the main character, Claire, is waiting to receive. Paying close attention to the opening sequence (see figure 4.5 image 1), in which Claire seems to be glad to get away from the city, combined with the apparent lack of urgency in her quest to get to the top of the peak, I started to consider that perhaps this was actually a way of setting up the player to appreciate the revelation that comes with the actual phone call.

Once Claire reaches the peak (see figure 4.5 images 2 and 3), she receives a call from her mom, who has just undergone surgery. Claire is clearly worried about the outcome of the surgery, suggesting that the desire to get away, and the seeming lack of urgency, actually reflects an attempt to avoid facing her fears about her mom's operation. After the phone call, Claire can catch an updraft from the hot spring just below the peak, and the player is treated to a long, soaring flight in which they can see all of the areas they have explored, mirroring Claire's relief at receiving her mom's call. This tension and relief is reinforced through the dialogue with Claire's aunt, back at the initial location in the game (see figure 4.5 image 4), where it becomes clear that Claire was very worried. Playing with an awareness of these various motivations, and how they encourage the implied player to engage with the game, enables the critic to uncover the close interdependency between the compositional, realistic and artistic motivations, and their connection with the ludic motivations. By *playing the right way*, the critic is deliberately and consciously attending is what the game is suggesting is the "right way" to play: to make the short hike into a long one. To digress. To stall for time. All in fear of being confronted with negative news about the outcome of Clair's Mom's operation. By shifting play strategies, I also was able to start to get a clearer sense of what the dominant might be in *A Short Hike* – the tension between trying to get to the peak and the lack of urgency to get to the peak, as manifest in the tension between encouraging the player to engage with the main game loop and at the same time there being an absence of any penalty for not engaging with the main game loop. In fact, as will be discussed below, this became even clearer when I engaged in yet another approach, that of playing playfully.

Playing *Playfully*

The forms of play we have discussed so far are what van Vught and Glas consider to be instrumental play. Going beyond this, they also suggest the possibility of the critic engaging in free play. The first form of free play, exploration, can involve trying out alternative ways of progressing in the game, or focusing on aspects of the game that are available based on the design of the game, but may not be suggested as the clearest way forward. As van Vught and Glas explain, "explorative play yields different results

Figure 4.6: Exploring various additional activities in *A Short Hike*.

from simply following intended or dominant paths through a game" (2018, 221). This can be seen as *playing playfully*, exploring the space of gameplay possibilities while not going as far in terms of pushing the boundaries as will be seen in transgressive play.

As an example of exploration, or playing playfully, there are many ways in which the player can approach playing *A Short Hike* that have no direct connection to the game's goals or the ways it suggests that the game should be played. There are a number of non-player characters around the island, many of whom will share their stories with Claire, and possibly ask for help with various tasks. This is an aspect of the game that I (Alex) paid little attention to when taking a rational and cooperative approach to play. However, when going back and playing further with more of an exploratory stance, I spent time trying these "side quests" (see figure 4.6, image 1). I also took time to enjoy the scenery (and the visual elements of the game that conveyed this scenery) (see figure 4.6, image 2). Both of these aspects of the play experience helped me to appreciate how the design of the game elements worked together to create the overall game aesthetic, that of the tension between the main character, Claire, simultaneously wanting to go on a short hike, but to make it something more like a long hike. This also fed into my understanding of the dominant, which is manifest as the tension between the core game loop and the lack of penalty for not engaging with the core game loop and is supported by the full range of other materials and devices within the game.

An important point to note here is that while I was exploring possible ways of playing the game that I had not tried when taking a rational or cooperative stance, I was still considering what the game elements were suggesting to me and combining this with my expectations as a player to decide what to do next. This is an attempt to balance the game as object and the game as process. It also inevitably requires some consideration of the context of play, as we will discuss further below.

Problematic Positions: Playing as an *Expert* and Playing *against the Grain*

Van Vught and Glas identify "going native" as either a potential play strategy, or perhaps the result of intensive, repeated study of a game. At a certain point, the player critic is likely to end up *playing as an expert*. Having developed an in-depth understanding of the game, the critic is able (or at least feels that they are able) to know what it would be like to play a game even without playing the game. This can be seen in Sharp's discussion of *Drop7* above. While he is playing to win, the description of his thought processes that we quoted earlier clearly show that he is playing through possible moves, in much the same way that an expert chess player will consider their current position in the game and the consequences of their potential moves from that position. For the critic, the danger here is that they may stop actually playing the game, and instead imagine possible paths through the text. This is problematic unless you are confident that your imaginings will exactly match how a game's formal elements will respond at any given time. This is not likely going to be the case, given the complexity of most videogames. While the critic can use these thought experiments to help guide their play strategy, it can also lead to conclusions that are more related to the critic's own mental model of the game than the actual form of the game.

It is also possible that playing as an expert will lead the player critic to seek out and inevitably take on transgressive play strategies. In their discussion of this play strategy, van Vught and Glas mention this, but do not directly tackle the seeming overlap with transgressive play. Examples of expert play that verge on or cross over into transgressive play include cheating (Consalvo 2009) and speedrunning (Snyder 2017; Brewer 2017). In both of these approaches, the player is using their expert understanding of how the game works to find ways to push the game beyond what it actually suggests to the player as possibilities for play. As van Vught and Glas explain, "transgressive play diverges from a game's intended or dominant repertoire of actions. Here, however, it usually involves creative use of game mechanics or exploitation of bugs" (2018, 222), something that can be seen as essentially *playing against the grain*. The intention here, at least in part, is to better understand the relationship between the materials in the game by finding the boundaries of play. Essentially, this is a way of finding the degree of free movement within the system, the amount of "play" that exists, and by doing so, get a better sense of how the system works.

While this is an interesting and potentially productive approach, it is also somewhat problematic for our formalist analysis. This is where we differ to some extent from van Vught and Glas. It is important to be aware that taking a loose approach to play runs up against the problem of overinterpretation (Eco 1990), in which the player critic can find connections between game elements that are more a result of their own play style than anything inherent in the game itself. While we emphasize the interrelationship of the game as object and the game as process and avoid what can be seen as a "procedural-ist" focus solely on the game rules, at the same time we must acknowledge, at least for this particular type of inquiry, that we are making the game the centre of our investigation, rather than the player. For a different type of analysis, such as one that examines how players are able to repurpose game systems to discover their own form of play (speedrunning is just one example), transgressive play is completely appropriate. But, as we discussed in chapter 1, it is important to keep in mind the underlying (epistemological) assumptions of the approach and connect it to a fitting methodological stance you are taking during analysis and remain true to that stance.

Considering How to Play

The strategies we have discussed above all involve considering what the game's constructed "implied player" is, and either working within this (playing for continuation, playing to win, and playing the right way), or gently pushing against this (playing playfully). In all of these approaches, the intention is to develop an understanding of the game's materials and how they interact. As mentioned above, some of these approaches more closely follow the notion of game as object as they focus on the materials themselves, whereas others have more of an emphasis on game as process, since play involves exploring or pushing against and beyond the boundaries of the system in motion. We have also cautioned that some approaches, such as playing as an expert or playing against the grain, while useful for some types of analysis, may not be appropriate for a formalist analysis as we have been describing in this book.

In addition, returning to our earlier discussion of the problem of variation and the potentially very wide possibility space of games, it may appear that taking a free play approach to play, runs counter to the need to keep the process of analysis manageable. While instrumental play carefully narrows down the play space, free play is doing just the opposite. It is important to maintain a focus on the overall objective of a formalist analysis, namely, to understand the relationship between the materials, identify those that are foregrounded, and work to develop an understanding of the resulting tensions that form the dominant. Keeping this in mind will help to make the analysis more tractable.

At the same time, it is worth noting that ultimately, your play strategy is largely determined by the iterative process of identifying the dominant. If you notice that a certain play strategy keeps yielding more interestingly unfamiliar devices that support a certain dominant structure, you are justified in further pursuing that strategy. The challenge is to determine at what point you have reached "saturation," and are no longer encountering completely new devices, suggesting that while you may not have exhaustively covered every element of the game, you have enough that you have confidence in your understanding of the dominant.

Finally, it is important to recognize that the critic may come to different understandings of the devices within a work, and the dominant present in the interaction between these devices, as the result of different playthroughs, depending on the play strategies they have adopted. It is also possible, or even likely, that different critics will come to different understandings of the dominant. What is important is that the critic makes clear their choice of play strategy/strategies, and clearly articulates how this led to their understanding of the dominant. This highlights the importance of documentation as a way to make the analysis rigorous and the process behind the conclusions that the critic came to clearly accessible to other critics. It is also important that the critic articulates and reflects upon the impact of context on this understanding. In the following two sections, we discuss first the question of context, and then the importance of documentation.

The Importance of Context

The discussion of strategies for "reading" above focuses on how you, as a player critic, should be making the moment-by-moment decisions that determine what action you will take next while playing a game. While it is possible to choose a specific strategy and attempt to use that strategy when playing the game, it is important to acknowledge that various forms of *context* also impact the play experience and may need to be deliberately brought to bear during play. In the process of carrying out the analysis, it is easy for the critic to become completely focused on the game itself, both as an object and as a process, without paying attention to the *context* of the game. This includes both the context of *production* and the context of *consumption*. To investigate the context, the critic is likely going to have to go beyond the game and the experience of playing the game and look to other sources for information. All of this is in service of helping the critic take on the appropriate stance as when playing, in the form of an understanding of the game's *implied player*.

Following our earlier discussion of games as object and games as process, and in line with van Vught and Glas (2018), here we consider first the importance of putting the *game* in context, and then the need to put *yourself*, as a player critic, in context.

Putting the *Game* in Context

Videogames, as with other media, are released and initially consumed at a particular moment in time and space. This can be seen as the "context" in which the game was originally played. To analyse a videogame, it is crucial that we are aware of that original context, even though we are inevitably playing the game in our own context. This is particularly important since our formalist approach to videogame analysis involves identifying which materials within a work are foregrounded, and therefore can be considered devices, and how these devices are in tension with the dominant. Since material is either foregrounded or automatized based on the player's expectations, and whether those materials follow the conventions of the form, this approach by its nature requires an understanding of what the implied player's expectations might be, and what the corresponding conventions were when that implied player would have been playing the game. This suggests that the two ways we are considering context – the context of the game and the context of the player critic – are actually inextricably interconnected. Putting the game in context, as played, also implies (to some extent) putting yourself as the player critic into that context (while being aware of your own context and background).

Context also changes over time. As discussed in chapter 2, it is important for a critic to understand a work both synchronically and diachronically. The synchronic or *in time* perspective involves being aware of the background against which the game existed when it was developed and released – what other game were being played, how players (and society more broadly) viewed those games, and what other social, cultural, technological and economic forces were at work at that moment in time. The diachronic or *over time* perspective focuses on how the various literary, artistic, and ludic systems change over time, and how a particular work serves to both reinforce and work against the prevailing conventions. Taking this into consideration helps a critic to determine both which materials are indeed devices, by virtue of their violation of convention, and which ones are mere design mistakes. In other words, looking at the system of norms over time allows us to see how devices fit into the overall trajectory of the development of the form of the videogame more broadly.

Genre and style can be seen as the sets of conventions that have developed over time and become automatized. This can impact what it is that the player, and the player critic, sees as devices, and what is identified as the dominant. One thing to consider is that devices can become conventionalized, but functions are more stable, and new devices may be brought in to replace the previous devices, not within a specific work, but within the space of videogames that are being developed and consumed. This can be seen as related to the development of new genres and styles. The development of genres, the shift of materials from devices back to materials, and the changes of what devices are used for specific functions and to satisfy specific motivations, e.g., the changing historical context, can also form part of the formalist analysis. This includes examining how the dominant within a given work changes over time, and how the dominant functions both against and in the context of other works.

For example, as mentioned in chapter 2 the emergence of walking simulators represented the development of a new, intriguing videogame form that has since become conventionalized over time. Understanding how a game such as *Dear Esther* (The Chinese Room 2012) fits into its context provides important insights into its position as an early walking simulator. Simply examining the materials, their tensions, and the ways in which some of those materials are foregrounded as devices may be problematic without both the synchronic and diachronic perspectives. In terms of the synchronic, without an understanding that when *Dear Esther* was first released, the term "walking simulator" was not commonly used, and the ways in which the game used spatial exploration as its primary game mechanics, a critic may see the walking mechanic as an automatized rather than a foregrounded material. The ways in which the game broke with the conventions of the first-person shooter need to be understood *in time*. While we are not shocked by a game that involves just walking around today, it was a major break with convention at the time it was first released. From a diachronic perspective, it is important for the critic to consider how this approach has become a convention, and how the critical and fan discourse around this game and others relate to the development of conventions and a distinct genre (Montembeault and Deslongchamps-Gagnon 2019). Again, just focusing on the game in isolation, without considering how it fits into the development of videogame conventions *over time*, runs the risk of overlooking (or conversely, over-emphasizing) the importance of what appear to be foregrounded or automatized materials within the game. This, in turn, suggests that by failing to take context into consideration, a critic may be making inappropriate assumptions about the implied player.

Putting *Yourself* (as the Player Critic) in Context

To be able to analyse a videogame, and particularly to examine the way a game can be seen in relation to both its original context and how the context has changed over time, it is also important to consider the context of the *player*. This involves both being aware of what the player of the game would have been expecting at the time the game was released, and how your own context as a player critic, such as your background, play experience, and personal expectations, may impinge on your analysis.

The first sense of putting the player in context is closely linked to our above discussion of putting the game in context, but from the perspective of process. Being aware of how a player would likely have viewed the game, and what expectations the player would bring to the game, requires an understanding of the game *in time* – what conventions were present in other games, how did people see those conventions, and how would this impact the choices a typical player would make as they play the game. Whichever of the play strategies the critic adopts, in addition to the affordances provided by the game materials, the critic needs to also consider how the player of the game in its original context would have perceived and responded to those affordances. Although it is not possible to completely play as a player would have played when the game was first released, it is important that the critic at least be mindful of this and attend to the possible impact of the implied player's original context while playing.

The other way that the player's context needs to be considered is in terms of the impact that the player critic's own previous gameplay experience and context of play will inevitably have on their analysis. Just as with the implied player, the actual player, in this case the player critic, exists in a particular moment in time, with a particular set of expectations and experiences that are brought to bear on the game during play. The player critic needs to be aware of, and reflect on, this positionality so as to move away from an analysis based on personal skills, preferences, experiences, background knowledge, etc. and towards an analysis based mostly on the qualities of the work.

Here we recognize the influence that Husserl's phenomenology had on the formalists, as we briefly discussed in chapter 2. Husserl's phenomenology involves the researcher undertaking a process of phenomenological reduction, or "removing the individual subject [...] from consideration" (J. Smith n.d.). As part of this process, referred to as the epoché or bracketing, "all judgements that posit the independent existence of the world or worldly entities, and all judgements that presuppose such judgements, are to be bracketed and no use is to be made of them in the course of engaging in phenomenological analysis" (Sawicki n.d.). This bracketing or "putting out of action" is combined with the reduction proper, "the 'moment' in which we come to the transcendental insight that the acceptedness of the world *is* an acceptedness and not an absolute" (Cogan n.d.). These two "moments" work together: "If the epoché is the name for whatever method we use to free ourselves from the captivity of the unquestioned acceptance of the everyday world, then the reduction is the recognition of that acceptance *as* an acceptance" (Cogan n.d.). This is similar to our suggestion that the player critic should be aware of, reflect on, and, where possible and appropriate, do away with the impact of their own experiences on their formal analysis of a game.

We acknowledge that it is not possible for the player critic to completely put aside, or bracket, their own experiences and preferences. In fact, this is something that we explicitly do not encourage. After all, we argued that the analysis should begin from the critic's own aesthetic experience and what the critic felt was intriguing about the game, and that the critic should start their analysis by playing the game as a player. Instead, what is important here is for the critic to be able to say with some certainty and rigour that the defamiliarizing experience they are describing comes from the inherent qualities of the game, and not just because they as a player have certain preferences, or very specific expectations and/or background knowledge. This is why it is important to be self-reflexive, to acknowledge that certain insights are derived from a more idiosyncratic "acceptedness" of the game and the world around us rather than a more shared understanding of the game's qualities. By consciously considering your own context and background and juxtaposing this with your understanding of the implied player's context and background, you sift out the more idiosyncratic experiences and aim for the more shared ones, while acknowledging that also these still occur in the interplay of game, player and context (they are still not absolutes). This is what you take into consideration as you play, and as you analyse the game, constantly reminding yourself of the interconnections between object, process, and context.

Example: Analysing *Paratopic* in Context

There are a number of ways in which the critic can attempt to understand the context of a game when undertaking a formalist analysis. This can include examining what other games were released at the time of the game's release, looking at the critical and popular discourse around the game, and being aware of how similar materials are used in other games both before and after the game being examined. To explore this, we turn again to one of our running examples, *Paratopic*.

Released in 2018, the game enjoyed some success, was nominated for the "Nuovo" award, received an honourable mention for "excellence in visual art," and won for "excellence in audio" in the Independent Games Festival (IGF) (Independent Games Festival 2019). The game's position as an IGF nominee/winner means that it is possible to look at the list of other nominees to get a sense of the games that were released around the same time. Notable games also represented at IGF include *Return of the Obra Dinn* (Pope 2018), *Hypnospace Outlaw* (Tholen et al. 2019) and *Minit* (Nijman et al. 2018). It is worth noting that many of these games, including the three mentioned here, employ a low-fi, retro visual aesthetic. *Return of the Obra Dinn* could also be roughly classified as a "walking simulator." This suggests that these approaches, shared by *Paratopic*, were very much in line with player expectations at the time. It would be reasonable, therefore, to consider these materials as automatized, something the critic should keep in mind when analysing the game. This is much different from how the critic should view these materials in a game such as *Dear Esther*, as discussed above.

There were a number of reviews of the game, both at the time of its initial release on PC and Mac, and again after the release of a Switch version in 2020. Contemporary reviews of a game can provide useful insights into how players (and game journalists) responded to the game on its first release, again giving some hints as to the nature of the implied player and the original play context. For example, the review for *Paratopic* in *The Verge* highlights several of the materials we identified in our earlier analysis:

> The game is less than an hour long and leaves many details unexplained, smash-cutting suddenly between scenes and characters. In these respects, it's a lot like the avant-garde cinematic games *Virginia* and *30 Flights of Loving*. But where those games smoothed out or removed obvious mechanical interactions, *Paratopic* includes standard old-school conventions like awkward text-heavy dialogue trees, only to send them in ominous directions (Robertson 2018).

This is useful, as it helps to clarify that some aspects of the game, while jarring, are not entirely unique. The frequent jump-cuts, for example, have appeared in previous games, for similar purposes. What is interesting here is the mention of the inclusion of "old-school conventions" which the developers then take "in ominous directions." This suggests that even though elements such as the dialogue trees may be familiar (or even seen as out-of-date) to players, it is reasonable to consider the particular way that the game uses them, as discussed in our earlier analysis, as foregrounded or defamiliarized.

There were also a number of articles written in the games press about the game soon after its release that included interviews with the developers. These can help to provide additional insight into the context of the game, what it was inspired by, and the intentions of the developer. It is, of course, important to approach statements by the developers with care, as they may or may not align with the actual gameplay experience. However, they are still a valuable resource when formulating your stance as a critic. One key insight from the various articles is the notion that the game's developers were trying to "fix," or at least "redefine," the walking simulator genre (Burford 2018). This suggests that there was a deliberate attempt to break with conventions. As Burford, one of the developers, writes:

> These games are called walking sims because that's all you do. You walk. You walk forwards. You consider the world around you, if you like, and you walk, and as you walk, a narrator tells you what's happening, and eventually, you stop walking and the game ends. If you're lucky, you might experiment with a few light puzzle elements. Some of the horror-themed walking sims, like Amnesia, have running and hiding mechanics as well, but in general, walking sims are very mechanics-light (2018).

Burford goes on to argue that what is missing in walking simulators is the "verbs," and that "to make a walking sim interesting, I reasoned, I'd have to make one with an awful lot of interesting verbs. In a sense, it would be more of an anti-walking sim" (2018). Burford connects this to a desire to avoid telling players what to feel, but instead "make them really feel it" by means of very specific interactions. This again aligns with the repetitive interactions and dialogue. Interestingly, Burford argues that they were attempting to "make a game that seemed like a walking sim on the surface, but that used its verbs to tell a story instead of exposition" (2018). While a critic analysing the game needs to be careful not to blindly follow these statements made by the developer, they are helpful in terms of contextualizing the game. In the end, however, the critic should focus back on the game itself, keeping the context in mind but as a background rather than the main focus of the analysis.

It is also important, as mentioned above, that the player critic put themselves in context. For me (Alex) as the player critic approaching a formalist analysis of *Paratopic*, I need to reflect on my own play preferences, play experiences, and expectations. I tend to play story-focused games with strong characters, having played *The Hitchhiker's Guide to the Galaxy* (Meretzky and Adams 1984) when it was first released, through to more recent games such as *Citizen Sleeper* (Jump Over The Age 2022). I have also played, and enjoyed, all the games mentioned above as IGF nominees in the same year as *Paratopic*. This suggests that as a player I resemble the typical player of *Paratopic* when it was first released. However, as mentioned at the start of this chapter, I was initially intrigued by *Paratopic* due to similarities that game journalists had pointed out to *Thirty Flights of Loving*. Here, I need to keep in mind that I have carried out both a close reading and an empirical study of *Thirty Flights of Loving* (Mitchell 2016; Mitchell, Sim, and Kway 2017), and that I made use of this game as an example in an earlier paper on poetic gameplay (Mitchell et al. 2020). As such, I would likely be highly attuned to possible similarities between these games. Because of this, as a player critic I need to remind myself to situate any observations I have of the possible devices in the work back into the game itself, rather than in my expectations as influenced by my previous academic work.

Actually *Doing* the Close Reading

While they provide extensive insights into the strategies involved, what van Vught and Glas (2018) don't discuss in detail is what you should actually be *doing* as you carry out a close reading. We have already suggested that this is an iterative process, involving first getting a sense as to why you want to analyse a particular game in the first place, and then working through the process of identifying the materials, considering which are foregrounded and which are automatized, what tensions are at work, and what this tells us about the dominant within the work. This, however, is the *analytical* process. Either before or (ideally) in parallel with this, you also need to be actually *playing* the game, and *collecting data* (e.g., keeping notes, recording play and/or commentary) about your play experience. Both Bizzocchi and Tanenbaum (2011) and Carr (2009; 2019) provide some suggestions as to how to do this. Here we draw from these approaches, but also ground our suggestions in a formalist perspective, as developed in this book so far. This is intended to help students and scholars who are new to the process to carry out a textual analysis of a videogame from a formalist perspective.

In the next section we will discuss the close playing experience, including the process of documenting your play sessions. That will be followed by a discussion of how you might approach writing up your analysis.

Playing the Game and Documenting Your Play

At the very basic level, the approach we are advocating in this book is in line with Aarseth's (2003) contention that the critic must *play the game* in order to analyse it. The question is, what does it mean to play the game for the purposes of analysis? As Aarseth asks, "how do we play?" (2003, 3). We have tried to answer many of the variations on this question above. Here, we want to address the very specific question of what the critic should be doing while playing.

At the start of this chapter, we argued that the analyst or critic should first identify why the game is of interest, before beginning to consider in more detail what the materials are, what is foregrounded, and what can be considered the dominant. This suggests that before engaging in analytical play, the critic should play at least once just to experience the game. Tanenbaum (2015, 139–40) encourages initially playing "authentically" without any data collection apparatus or specific focus on the research problem, before then playing again as a researcher. They propose that this initial playthrough can provide a point of reference to help attend to the possible issues that may arise due to the act of playing to analyse the game. If at any point the researcher begins, for example, to wonder about their experience and whether they are over-analysing, it is possible to think back to that original, "naive" playthrough as a baseline. Similarly, Carr describes the process of close reading as involving "playing through the game several times and then engaging in a closer consideration of particular moments within the game through forms of fragmentation (repeated play, taking and reviewing screenshots)" (2019, 711).

In practice, particularly for a very long game, it may be difficult to engage in multiple playthroughs. It also may be difficult to completely avoid engaging in some form of analysis during a first playthrough, despite your best efforts, unless your decision to analyse the game came about as the result of, rather than before, your first playthrough. Regardless, the principle is sound, and is something that we would advise if at all possible.

Once the researcher decides to play the game analytically, the question is *how* this should be done. A number of questions arise: How much should play be dictated by particular research questions? How much attention should the researcher pay to playing as opposed to data collection and analysis? What form of data collection is appropriate to support the process of close reading and a formalist analysis of the game? In fact, should any actual analysis be done during play, or should this be limited to post-game reflection? All of these are challenging questions and are somewhat different from the challenges involved in close reading of a novel or a film, due largely to the participatory nature of play.

Following on from our discussion of the various strategies that can be adopted for "reading," the critic can make use of a particular reading strategy to decide what to do next as they play. For Tanenbaum (2015), this involves deciding on a number of "analytic lenses," and keeping these in mind while playing. This also helps focus note taking and data collection, as will be discussed below. For example, in their analysis of the *Mass Effect* (Bioware 2007) trilogy, Tanenbaum prepared a series of "cheat sheets" (2015, 141) summarizing their chosen analytic lenses, and also providing reminders to take screenshots and write notes at various intervals. An important point here was that while the initial lenses were grounded in the previous literature, as they played the game, Tanenbaum found it necessary to revise these lenses. This emphasizes the iterative nature of close reading and textual analysis, in which the text (e.g., the game) itself is the main focus. Theory can provide a starting point, but the analyst must be open to changing their focus as they play the game, to avoid predetermining the findings. It is also important, as we will discuss below, that the researcher be reflective and open about these revisions. As Tanenbaum explains:

> One critique that might be leveled at close reading is that the theorist over-determines the theoretical outcomes by intentionally or unknowingly encoding bias into the primary investigative frame: the analytical lenses. In practice, however, when confronted with the realities of a text some lenses succeed while others fail. Acknowledging and learning from those failures is important to the validity and rigor of the close reading process (2015, 147).

Tanenbaum describes the process of actually playing the game while engaging in analysis, which in addition to data collection during the play session, also involved doing a detailed "debrief." A rigorous documentation of the playing strategy and reflection on the contexts grounds the formalist analysis in empirical data and a shared (but changing) historical background, which keeps the analysis from becoming idiosyncratic. Following Bordwell (2008), Tanenbaum sees poetics as an empirical undertaking (2015, 135). As they argue, "[c]entral to this process is a systematic commitment to treat the text as a site for data collection and to rigorously ground the argument in the available data" (2015, 135–36).

Furthermore, Tanenbaum develops a rigorous approach to data collection during a close reading. A central question here is what is the purpose of the data collection? Generally, there will likely be two main purposes: 1) as an aid in recall while carrying out the analysis, since it is often difficult or impossible to jump back into the moment of the game being analysed, and 2) as a source of details for retelling and argumentation. For Tanenbaum's analysis of *Mass Effect*, they chose to focus on screenshots, save game files, and journaling. There were a number of reasons behind this, one key consideration being the amount of storage required to manage the amount of video resulting from a full recording of the playthrough, given the length of the trilogy. While data storage may not be such an issue as the cost of storage media drops, there is still the question of making sense of and accessing masses of video data. As they discuss, some researchers, such as Perron, Arsenault, Picard and Therrien (2008), feel that full video recordings are important, particularly when there are multiple researchers involved in a project. However, even full video doesn't completely capture the experience.

Here it again may be worth considering what the purpose of data collection is. For example, if the full process of interaction is required (physical engagement with controls plus in-screen actions), possibly because the analysis will be focusing on specific relationships between player action and game response, perhaps more than the on-screen actions need to be captured, then, it may be worth looking at how, for example, the speedrunning community often record both a video of the player's hands manipulating a controller together with the on-screen action, as they are interested in the specific moves being performed and whether the speedrun was legitimate (Ritchie 2021). This may be of interest to the formalist critic if the player's physical actions on the controls are an important part of the materials under consideration. In Tanenbaum's case, they initially planned to take manual screenshots based on their analytic lenses, and a number of heuristics based on in-game circumstances. However, this became problematic in terms of their focus of attention, leading them to adopt an automated system of screenshots. This was accompanied by note taking at regular intervals, capturing the key reactions close to the moment (but not in the moment). They also engaged in a more detailed "debrief" after completing the game, as a form of post-play reflection. With careful organization, the combination of notes, post-play reflection, and screenshots provides a fairly detailed record of the play experience.

As mentioned above, taking detailed notes at certain points during play, and at the end of play, can allow the researcher to capture their experience at a slight remove from the play experience, balancing the danger of disrupting the play experience against the problem of waiting too long and losing the ability to clearly recall the experience. This is somewhat similar to the practice of writing "thick descriptions" in ethnographic or autoethnographic research (Tracy 2020). However, Tanenbaum argues that given the length of gameplay in many games, "this technique does not scale well when the phenomenon under study occupies hundreds of hours of experience" (2015, 140). It could be argued, however, that ethnographic researchers who spend years in the field have had similar masses of data to deal with. What may be worth considering here is how other researchers who are faced with large amounts of experiential data manage this. Given the similarities between the data collected in ethnographic or auto-ethnographic research and the data accumulated in a close reading of a game, it may be worth exploring the tools used by these research communities as a means for organizing and annotating rich media data during close readings.

For example, Wolfinger (2002) distinguishes between two different note-taking strategies in ethnographic research. First of all, researchers can take a so-called *comprehensive note-taking* strategy, in which the researchers "systematically and comprehensively describe everything that happened during a particular period of time" (Wolfinger 2002, 90). To structure this, one may use specific guiding questions or decide to take notes temporarily starting at the beginning and ending at the end. While thorough, this strategy risks either becoming an unmanageable amount of work since the aim is to note down as much as possible from beginning to end, or blinding the analyst to interesting elements that fall outside the scope of the guiding questions. We therefore find more use in Wolfinger's second strategy, in which notes are taken on the basis of what they call *salience hierarchy*. Here, the researcher "can start by describing whatever observations struck them as the most noteworthy, the most interesting, or the most telling" (Wolfinger 2002, 89). In the case of the formalist critic, saliency is determined by which devices become foregrounded as the more intriguing ones due to the fact that they challenge the critic's expectations as a player. While this strategy risks becoming more idiosyncratic (what is interesting to you, may not be interesting to someone else), that could be overcome by familiarizing oneself with the context of the game and game genres in time and over time and being open about the context of oneself as a player critic and juxtaposing that position with the position of the implied player.

In summary, when playing the game, we recommend the following:

1. First, play the game *as a player*. This will both enable you to consider what it is about the work that is intriguing (see section above), and also provide a "baseline" against which you can compare, and check, your later, analytic play.

2. Once you have determined what it is that intrigues you, then you return to the game and play one or more times, from an analytic perspective. Here, you should be collecting data, and playing based on a (combination of) specific play strategy/strategies, as described earlier in this chapter.

3. During play, find a balance between playing the game and capturing data. Depending on the type of gameplay involved, this may require some form of video recording or automated screenshot collection or may be done manually. Similarly, note-taking can be done at set intervals in a game that requires constant input from the player, such as a first-person shooter, or as and when the player critic has insights, if the game allows for this.

4. Regardless of the in-game data collection strategy, journaling is an important practice. Take notes on the play session as soon as you finish. You can also iteratively refine your focus and your understanding of the game, using this to guide subsequent play sessions. This may include a shift in what you currently think of as the dominant. It may also involve a change in play strategy as a result of this shifting focus. Documentation should be reflective, capturing any of these changes in focus and play strategy, and the rationale behind them.

How to Write about Your Analysis?

Having carried out the close readings, with careful attention to capturing data that can be used both for further analysis and to provide "evidence" for your claims about the game, the next question is: how to write your analysis? How should you talk about what you have found out about the ways the game materials work together, create a sense of the dominant, and are in tension with each other? Should you write in the first person, acknowledging your presence as a player-researcher, or in the third person, attempting to maintain some academic distance? How do you bring in the documentation and data you have accumulated as part of your argument? Part of what you need to consider here is the audience for the analysis – are you writing a journal article? A student report? An extended manuscript or dissertation? This will to some extent determine, for example, how much detail you are able to provide, and what style to adopt.

Another important consideration is how to address the issue of the *validity* of your analysis. The use of detailed descriptions of gameplay together with other media such as screenshots or sequences of screenshots relates closely to the issue of validity in close readings. As Tanenbaum argues, "the burden of proof in my own presentation of the material lies in making certain that I've provided sufficient contextual information about the experience to guide someone else to discover the same material that I discuss in my critique" (2015, 140). To address this, Tanenbaum makes use of a combination of screenshots, frame-by-frame sequences of visuals, and thick descriptions. As they mention, there is some need to consider how much is too much. Will providing detailed explanations of gameplay help the reader to visualize the play experience, or will it distract them from the argument being made? Will it emphasize the personal nature of the observations in a manner that highlights the empirical grounding and experiential nature of the analysis, or will this instead encourage the reader, or the reviewer, to feel that the textual analysis is just "someone playing the game," as a reviewer of one of this book's author's published papers contented?

To help us consider the amount of detail to provide, and the way to handle the inclusion of personal details, we can compare two descriptions of gameplay from two very different approaches to analysis. A classic example of a detailed autoethnography of gameplay, Sudnow's study of playing *Breakout* provides an extreme example of rich-thick description of gameplay. For example, the following passage describes their process of developing an understanding of the paddle controller when they first began playing the game:

> Within fifteen minutes I'm no longer conscious of the knob's gearing and I'm not jerking around too much. So far so good. Slow down, get rid of the neighbor, get a little rhythm going, and in no time at all you've got a workable eye hand partnership, the calibrating movement quickly passes beneath awareness, and in the slow phase the game is a breeze, doesn't even touch the fingering you need for 'the eentsy, weentsy spider went up the water spout....' Here I was lobbing away with a gentle rhythm, soon only now and then missing a shot through what seemed a brief lapse in attention rather than a defect in skill (Sudnow 1983, 30).

Here, the experience is very personal, and the descriptions are clearly in line with what one would expect from an ethnographic account. Sudnow also selectively includes both screenshots and illustrations of the controllers being used to play the game. This is very descriptive, but also begins to introduce the overall argument of the book, which focuses on the ways the player, in this case Sudnow, becomes connected to and immersed in the play experience. Here the analysis focuses more on the player-game relationship, very much at a visceral, embodied level.

In contrast, in the analysis of *Thirty Flights of Loving* (Blendo Games 2012) mentioned in chapter 2, Mitchell also provides detailed descriptions of their play experience, interspersed with analysis of the various "poetic gameplay" devices they are identifying. For example, to introduce the ways in which the game disrupts the player's expectations for navigational controls, they describe the following sequence:

> The cutscene showed, in rapid succession, a series of non-interactive shots illustrating the professions of the characters, in a sequence that felt very much like what might be seen in a 'heist film' (see figure 1). This sequence was unsettling in two ways. In most games, approaching a character and choosing to interact by pressing the 'E' key triggers a dialogue with the character, rather than a cutscene. This unexpected response to interaction was in direct opposition to my expectations (2016, 4).

Again, there is a description of the play experience, accompanied by some explanation of how the player critic felt about and reacted to the game's formal elements. The account is personal, acknowledging the specific nature of the observations being made, but the focus remains on the game, rather than the player. Here, there is an accompanying set of images from the game. A key point to note is that an argument is being made – the details of gameplay are not simply descriptive but lead into the subsequent argumentation. These descriptions and images provide the "evidence" for what is being argued through the course of the paper.

Another issue to consider is how familiar the target audience is with textual analysis and "close readings." Many critical discussions of games are actually taking a formalist, textual analytic, close reading approach without explicitly foregrounding this, perhaps seeing this as a given. However, given the specificity of this methodology, it may be of value to consider explicitly signalling the approach being taken. Again, this may also depend on the purpose of the paper and the audience. For a student paper, or for a dissertation, it may be important to include reflection on the methodology, to highlight to the readers (and potential examiners) that you are consciously undertaking a particular approach to analysis, and not just "playing the game." In a journal article or conference publication, on the other hand, it may be more appropriate to simply focus on the analysis. However, this may also depend on the familiarity of the scholarly community with the approach taken. There are various degrees to which the nature of the method taken can be articulated. For example, in an early formalist analysis of *Kentucky Route Zero* (Cardboard Computer 2013), Mitchell simply stated that they were carrying out a close reading, while at the same time providing detailed background on the formalist perspective being taken (2014, 162). In the analysis of *Thirty Flights of Loving* mentioned above, in addition to stating that the analysis was the result of a close reading, Mitchell also connected the analysis to Bizzocchi and Tanenbaum's (2011) description of the approach, explicitly stating the analytical lenses used in the analysis. As discussed in chapter 1, some degree of acknowledgement of the methodological stance being taken can help the critic to situate their work and make clear the type of claims they are (and are not) making.

It is also important to make clear the roles of the authors in a given paper. If multiple authors worked together to analyse a game, did they all engage in the close reading? There are examples of close readings where the roles and backgrounds of the authors are explicitly mentioned (Mitchell and Kway 2020; Mitchell, Kway, and Lee 2020). However, other published papers make no mention of the methodology, focusing entirely on the discussion of the games. For example, Gasque et al. (2020) only make mention later in the paper that the authors "mapped our own experience of one playthrough of the game," suggesting that the analysis is based on their own playthroughs of the game. They also mention that, for example, "[t]hroughout the session, we spent the bulk of our time in the temporal middle of the story." However, there is no indication of who "we" refers to. Is this both authors? The first author? Do the authors have equal experience with games? In this case, the second author is very senior, and would likely have a very different perspective on games than the first author. While this doesn't in any way diminish or invalidate the contribution of the paper, it might have been useful to include some reflection on this in the paper.

This highlights that it is particularly important to consider, as you are writing and potentially publishing your analysis, how much of *yourself* can and should appear in the analysis. It is important to be reflective, and to make clear your own positionality and potential biases when playing the game, given the observations are all ultimately filtered through your own experience. However, this can also make the close reader vulnerable, as you are part of the analysis yourself, and by writing, and publishing, the analysis you are revealing something about yourself in public. This is both a strength and a possible danger of the methodology. As Stang argues:

Close reading centralizes the scholar's perspective, subjectivity, and experience, which is particularly important when the scholar occupies a less privileged subject position and can speak to systemic oppression as it is intertwined with mediated content. The closeness, intimacy, and vulnerability of close reading is what makes it compelling as a method. On the other hand, choosing not to publish this kind of work or make these kinds of videos means choosing safety. Feminist critics and journalists put themselves at risk every time they publish and we as academics often remain relatively safe publishing in academic journals (Stang 2022, 7–8).

There are at least two issues here. The first is how you reflect on your own experiences and positionality, and the second is how much care you need to take not to compromise your own safety by doing so.

In summary, when writing about your analysis, we recommend that the following issues be kept in mind:

1. What is the purpose of the analysis? Who is the audience?
2. How will you approach the question of "validity"?
3. How explicitly will you identify and articulate your methodological stance?
4. What are the role(s) of the author(s) and how will you reflect on this?
5. How much of yourself as a critic do you reflect in the analysis, and what impact might this have on your own personal safety within the academic community, and beyond?

Beyond Close Readings: Taking a Formalist Stance with Other Approaches

Finally, we suggest ways that these formalist considerations can be used as a focus point for other types of game analysis, such as qualitative player studies. What we highlight here is that studies can, for example, be designed to identify the dominant and consider the devices at work, but do this through, for example, observation of players rather than close readings. This is worth considering as a way of gaining deeper insights and new perspectives on the phenomena under consideration. This is comparable to, for example, Miall and Kuiken's (1994) empirical studies of foregrounding, defamiliarization and affect in short stories, which is clearly grounded in the same theoretical frameworks as our work.

One way to approach this is to undertake observational studies of player responses to games, which can involve having players play through a game under study, and then ask the players to describe or explain their responses to the game through a process of retrospective protocol analysis (Ericsson and Simon 1993; Knickmeyer and Mateas 2005). As with close readings, the focus is on looking for the dominant and how other elements relate to it, and the resulting aesthetic experience. Examples of this approach include Mitchell et al.'s empirical study of poetic gameplay (2017), and Neo and Mitchell's study of player response to interactive comics (2019).

An important point to make here is that we agree with Mortensen and Jorgensen that "it is a fallacy to claim that game analysis through self-play and observing actual players are two incompatible paradigms" (2020, 9). As they argue, "our own play will only enable a very limited understanding based on the researcher's own cultural and social predispositions" (2020, 11). This, as they go on to point out, does not invalidate the importance of close readings as a methodology, but instead suggests that taking a multiple player perspective, including studies of player responses to games, is an important way to deepen our understanding of games as a meaning-making object and process.

Conclusion

In this chapter we have explored ways in which a formalist stance can be used as the foundation for a flexible methodology for videogame analysis. This involves starting from the notion of the dominant, identifying what it is that is of interest in a game, and what tensions are at work. When undertaking this type of analysis, we argued that it is important for the player critic to carefully consider their play strategies, as this will impact the outcome of the analysis. We also emphasized the importance of context, both of the game and of the player, when conducting the analysis. Following these discussions, we provided some details as to how to go about conducting a close reading or close playing of a videogame. We closed by suggesting that a formalist perspective can be taken as part of other approaches to analysis, such as observational studies of player response to games. A key thread running through this chapter is the importance of taking a deliberate and conscious stance in terms of both the theoretical and methodological approach being taken as part of the analysis of a videogame.

Having explored videogame formalism as a methodology, in the next chapter we will work through two extended examples of game analysis using this approach, to demonstrate the concepts developed in the book.

References

Aarseth, Espen. 2003. "Playing Research: Methodological Approaches to Game Analysis." In *MelbourneDAC, Proceedings of the 5th International Digital Arts and Culture Conference*. Melbourne, Australia: RMIT University.

Aarseth, Espen. 2014. "I Fought the Law: Transgressive Play and the Implied Player." In *From Literature to Cultural Literacy*, edited by Naomi Segal and Daniela Koleva, 180–88. London: Springer.

Arbitrary Metric. 2018a. "Paratopic." Steam. 2018. https://store.steampowered.com/app/897030/Paratopic/.

Arbitrary Metric. 2018b. "Paratopic [MacOS Game]." Arbitrary Metric.

Bioware. 2007. "Mass Effect [Microsoft Windows Game]." Electronic Arts.

Bizzocchi, Jim, and Teresa Jean Tanenbaum. 2011. "Well Read: Applying Close Reading Techniques to Gameplay Experiences." In *Well Played 3.0. Video Games, Value and Meaning*, edited by Drew Davidson, 262–90. Pittsburgh: ETC Press.

Blendo Games. 2012. "Thirty Flights of Loving [MacOS Game]." Blendo Games.

Bopp, Julia Ayumi, Elisa D. Mekler, and Klaus Opwis. 2016. "Negative Emotion, Positive Experience?: Emotionally Moving Moments in Digital Games." In *Proceedings of the 2016 CHI Conference on Human Factors in Computing Systems*, 2996–3006. New York: ACM.

Bordwell, David. 2008. *Poetics of Cinema*. New York: Routledge.

Brewer, Christopher G. 2017. "Born to Run: A Grounded Theory Study of Cheating in the Online Speedrunning Community." MA Thesis, The University of Southern Mississippi.

Burford, Doc. 2018. "How I Attempted to Redefine the 'Walking Sim' With Paratopic." *USgamer*, September 6, 2018. https://www.usgamer.net/articles/how-i-attempted-to-redefine-the-walking-sim-with-paratopic.

Cardboard Computer. 2013. "Kentucky Route Zero [MacOS Game]." Annapurna Interactive.

Carr, Diane. 2009. "Textual Analysis, Digital Games, Zombies.' In *Proceedings of the 2009 DiGRA International Conference: Breaking New Ground – Innovation in Games, Play, Practice and Theory*. London: Digital Games Research Association.

Carr, Diane. 2019. "Methodology, Representation, and Games." *Games and Culture* 14 (7–8): 707–23.

The Chinese Room. 2012. "Dear Esther [MacOS Game]." The Chinese Room.

Cogan, John. n.d. "The Phenomenological Reduction." In *Internet Encyclopedia of Philosophy*. Accessed June 13, 2023. https://iep.utm.edu/phen-red/.

Cohen, Ethan, dir. 2008. *No Country for Old Men*. Paramount Pictures.

Consalvo, Mia. 2009. *Cheating: Gaining Advantage in Videogames*. Cambridge, MA: MIT Press.

Csikszentmihályi, Mihály. 1990. *Flow: The Psychology of Optimal Experience*. New York: Harper and Row.

Dinosaur Games. 2017. "Desert Bus VR [Microsoft Windows Game]." Gearbox Software, LLC.

Eco, Umberto. 1990. *The Limits of Interpretation*. Bloomington, Indiana: Indiana University Press.

Ericsson, Karl Anders, and Herbert Alexander Simon. 1993. *Protocol Analysis: Verbal Reports as Data*. Revised Edition. Cambridge, MA: MIT Press.

Gasque, Terra M, Kevin Tang, Brad Rittenhouse, and Janet H. Murray. 2020. "Gated Story Structure and Dramatic Agency in Sam Barlow's Telling Lies BT – Interactive Storytelling." In *Interactive Storytelling: 13th International Conference on Interactive Digital Storytelling – ICIDS*, edited by Anne-Gwenn Bosser, David E. Millard, and Charlie Hargood, 314–26. Cham: Springer International Publishing.

Imagineering. unreleased. "Penn & Teller's Smoke and Mirrors [Sega Genesis Game]." Absolute Entertainment.

Independent Games Festival. 2019. "IGF 2019." Independent Games Festival (IGF). July 19, 2019. https://igf.com/2019.

Iser, Wolfgang. 1980. *The Act of Reading: A Theory of Aesthetic Response*. London: The Johns Hopkins University Press.

Jakobson, Roman. 1987. *Language in Literature*. Edited by Krystyna Pomorska and Stephen Rudy. Cambridge, MA: Harvard University Press.

Jump Over The Age. 2022. "Citizen Sleeper [MacOS Game]." Fellow Traveller.

Juul, Jesper. 2005. *Half-Real: Video Games between Real Rules and Fictional Worlds*. Cambridge, MA: MIT Press.

Knickmeyer, Rachel Lee, and Michael Mateas. 2005. "Preliminary Evaluation of the Interactive Drama Facade." In *CHI '05 Extended Abstracts*, 1549–52. New York: ACM.

Lantz, Frank. 2009. "Drop7 [Mobile Game]." Zynga.

Leino, Olli Tapio. 2010. "Emotions in Play: On the Constitution of Emotion in Solitary Computer Game Play." PhD Thesis, IT University of Copenhagen, Innovative Communication.

Lynch, David, dir. 1990. "Twin Peaks."

Meretzky, Steve, and Douglas Adams. 1984. "The Hitchhiker's Guide to the Galaxy [MS DOS Game]." Infocom.

Miall, David S., and Don Kuiken. 1994. "Foregrounding, Defamiliarization, and
    Affect: Response to Literary Stories." *Poetics* 22 (5): 389–407.

Mitchell, Alex. 2014. "Defamiliarization and Poetic Interaction in Kentucky Route
    Zero." *Well Played: A Journal on Video Games, Value and Meaning* 3 (2): 161–78.

Mitchell, Alex. 2016. "Making the Familiar Unfamiliar: Techniques for Creating
    Poetic Gameplay." In *Proceedings of the First International Joint Conference of
    DiGRA and FDG 2016*. Dundee: Digital Games Research Association.

Mitchell, Alex, and Liting Kway. 2020. "'How Do I Restart This Thing?' Repeat
    Experience and Resistance to Closure in Rewind Storygames." In *Interactive
    Storytelling: Proceedings of ICIDS 2020*, edited by Anne-Gwenn Bosser, David E.
    Millard, and Charlie Hargood, 164–77. Cham: Springer International Publishing.

Mitchell, Alex, Liting Kway, and Brandon Junhui Lee. 2020. "Storygameness:
    Understanding Repeat Experience and the Desire for Closure in Storygames."
    In *Proceedings of the 2020 DiGRA International Conference: Play Everywhere*.
    Tampere: Digital Games Research Association.

Mitchell, Alex, Liting Kway, Tiffany Neo, and Yuin Theng Sim. 2020. "A Preliminary
    Categorization of Techniques for Creating Poetic Gameplay." *Game Studies* 20 (2).

Mitchell, Alex, Yuin Theng Sim, and Liting Kway. 2017. "Making It Unfamiliar in
    the "Right" Way: An Empirical Study of Poetic Gameplay." In *Proceedings of
    the 2017 DiGRA International Conference*. Melbourne, Australia: Digital Games
    Research Association.

Montembeault, Hugo, and Maxime Deslongchamps-Gagnon. 2019. "The Walking
    Simulator's Generic Experiences." *Press Start* 5 (2): 1–28.

Mortensen, Torill Elvira, and Kristine Jørgensen. 2020. *The Paradox of Transgression
    in Games*. New York: Routledge.

Neo, Tiffany, and Alex Mitchell. 2019. "Expanding Comics Theory to Account for
    Interactivity: A Preliminary Study." *Studies in Comics2* 10 (2): 189–213.

Nijman, Jan Willem, Kitty Calis, Jukio Kalio, and Dominik Johann. 2018. "Minit
    [MacOS Game]." Devolver Digital.

O'Connor, Alice. 2018. "Paratopic Is Some Fine Low-Fi Vignette-y Horror."
    RockPaperShotgun, March 15, 2018. https://www.rockpapershotgun.com/
    paratopic-vignette-horror-game-released.

Perron, Bernard. 2018. *The World of Scary Video Games: A Study in Videoludic Horror*.
    New York: Bloomsbury Publishing USA.

Perron, Bernard, Dominic Arsenault, Martin Picard, and Carl Therrien. 2008.
    "Methodological Questions in 'Interactive Film Studies'." *New Review of Film
    and Television Studies* 6 (13): 233–52.

Pope, Lucas. 2018. "Return of the Obra Dinn [MacOS Game]." 3909 LLC.

Quantic Dream. 2010. "Heavy Rain [Playstation 3 Game]." Sony Computer
    Entertainment.

Ritchie, Stuart. 2021. "Why Are Gamers So Much Better Than Scientists at Catching Fraud?' *The Atlantic*, July 2, 2021. https://www.theatlantic.com/science/archive/2021/07/gamers-are-better-scientists-catching-fraud/619324/.

Robertson, Adi. 2018. "Paratopic Is a Short, Grimy Horror Game with a Style Straight out of 1998." *The Verge*, April 29, 2018. https://www.theverge.com/2018/4/29/17228744/paratopic-horror-exploration-game-tapes-review.

Robinson-Yu, Adam. 2019. "A Short Hike [MacOS Game]." Adam Robinson-Yu.

Robinson-yu, Adam. n.d. "A Short Hike." Accessed June 28, 2022. https://ashorthike.com/.

Rockstar Studios. 2019. "Red Dead Redemption 2 [Playstation 4 Game]." Rockstar Games.

Salen, Katie, and Eric Zimmerman. 2004. *Rules of Play: Game Design Fundamentals*. Cambridge, MA: MIT Press.

Sawicki, Marianne. n.d. "Phenomenology." In *Internet Encyclopedia of Philosophy*. Accessed June 13, 2023. https://iep.utm.edu/phenom/.

Sharp, John. 2010. "The Purpose and Meaning of Drop 7." In *Well Played 2.0: Video Games, Value and Meaning*, edited by Drew Davidson, 48–55. Pittsburgh: ETC Press.

Smith, Joel. n.d. "Edmund Husserl (1859–1938)." In *Internet Encyclopedia of Philosophy*. Accessed June 13, 2023. https://iep.utm.edu/husserl/.

Smith, Jonas Heide. 2006. "Plans and Purposes How Videogame Goals Shape Player Behaviour." PhD Thesis, The IT University of Copenhagen.

Snyder, David. 2017. *Speedrunning: Interviews with the Quickest Gamers*. McFarland.

Stang, Sarah. 2022. "Too Close, Too Intimate, and Too Vulnerable: Close Reading Methodology and the Future of Feminist Game Studies." *Critical Studies in Media Communication* 39 (3): 230–38.

Sudnow, David. 1983. *Pilgrim in the Microworld*. New York: Warner Books.

Szabó, Judit. 2022. "Fear and Agency in Survival Horror." In *Negative Emotions in the Reception of Fictional Narratives*, 43–62. Paderborn: Brill | mentis.

Tanenbaum, Teresa Jean. 2015. "Identity Transformation and Agency in Digital Narratives and Story Based Games." PhD Thesis, Simon Fraser University.

Tholen, Jay, Mike Lasch, Xalavier Nelson Jr., and Corey Cochran. 2019. "Hypnospace Outlaw [MacOS Game]." No More Robots.

Thompson, Kristin. 1988. *Breaking the Glass Armor: Neoformalist Film Analysis*. Princeton, New Jersey: Princeton University Press.

Tracy, Sarah J. 2020. *Qualitative Research Methods: Collecting Evidence, Crafting Analysis, Communicating Impact*. 2nd ed. John Wiley & Sons.

Tyack, April, and Elisa D. Mekler. 2021. "Off-Peak: An Examination of Ordinary Player Experience." In *Proceedings of the 2021 CHI Conference on Human Factors in Computing Systems*, 1–12. New York: ACM.

Vught, Jasper van. 2016. "Neoformalist Game Analysis: A Methodological Exploration of Single-Player Game Violence." PhD Thesis, University of Waikato.

Vught, Jasper van, and René Glas. 2018. "Considering Play: From Method to Analysis." *Transactions of the Digital Games Research Association* 4 (2).

Wardrip-Fruin, Noah. 2009. *Expressive Processing: Digital Fictions, Computer Games, and Software Studies*. Cambridge, MA: MIT Press.

Wolfinger, Nicholas H. 2002. "On Writing Fieldnotes: Collection Strategies and Background Expectancies." *Qualitative Research* 2 (1): 85–93.

5. Applying Formalism

Abstract: In this chapter, we apply the formalist approach to videogame analysis, for which we laid the groundwork in chapters 1–3 and further described in chapter 4, to two case studies: *Kentucky Route Zero*, which is often considered to be an art game, and *The Legend of Zelda: Breath of the Wild*, a mainstream AAA game. We demonstrate in detail the steps involved in the process, from the initial aspects of the game that intrigue the player critic, through to the identification of devices, defamiliarization, and the dominant. We provide examples of how this process starts from the player's aesthetic experience and takes the context of play into consideration. Through the analysis of these two very different games, we demonstrate the range and diversity of possible applications of our videogame formalism.

Keywords: case studies, formalist analysis, art game, AAA game

The methodological and theoretical pointers described in the previous chapters provide a strong foundation for formalist videogame analysis. Here, we demonstrate how a formalist analysis would function, showcasing the flexibility and range of applications of a formalist analysis by discussing and analysing in detail two games: an art game: *Kentucky Route Zero* (Cardboard Computer 2013), and a mainstream AAA title: *The Legend of Zelda: Breath of the Wild* (Nintendo 2017). This demonstrates both the range and diversity of applications of the concepts and tools of a formalist analysis, which, as we have stressed before, are not to be seen as a recipe for analysis but rather a set of tools applied, in context, to each game as needed.

Kentucky Route Zero

As an example of applying our approach to a formalist analysis of a videogame, we will now present a detailed analysis of *Kentucky Route Zero* (Cardboard Computer 2013), a game that is often considered an example of an art game.

Mitchell, A. and J. van Vught, *Videogame Formalism: On Form, Aesthetic Experience, and Methodology*. Amsterdam: Amsterdam University Press, 2024
DOI 10.5117/9789463720663_CH05

This type of game is perceived as somehow different from the mainstream, often as the result of the violation of expectations most players bring to videogames (Bogost 2011; Sharp 2015). As such, an art game readily lends itself to a formalist analysis, particularly in terms of the application of concepts such as defamiliarization. This analysis will allow us to provide an initial demonstration of how the tools provided by a formalist approach can be applied to videogames.

Kentucky Route Zero is a "magical realist adventure game about a secret highway running through the caves beneath Kentucky, and the mysterious folks who travel it" (Cardboard Computer 2020). The game initially focuses on Conway, a delivery driver working for an antiques shop, who is on the way to make a final delivery to "5 Dogwood Drive" somewhere on the elusive "Route Zero" in Kentucky. Gameplay largely involves point-and-click movement around and interaction with the game world. This is combined with conversational interaction with non-player characters, which usually involves dialogue choices which result in different responses. As the game progresses, several other characters are encountered, including Shannon, Ezra, Johnny, and Junebug, whom the player will also have the opportunity to control, as will be discussed in detail below. The player also can move between game locations using several variations of a map interface. The game was originally funded through a Kickstarter campaign in January and February 2011, and targeted to Windows, MacOS and Linux. Intended to be released in five "acts," the first act was released in January 2013, with "the rest coming every 2–3 months throughout 2013" (Elliot 2011). The actual release schedule was much more drawn-out: acts were released sporadically over the next few years, with additional, free "interludes" released between episodes. The final act, together with a combined release labelled the "TV edition" (on Switch, PlayStation 4, and Xbox One), was released in 2020. In this section, I (Alex)[1] will describe my process of analysing the game, including my choice of play strategies, and I will systematically step through the various stages of our approach to a formalist analysis of a videogame as outlined in chapter 4.

What Is It about the Game That Intrigues Me?

I first came across *Kentucky Route Zero* in 2014, after Act II was released. I was initially intrigued both by the visual style and the reference to magic realism. I was also familiar with an earlier game developed by Cardboard

---

1   Note that when discussing specific play experiences, we will use the first person to acknowledge that this is the experience of one or the other of the authors. In this section, we focus on the first author's experiences.

Computer, *Balloon Diaspora* (Cardboard Computer 2011), which contained some interesting dialogue mechanics that seemed to be deliberately de-familiarizing the player's sense of agency. I was curious as to where these ideas might have been taken in a longer game such as *Kentucky Route Zero*. As described in my early analysis of the game (Mitchell 2014), the game initially appears to be a point-and-click adventure game, albeit one with a very cinematic feeling, stylized art, and poetic text. However, the player's expectation that this is a typical adventure game is quickly undermined:

> The standard pattern in point-and-click adventure games is to place puzzles in the way of the player, forcing the player to solve the puzzle before she can move on. In *Kentucky Route Zero*, the only explicit puzzles that appear are in the first few minutes of the game, and even then, the puzzles seem impossible not to solve. Instead, they seem to be placed in the player's path to first make the gameplay seem familiar, and then to gradually undermine that familiarity as the player starts to wonder what, exactly, was the point of these puzzles. And that wondering, in itself, may be the point (Mitchell 2014, 168).

It was this deliberate undermining of expectations that drew me to the game. I would return to *Kentucky Route Zero* several times over the next few years, as the subsequent acts were released. Beyond the defamiliarization of the puzzle mechanics, the game also seemed to be questioning the very form of the game itself, as it often seemed to be "peeling back the borders of the game world to reveal the stage on which the action is taking place," which served to "defamiliarize the experience and question what exactly are the bounds of what makes something a 'game'" (Mitchell 2016, 13). At times it even seemed to be pushing beyond the boundaries of the game, to the point where "elements of the game world were manifest as actual events or objects outside of the game" (Mitchell et al. 2020). In my earlier work, I have identified a number of poetic gameplay devices that I was encountering in the game, including "imperfect information," "reference to the game from the player's world," "import of other forms into the game," and "ludic intertextuality" (Mitchell et al. 2020).

All of this has served to keep me intrigued by the game over the past eight years, as the acts and interludes were progressively released, together with a number of additional related materials. It is this ongoing intrigue that suggests to me that the game is worth examining in detail from a formalist perspective. For the current analysis, I was particularly intrigued as to how the various motivations beyond the ludic feature in the experience of playing the game, and what additional insights I could develop by taking a more rigorous look at the devices in the game, and how they work together to form the dominant.

What Play Strategies Did I Employ?

For an episodic game that was released over a period of eight years, it is difficult to directly follow the approach we described in chapter 4, namely, to first play the game as a player, and then return to the game with specific play strategies. In fact, I have played parts of the game numerous times, both as a player and a critic, revisiting earlier acts and interludes as each new act was released. In each playthrough, I would notice new elements of the game being made unfamiliar and make connections and see tensions at work that I had not previously noticed. In my early encounters with the game, particularly my first playthrough of Act I, I was likely engaging in some combination of *playing for continuation* and *playing to win*. However, I quickly realized that, even with the first puzzle, there is no way to "lose" the game – the main difficulty is what Jagoda (2018) refers to as interpretive difficulty, which emerges very much from the extensive foregrounding and defamiliarization within the work. There is little in the way of mechanical difficulty – although there are moments where the player needs to determine, for example, where the next trigger for a scene is on the map of the underground highway after which the game is named, it is very unlikely that the player will be unable to progress, and there is definitely no way that the player can "lose" the game. As a result, I very soon found myself adopting a strategy of *playing the game the right way*, even during my first playthrough of some of the later acts and interludes.

Although the game involves a number of choices, often in the form of dialogue, the main consequence of these choices is what the player experiences in terms of the resulting text. While these choices for the most part do not have any impact on what happens in the game, there are lengthy sequences, particularly in Act IV, which the player (possibly unknowingly) needs to choose between, with the path not taken only accessible by replaying the entire act. At other points, there is information scattered around the map, and optional conversations that require the player to actively seek out the trigger points in a location. Having realized this on a second playthrough of Act IV, I found myself deliberately trying to find additional information, engaging in what could be seen as *playing playfully*, so as to find all the information I may have missed on previous playthroughs. This iterative adjustment of play strategies was a response to my ongoing, and constantly updating, understanding of what tensions are at work in the game, and how they form the dominant. Although I was not consciously attending to these concepts in my earlier analysis, as I was focusing entirely on the individual poetic gameplay devices, my play strategy was still somewhat determined by an attempt to maximize my ability to identify new devices.

Preparing for this most recent analysis of the game, I replayed the game from Act I through to the end of the final interlude, *The Death of the Hired Man*, also looking at the various external materials such as the in-game character Junebug's album on Bandcamp, as will be described below. I also played Act IV a second time, since many of the choices in that act lead to mutually exclusive paths through the game. During this process, I was largely focused on playing playfully, trying to find as many additional paths and pieces of information as possible.

Although the game is now available on a range of consoles (in the "tv edition") and on mobile (through Netflix), I played the game on a MacBook Pro using a mouse and keyboard, partly for convenience but also for consistency with my earlier playthroughs, which were all on a MacBook Pro. Throughout my analysis playthrough, I recorded each play session, and took detailed notes at the end of each session. The playthrough took a total of seventeen play sessions, each lasting between thirty minutes and ninety minutes. Most acts took between two to three sessions to complete, other than Act V which was completed in a single session. Interludes also took a single session each. The video recordings, after compression, totalled just under 6 GB. While writing the detailed analysis below, I referred back to my notes, and also skimmed through the videos for reference. The screenshots included in the analysis are all stills taken from these video recordings, occasionally cropped to focus on specific elements of the scene.

Identifying the Materials

To begin considering the tensions at work within *Kentucky Route Zero*, and eventually come to some understanding of the dominant, I started by looking at the materials that make up the game and tried to understand their functions. In this process, I inevitably started to notice materials which are foregrounded (and therefore can be considered to be devices), and where they are in tension with each other. I will start by discussing the materials I encountered as I began playing the game for my analysis playthrough.

Paratexts (Genette 1997; Švelch 2020) are elements of the game that are not actually *in the game* but that the player can encounter when preparing to play the game, during or in between play sessions, or after play, and that will impact the experience and "reading" of the game material. These

Figure 5.1: Introductory splash screen sequence in *Kentucky Route Zero*, including the fictional WEVP-TV logo (all screenshots of *Kentucky Route Zero* are by the first author).

paratexts include things such as a Steam page or back-of-the-box text, and while engaged with the software outside of the game proper, such as splash screens, menus and option screens. The paratext helps to set the tone for the game, particularly for the first-time player.

When starting a new playthrough of *Kentucky Route Zero*, I first encountered a series of *splash screens*[2] (see figure 5.1), each containing a line of text: "Annapurna Interactive," the publisher that Cardboard Computer worked with to release the complete game and the "tv edition"; "WEVP-TV," the name of a fictional television station within the game world, accompanied by a logo of a hand with an eye on its palm; and "A game by cardboard computer" in cursive text. All of these splash screens are rendered such that the image wavers slightly, with the background shown with a slight grey gradient which also wavers, reminiscent of a slightly out-of-tune channel on an analogue television. These screens are accompanied by *audio that resembles static*, ending with a sound reminiscent of the changing of a slide on a manual slide projector. The final splash screen shows the title of the game, rendered crisply in a serif font, with no accompanying audio.

Despite these paratexts being outside of the game world, these materials do not simply function as a way to transition the player from outside to inside

---

2   In this section, as I am focusing on identifying the materials in the game, I will indicate materials in *italics*.

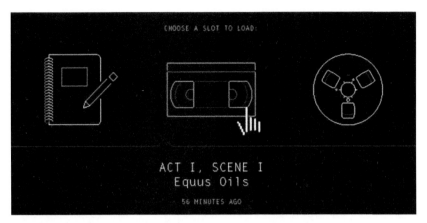

Figure 5.2: *Kentucky Route Zero* loading screen.

the game. They also have both a compositional and an artistic motivation. The compositional motivation comes through the use of the "WEVP-TV" logo, which is actually the logo of a TV station within the game world. This begins the process of world-building. The artistic motivation can be seen in the fact that these materials start to set the tone or feel of the game. In addition, the inclusion of the logo of an in-game organization in the splash screens, on equal footing with the game's publisher and developer, is the first of many moments where the boundaries between the game world and the player's world start to become blurred.

The last splash screen is replaced by a "loading screen," which is titled "CHOOSE A SLOT TO LOAD." Here, I was presented with three icons: a sketchbook, a VHS tape, and a reel-to-reel audio tape (see figure 5.2). The icons are rendered in a way that resembles an old vector-based computer display. Moving the mouse cursor, which is styled as a hand with a pointing finger much like a pointer on an old computer, over an icon changes the lines to a CRT green and is accompanied by low pitched "buzzing" audio feedback. Clicking on an icon is accompanied by a clear "clicking" sound. The *visual style* of the user interface shown here, and the accompanying interaction style, is continued throughout the game. As with the title screens, these materials don't simply form part of the functionality of the user interface, but the specific visual style suggests an artistic motivation related to creating the overall artistic shape of the game.

Upon choosing a new "slot," I was given the choice to "Start" or go "Back," rendered in orange in the same font as the loading screen. Choosing "Start," the screen was replaced by the text "ACT I, SCENE I" in white sans serif font on a black background, followed by "EQUUS OILS" in the same serif font as

Figure 5.3: Establishing the point-and-click conventions of the game *Kentucky Route Zero* in Act I, Scene I.

the main game title screen. This sequence is consistent visually with the initial title sequence. However, this first scene is designated "Act I, Scene I," rather than for example "Episode 1, Chapter 1," as is often the case in games such as *The Walking Dead* (Telltale Games 2012) and *Life is Strange* (Dontnod Entertainment 2017). This suggests a transtextual connection closer to theatre, for example, rather than television as is the case in many episodic games.

In the first scene, "Equus Oils," the game establishes the basic materials that it is composed of (see figure 5.3). The *visual presentation* is similar to that of a typical adventure game, with the game world presented from a side-scrolling perspective that is, for the most part, continuous, without any camera cuts, within a given "level" (scene). There is a cinematic quality to the *camera movement*, with the scene starting with the camera panning down smoothly from a shot of the setting sun to the Equus Oils gas station. When a dialogue box is shown, the camera also smoothly zooms in to focus on the characters and the dialogue box, and the camera smoothly zooms out again when the dialogue box is closed. The *ambient audio* also has a cinematic quality, with crickets chirping in the distance, the rumbling of Conway's truck, and distant sounds of passing traffic all helping to give the scene a sense of depth.

Interaction consists of clicking on a location within the scene, which causes the currently controlled character (initially Conway) to walk towards that location. Icons such as an "eye" (examine) or a "dialogue box" (talk) indicate actions that can be taken on objects within the scene. Clicking on the "eye" icon shows a text description of the selected object, whereas

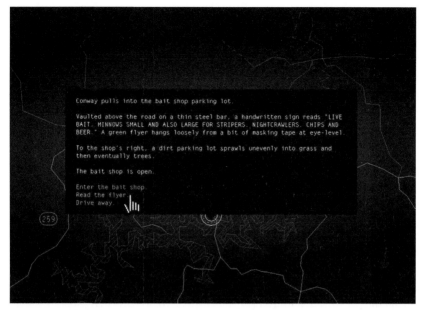

Figure 5.4: Text-based interaction accessed from the map interface: "Bait Shop."

clicking on the "dialogue box" icon brings up a dialogue, showing lines spoken by the selected character, and a set of options, in orange, that the player can choose from. These options are usually *dialogue choices*. The visual style of these text boxes, and the interaction style, is consistent with the loading screen described above.

In addition to the point-and-click interaction described above, *Kentucky Route Zero* also has a *map-based interface*, where initially the player drives around various surface roads in Conway's truck. In later acts the player will fly across the same surface roads on the back of Julian, a giant eagle, drive Conway's truck around the subterranean highway that is Route Zero (referred to as "the Zero" in the game), or sail along the underground Echo River in the Mucky Mammoth, a tugboat introduced at the end of Act II. The map allows the player to move between locations, which generally trigger new Scenes within the current Act or occasionally involve either short point-and-click sequences, such as "Airplane" and "Wreck" in Act I, or purely text-based interaction, such as "Diner" or "Bait Shop" in Act I (see figure 5.4). These text-only sequences are very similar to the dialogue interaction in the point-and-click scenes, with the addition of detailed descriptions of the location, much like a text adventure. In addition, the choices are often actions, rather than dialogue choices, much like when the player is interacting with an object in the point-and-click scenes.

The game initially seems to *progress linearly* for the most part. Although there are some moments in Act I where the player can explore the map and encounter certain optional scenes, such as "Airplane" and "Diner," after completing the puzzles at Equus Oils, the player still needs to first head to the Marquez Farmhouse to speak to Weaver, only after which can the player visit Elkhorn Mines, the possible onramp to the Zero. After this, the player can return to the Marquez Farmhouse, fix Weaver's television, and reveal the actual onramp to the Zero, ending Act I.

Finally, the game introduces what appears to be a typical *puzzle mechanic*. Speaking to Joseph in the first scene, I discovered that Conway, the character I was controlling, is in the midst of delivering some antiques to "Dogwood Drive" but is not sure how to get there. Joseph says that to get there Conway will have to take the Zero, the highway after which the game is named. The Zero is difficult to find, but the directions can be found on Joseph's computer. Unfortunately, the power is out, and to use the computer Conway needs to go down into the basement to reset the circuit breaker. This seems to be following the typical pattern of an adventure game: to solve the overall puzzle of the game (deliver the antiques to Dogwood Drive), the player first has to solve a series of smaller puzzles: find a missing game piece to get past Emily, Ben and Bob, the people in the basement, so as to reset the circuit breaker to access the computer, and then access the computer to find the address.

What Tensions Are at Work, and What Is Foregrounded?

What I have described above seems to be framing the player's experience as that of playing a traditional point-and-click adventure game, albeit one with a very distinct visual style. However, almost every aspect of the game is eventually made strange to a greater or lesser extent. This foregrounding of the various materials was hinted at in the inclusion of the fictional "WEVP-TV" logo in the splash screens, together with the splash screens for the publisher and developer, suggesting that this fictional TV station has the same status as these real organizations. This foreshadows the later blurring of boundaries between the real world and fictional world throughout the game. My inclusion of possible motivations for these materials also suggests that they may in fact be devices. I will now examine how each of the sets of materials described above are foregrounded.

Visual Presentation, the Camera, and the Use of Music
The side-scrolling visual presentation is usually maintained, although in the "Airplane" optional sequence mentioned above the camera perspective is

Figure 5.5: The camera zooming in during the Marquez Farmhouse scene.

shifted to a slightly angled overhead view. This manipulation of the camera is more pronounced in Act I, Scene II. As Conway made his way up the hill to the Marquez Farmhouse, and then entered the second storey room to talk with Weaver, the camera smoothly zoomed in without any cuts, the front wall of the house becoming see-through so that I could see the interior rooms. After I chose to set up Weaver's TV, the camera zoomed in even further, and the lighting changed to a greyish-blue, much like a black-and-white TV. The back wall of the house seemed to open up, with a barn and some horses visible through the wall (see figure 5.5). A vague image was seen on the TV. When I selected to interact with the TV, the camera zoomed in even further until only the barn and horses were visible. After a few moments, Weaver spoke, telling Conway that he spaced out. After a short conversation, in which Weaver seems to be saying goodbye, the camera zoomed out, the wall closed, and the scene returned to normal, with Weaver having disappeared.

This use of the camera zooming in as a way to portray shifts in consciousness, while very unexpected at this moment, comes to be used frequently throughout the game. For example, similar zooming in and out of the camera is used at the end of Act II, when Conway is being tended to by Dr. Truman. However, while this might potentially undermine the degree to which it is foregrounded, the game repeatedly plays with and again foregrounds the way the camera is used. For example, in the same scene, as Conway walked back down to his truck, the camera continued to pan out, beyond the truck, until shadowy figures became visible between the camera and the main scene. These figures appeared to be musicians who are playing the

Figure 5.6: The camera pulls back until the musicians can be seen playing.

music that accompanied the scene (see figure 5.6). This breaks the player's expectation that this music is non-diegetic, and as with the WEVP-TV logo, begins to break the boundaries of the game world.

In addition to zooming, the orientation and position of the camera is also used to de-automatize the player's assumption about the side-scrolling nature of the game. The "Airplane" sequence mentioned above is one example. This becomes more radical in the first interlude, *Limits and Demonstrations*, where instead of a fixed camera angle, the camera seems to be suspended in the middle of a large hall, in this case an art gallery. The camera stays stationary, but pans to follow the three characters, Emily, Ben and Bob. A similar approach will be used in several scenes in Act II, in particular in "The Museum of Dwellings." A variation where the camera moves around a stationary point as characters change location can be seen in the scenes in Act III set in the "Hall of the Mountain King." There are also scenes, such as Act IV, Scene V: "The Radvansky Centre," where the entire scene is rendered in black-and-white, as if shot through a surveillance camera. This foregrounding of the use of the camera becomes more unusual in the second interlude, *The Entertainment*, where the player is placed in the centre of a 3D environment with the camera positioned at eye level, as if the player is seated at a table. The camera is fixed in place, and the player is only able to look around. The scene progresses as the player focuses on the main action taking place in the scene, otherwise the action is paused as the player examines other aspects of the scene. This use of the camera is taken to the extreme in Act V, where the entire act consists of the camera locked

Figure 5.7: Distorted positioning of objects in 3D space in Act II, Scene V: "A Forest."

in place above the centre of a flooded town, focused on the movements of a cat that the player controls. Finally, in the final interlude, *The Death of the Hired Man*, the entire scene consists of the camera remaining stationary and focused on a TV set on a shelf above the bar in "The Lower Depths."

There are moments where the position of the camera with respect to the scene is made strange. The earlier moment when the camera pulls back and shows the musicians is one example. There are also times where the depth of the objects in 3D space seems to be deliberately incorrect, such as during Act II, Scene V: "A Forest," where there are moments where the trees seem to be both in front of and behind the main focus of the scene, in this case Ezra's brother, the giant eagle Julian (see figure 5.7), echoing Magritte's *Le Blanc-Seing* (1965). In fact, at certain moments in this scene the musicians can again be seen between the camera and the main scene. Later, as Conway is put under anaesthetic, the walls pull back, and the same forest becomes visible through the back wall. The text in the dialogue box is increasingly distorted, and as the Act ends, the camera tilts sideways and abruptly cuts to black.

From a typical side-scrolling camera that follows the player's character in much the way the player would expect of a point-and-click adventure game, the camera has been repeatedly defamiliarized. Similarly, the position of music as non-diegetic has been repeatedly defamiliarized. As I will discuss below, this unusual use of the camera and music is often linked to and works together with various other devices, such as breaking of the boundaries of the game, shifting locus of control, and non-chronological sequencing of events.

Interaction, Choices, and Locus of Control

The discussion so far has focused on the various non-interactive materials that make up *Kentucky Route Zero*, and the way that they are foregrounded so as to become devices. I will now discuss the ways that interaction, and in particular the choices the player is given and the character that the player is controlling, is also made strange.

In most adventure games, dialogue choices are one of the main forms of interaction. Players generally expect to be presented with choices as to how the character they are controlling will act, and the ability to select one of these choices and then see the results of that choice played out. In *Kentucky Route Zero*, this expectation is frequently undermined. For example, in the very first scene of the game, in Act I, Scene I, Conway engages in conversation with Joseph, the owner of Equus Oils. In the very first conversation, Joseph asks Conway the name of his dog, to which the player must reply, "His name is Homer," "Her name is Blue" or "Just some dog. I don't know his name." This interaction determines the dog's name. From this point onwards, the dog is referred to as "Homer," "Blue" or "Dog," depending on the option the player selected. Otherwise, there is no discernible impact on the game or the story. There is also no information given to the player as to how to make this choice, as the player has no idea yet who Conway is, or anything about his dog.

Similarly, in one of the early scenes in Act III, the main characters Conway, Shannon and Ezra are stranded when Conway's truck stalls. They call a tow truck, and Shannon has a conversation with the tow truck company's operator. Interestingly, rather than being able to choose what is said by Shannon, one of the characters that I had been controlling so far, I was instead asked to decide how the tow truck operator responds. To complicate matters, the tow truck operator's responses are not shown clearly, with options such as "(inaudible, irritable)," "(inaudible, sleepy)" and "(inaudible, confused)" presented to the player (see figure 5.8). This obscuring of the choices available to the player draws attention to the fact that, in many adventure games, players do not actually have enough information to make a decision. Here, this is very much the case, as the choices themselves are not visible, and I was making choices on behalf of an unnamed, and previously unknown, character.

The strategy of defamiliarizing the choices presented to the player is also used later in the same scene, where the minor characters Johnny and Junebug

Figure 5.8: Inaudible dialogue options and an unknown speaker.

Figure 5.9: Unclear choice of dialogue sequences: headlight, sidecar or brake disc?

are seen riding a motorcycle and sidecar towards the bar "The Lower Depths." During this scene, I was able to trigger a number of dialogue sequences. The choice of which dialogue sequence to activate was presented as a set of options related to aspects of the scene, such as "Headlight," "Sidecar," and

"Brake Disc" (see figure 5.9), without any immediately obvious connection to the resulting dialogue, and certainly with no indication at the time of making a choice what options might be appropriate. Again, this encourages the player to consider how much control the player actually has over the choice of dialogue, and how important these choices may or may not be to the experience of the game.

It is also worth noting that this is the first time I had seen these two characters, so I had no idea who they are or how to make a choice on their behalf. These choices also seemed to be somewhat inconsequential. For example, when Johnny and Junebug later encounter Conway, Shannon and Ezra and offer to give them a ride on their motorcycle, Junebug mentions the name of the bike, and several options are shown. Here, I was asked to make this decision without any background information to base it on, a decision that does not have any impact on the overall narrative of the game but, much like the naming of the dog, will show up later when the bike is mentioned.

An important point to make here is that these instances of foregrounding and defamiliarization, in terms of the player's ability to make choices, the (lack of) consequences of those choices, and who they are controlling, is something that is gradually built up over the game. Although the materials in the game are being foregrounded, there is a pattern being established. The withholding of information about choices, the seeming lack of consequences for choices, and the switching of locus of control are not a one-off defamiliarization. Instead, they are introduced and then repeated with variations throughout the game. The player's blind choice of the name of Junebug's bike directly mirrors the need to name Conway's dog in the first scene. And the conversation between Shannon and the tow truck operator even more directly mirrors the player's first encounter with Shannon in Act I, Scene III, where the player was suddenly put in control of Shannon and asked to make choices for her based on an inaudible response from her phone, and then talk with Conway, who is initially labelled "Stranger" (see figure 5.10).

There are two key observations to make here. First, while the repetition of devices might suggest that the player will become accustomed to the devices, and therefore no longer find them defamiliarizing, this is an important part of the player's experience. Repeating devices prevents the game from becoming chaotic and incoherent. Instead, the player is initially disoriented, but then through the process of refamiliarization the player learns the new conventions of the game, and gradually incorporates them into their process of sense-making around the game. At the same time,

Figure 5.10: The player's first encounter with Shannon, and the accompanying shifting of locus of control.

there is the danger that these devices will become automatized. However, in *Kentucky Route Zero*, over the course of the game, these same devices are again defamiliarized, carefully and repeatedly, constantly pulling the player back out of automatization.

This can be seen as the difference between the type of short, "lyric" poetic game that Magnuson (2019) talks about, and a long-form game such as *Kentucky Route Zero*, in which it is not possible to just defamiliarize materials once and expect the effect of the foregrounding to persist across the game. In particular, for an episode game such as *Kentucky Route Zero* which was developed and released over several years, devices are likely to become conventionalized. However, the game cannot keep arbitrarily throwing new forms of foregrounding at the player, as this is likely to impact the coherence of the game experience. What we see in *Kentucky Route Zero*, instead, is a progression in the devices, as the materials are foregrounded, and then once they are refamiliarized, they are carefully once again foregrounded in a manner that is, on hindsight, consistent with the underlying motivation behind the original foregrounding. This is something that can be seen through a focus on the dominant. I will return to this below as I discuss the dominant in *Kentucky Route Zero*.

An example of this progression in the foregrounding of materials can also be seen in the way that *Kentucky Route Zero* explores different ways of shifting the locus of control. In Act II, Scene IV: "The Museum of Dwellings," I initially saw Conway, Shannon and the dog, whom I had named Blue,

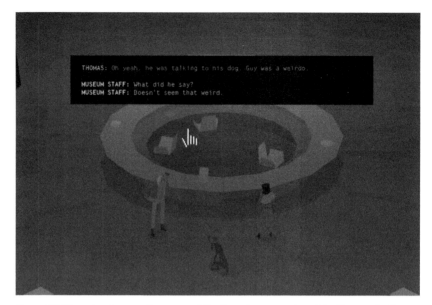

Figure 5.11: Observing Conway, Shannon and Blue from the perspective of the Museum Staff.

standing in what appears to be the information counter in the middle of a museum. An "eye" icon is seen on the counter, and "dialogue" icons appear over Shannon and Blue. On seeing this, I assumed that I was controlling Conway, and that I could have Conway look at the counter or talk to Shannon or Blue. However, on clicking on Blue, I instead saw a dialogue box in which I seemed to be controlling a character named "Museum Staff," who was talking to another character, "Thomas" (see figure 5.11). This continues throughout the scene – although I can control where Conway and the others walk, all dialogue is from the perspective of the Museum Staff interviewing various other characters who seemingly observed the main characters' visit to the museum.

This builds upon the previous changes in locus of control and defamiliarization of dialogue choices, but also takes it one step further, ensuring that if the player had become familiar with the previous use of this device, they would again feel that the device has been foregrounded, but in a way that is consistent with the previous defamiliarization.

Non-chronological Presentation of Events
In addition to re-defamiliarizing the player's experience of locus of control and choice, the scene in "The Museum of Dwellings" also begins to introduce another device, that of the use of interactive flashbacks and non-chronological play sequences.

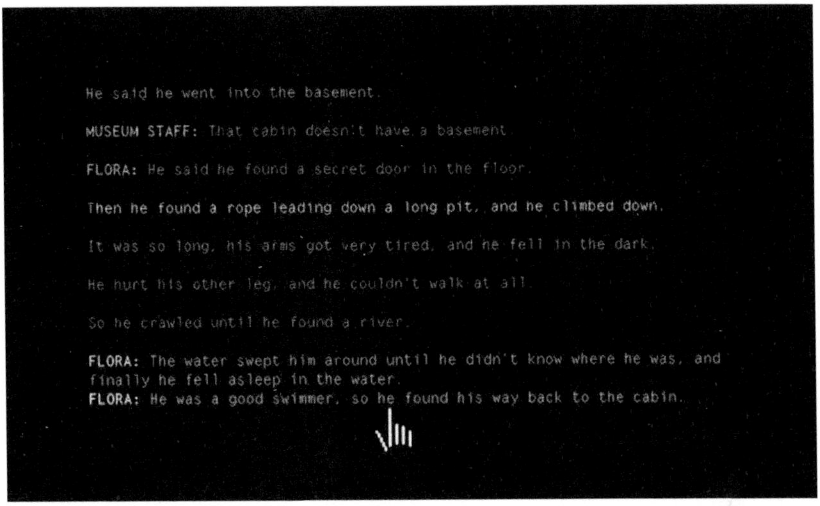

He said he went into the basement.

MUSEUM STAFF: That cabin doesn't have a basement.

FLORA: He said he found a secret door in the floor.

Then he found a rope leading down a long pit, and he climbed down.

It was so long, his arms got very tired, and he fell in the dark.

He hurt his other leg, and he couldn't walk at all.

So he crawled until he found a river.

FLORA: The water swept him around until he didn't know where he was, and finally he fell asleep in the water.
FLORA: He was a good swimmer, so he found his way back to the cabin.

Figure 5.12: Making decisions as Flora about what Conway told her he had done in the basement.

At certain moments in the conversation, for example when the Museum Staff are interviewing Flora about her conversation with Conway, the point-and-click scene fades to black, and only the dialogue is visible (see figure 5.12). During this sequence, I could make choices about what Conway told Flora he had done in the basement of one of the houses in the museum. Note that here I was controlling Flora, not the Museum staff, so control had again shifted. Also, the choices I was making were directly determining Flora's responses, but they were also indirectly determining what Conway said he had done, and thus what Conway had actually done, at some earlier point in time from Flora's perspective, but (given that I was controlling Conway's movements around the museum) that were happening at that exact moment from my perspective. This complex interweaving of flashbacks and the present is clearly not what most players would expect from a game, where players generally expect a direct correspondence between play time and game time (Juul 2004; Mitchell et al. 2020).

This sequence provides a starting point for a more complex defamiliarization of both control and time in what is possibly the turning point in the game, which occurs in two scenes in Act III, both titled "Where the Strangers Come From." In Scene VII: "Where the Strangers Come From," Ezra, Shannon and Conway are looking for a mysterious group of "strangers," as they have been told that the strangers will be able to help repair the computer Xanadu that they need to access to get in touch with Lula Chamberlain, who they believe will be able to get them the address to Dogwood Drive, so that Conway can complete his delivery. Reaching a churchyard where the strangers are said to be found, unexpectedly the two main characters, Shannon and Conway, go off into the church but the player's control is given over to a third character, Ezra, who stays behind together with Johnny and Junebug. As Ezra, I was able to explore the graveyard outside the church, and read the inscriptions on the graves, but not take part in the main action of the scene, which occurs off-screen. After some time, Shannon and Conway emerge from the church. When Junebug asks what happened, Shannon answers, "It wasn't ...," and Conway says: "It doesn't matter." The scene ends, with the player as unaware of what has happened as Ezra, Johnny and Junebug.

This withholding of information, and refusal to allow the player to take control of the main characters, is similar to what I had experienced in earlier scenes. However, in this case, the entire scene seems to have happened beyond my control or even awareness. Interestingly, the player is eventually given access to this information through an extended, interactive flashback. In Scene XI, while the characters are waiting for a ferry at the Bureau of Reclaimed Spaces, Junebug once again asks, "Alright, what happened?" In response to this, I could choose to have Shannon say, "What?," "Nothing.," or "(To Conway) Up to you." Regardless of the player's choice, Conway will say, "It's OK. You can tell them. It doesn't matter anymore," after which the scene transitions to Scene XII: "Where the Strangers Come From." The new scene begins in exactly the same manner as Scene VII. However, this time I was controlling Conway, and the camera followed Conway and Shannon down into the church. I then proceeded to play through the earlier scene, which had previously happened off-screen.

Embedded within this playable flashback sequence is another, nested flashback. Towards the end of Scene XII, Conway is discussing taking on a job as a driver (see figure 5.13). During this dialogue, I was given a seemingly incongruous option: "Conway had to get off the highway – too loud, too murky," which is presented in italics. Choosing this option causes the main scene to fade, and the game to switch to a text-only flashback embedded within the current flashback. Interestingly, I could make choices within this nested flashback, determining which parts of these fragmented memories Conway focuses on. These memories help to flesh out Conway's character. Essentially, I was making decisions about the past, within the flashback, that change the nature of the main character in the present. This builds upon the devices introduced earlier, so I was able to recognize what was happening, but it was taken one step further, allowing me to actually play through a scene from the "past" (from the perspective of the main timeline in the

Figure 5.13: Entering the nested flashback in Act III.

game). This building upon the earlier foregrounding of the non-chronological presentation of events serves to foreground these devices coherently but unexpectedly once again.

Breaking of Boundaries

The final set of devices that I observed in *Kentucky Route Zero* is, once again, foreshadowed from the very start of the game, in the form of the fictional WEVP-TV logo. Throughout the game, there are instances of a gradual breaking down of boundaries. This takes the form of both the game incorporating other, non-game forms, and elements of the game seeming to slip out into the player's world.

A clear example of the game incorporating decidedly non-game elements is seen in the song sequence in Act III, Scene III: "The Lower Depths." As I have described elsewhere (Mitchell 2016), in this scene, Ezra, Shannon and Conway arrive, together with Johnny and Junebug, at the bar after which the scene is named. In the middle of the scene, Johnny and Junebug perform a song, "Too Late to Love You." There are a number of ways in which this sequence is unusual, serving to create a sense of defamiliarization. As the song begins, the roof of the bar rises up into the sky, and Johnny and Junebug's costumes change. The overall effect of this transformation is to give the feeling that you are no longer playing a game, but instead watching a performance on a stage, with the characters played by actors.

Figure 5.14: Interactive song sequence in Act III, Scene III: "The Lower Depths."

The transition here echoes and builds upon the transition seen in Act I, Scene II: "The Marquez Farmhouse."

The interaction provided to the player during this sequence is also somewhat unusual. Before each verse of the song, I was presented with a choice, in a manner very similar to the dialogue choices presented elsewhere in the game (see figure 5.14). Selecting an option, rather than triggering a dialogue response, selects the next verse that Junebug will sing. As she sings each verse, the lyrics are shown, with the current word being sung highlighted in green, much like a karaoke machine. Once the song ends, the roof comes back down, and everything returns to normal. But the sense of strangeness created by this sequence lingers.

This is an example of the game incorporating very non-game-like sequences. Similar examples of non-game-like interactions can be seen throughout the game. For example, in Act IV, Scene III: "The Rum Colony," if the player chooses to stay on the Mucky Mammoth, Shannon watches several tapes on an old video cassette player. The selection and "viewing" of the videos is done entirely through text. This not only breaks the visual point-and-click nature of the game but does so in the context of interacting with a simulation of a visual medium, a video cassette recorder. There is a blurring and swapping of modalities here: Shannon is viewing a video tape, but the player is "seeing" this through text.

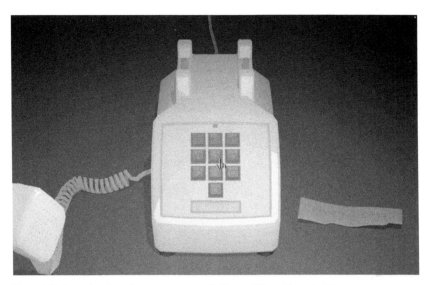

Figure 5.15: Accessing the voice response menu in *Here and There Along the Echo.*

The disruption of boundaries is taken to an extreme in the third interlude, *Here and There Along the Echo*, originally released after Act III. This interlude consists of an interactive rendering of an old touch-tone phone. The interaction consists entirely of dialling a phone number (originally provided on a simulated postcard on the *Kentucky Route Zero* website but shown on an on-screen scrap of paper in the final version), and then navigating through a voice response menu (see figure 5.15). The menus provide information about various sites along the Echo River, and also give advice as to how to handle situations such as "if you are holding a snake right now," or "if you don't remember dialling this number." This interlude pushes the defamiliarization of interaction one step beyond what has been discussed so far. The interaction style – that of navigating a voice response menu – is certainly not what is usually expected in a game and does not follow from anything I had experienced in the game to this point. The content is also unusual. Some of it provides insight into the Echo River, a location in the world of *Kentucky Route Zero* that will be of importance in Act IV. However, some of it, such as the instructions on how to deal with discovering that you are holding a snake, are surreal and never actually occur anywhere else in the game, but still do fit within the magical realist setting of the larger game.

There is, however, one more way in which the interlude makes the experience of play unfamiliar. This is through a bleeding over into the real world. This was done through the sale, on eBay, of a "Weird Telephone, only dials one number" (see figure 5.16). The only number the phone can dial is the

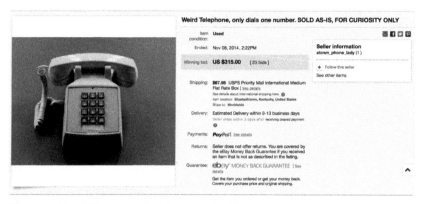

Figure 5.16: "Weird Telephone, only dials one number," for sale on eBay.

number featured in the interlude. Once this number is dialled, the phone allows you to access, through a physical interface, the same voice response menu as in *Here and There Along the Echo*. This effectively breaches the boundary of the world of the game, bringing an artefact from the game world into the real world.

As a final point on this interlude, it turns out that when I exited from the voice response menu in the digital version of *Here and There Along the Echo*, I encountered a brief dialogue-based interaction where it became clear that Emily, Ben and Bob, the characters I first encountered in the basement of Equus Oils in Act I, Scene I, and had later seen in *Limits and Demonstrations*, are the characters I was controlling as I interacted with the virtual phone. The phone's voice response menu also makes an appearance in one of the scenes in Act IV, where the characters stop at a floating phone booth on the Echo River, and I had the opportunity to access some of the messages found in a section of *Here and There Along the Echo*.

This strategy of overlapping the game world with the player's world has been used, to varying degrees, as an extension or supplement to several earlier interludes: the scripts for the plays featured in *The Entertainment*, for example, are available for order from Lulu (Cardboard Computer n.d.), and the artist/curator Lee Tusman curated an exhibit of the character Lula Chamberlain's work (Tusman 2013) in parallel with the release of the first interlude, *Limits and Demonstrations*, which also featured Lula Chamberlain's work in a virtual exhibition. There are also a number of examples not directly associated with the interludes, including the release of a music album by the character Junebug (Junebug and Ben Babbitt 2020), and the characters Johnny and Junebug appearing on late-night TV on WEVP-TV (Cardboard Computer 2016) (see figure 5.17).

Figure 5.17: Johnny and Junebug appear on WEVP-TV's "Night Noise with Rita," used by permission of Cardboard Computer.

Stepping Back: What Is the Dominant?

In the above sections, I have analysed the various materials used in *Kentucky Route Zero* and explored where these materials are foregrounded and therefore transformed into devices. I have also discussed both how these devices work together, and how the game repeatedly introduces these devices and then, once the player has become accustomed to them, once again foregrounds them. This is leading us towards a discussion of the dominant, and hopefully a sense as to what it is that creates the player's aesthetic experience in the game, and how the player can make sense of this experience.

The use of defamiliarization throughout the game can be seen as building towards the final Act, where all of the techniques seen so far are brought to bear and are yet again foregrounded. This reflects a number of elements of the context of the game that I have alluded to but have not discussed in detail. One key point is that the game was developed over a period of eight years, from 2012 when the Kickstarter campaign was completed, through to 2020 when Act V and the complete "tv version" was released. Over this time, there were many changes to what players would expect of a game, and many changes to what the developers, Cardboard Computer, were able to do both from a design and a technical standpoint. The game clearly reflects both of these progressions. By the end of the game, all of the devices that were introduced over the course of the game had come to contribute to the overall experience: the use of visual presentation, the camera and music; changing the locus of player control; undermining of expectations for dialogue choice; non-chronological play sequences; and breaking the boundaries of the game. In this final section, I will first discuss the interlude between Acts IV and V, *Un Pueblo De Nada*, and then Act V and the final interlude, *The Death of the Hired Man*, and use this discussion to show how the dominant becomes clearest upon considering the final act and final two interludes in relation to the rest of the game.

The interlude *Un Pueblo De Nada* makes use of a number of the devices that we have seen so far, while at the same time making alterations to the interaction style. Similar to *Limits and Demonstrations*, the camera is fixed in the middle of a 3D space, and the player's interactions cause the camera to pan around that space. Here, however, the presentation is much more like a traditional 3D game, with the characters much closer to the camera as opposed to the somewhat distant positioning in the rest of the game. I was controlling Emily, and it quickly became clear that the action was taking place in the WEVP-TV studio. Emily is working the camera for "The Evening Broadcast," which turns out to be the last programme broadcast by the station before it is destroyed in a flood. Interestingly, a live-action version of the broadcast can be found both on the Cardboard Computer YouTube channel,[3] and on the WEVP-TV website.[4] This video mirrors what is happening in the interlude (see figure 5.18), once again serving to foreground the barriers between the game world and the real world, and doing it in a way that goes beyond what I had experienced in the game so far.

The various forms of defamiliarization and foregrounding seen throughout the game all come together in Act V, where the player's control is shifted to a cat who roams the town where the main characters have ended up, having finally completed Conway's mission to deliver the antiques to Dogwood Drive, although Conway has not managed to make it to his destination. As the cat, I could interact with all of the characters who had been encountered so far, plus a few who were new to the final Act. By this point I was familiar with the shifting locus of control and the frequent flashbacks. These happened more and more frequently and served as a way to bring together the many characters I had encountered. There were some new interactions introduced here, including the ability for the cat to meow in a number of different ways. There were also a number of passages in text, triggered when the cat approaches the mysterious black silhouetted figures who are wandering the

3   https://www.youtube.com/c/CardboardComputer/videos
4   http://wevp.tv/vdb/

Figure 5.18: "The Evening Broadcast," in-game version (left) and live-action version (right), used by permission of Cardboard Computer.

town, where interaction is through clicking on in-line hyperlinks, rather than dialogue choices. As with previous text-based flashbacks, the main scene is dimmed, but here it does not fade completely to black. These subtle alterations to the interaction draw attention to themselves but remain consistent with the trajectory of alterations to the devices throughout the game.

Act V is a single scene, only divided by three title cards that momentarily appear and display what appears to be a scene break, but without the scene numbers from the previous acts, and without a change of setting. Interestingly at least one of these, the final, is written in the first person: "THEN WE BURIED THE HORSES." The act culminates in a funeral held for the "Neighbors," horses that lived in the town and were killed in the flood that destroyed the WEVP-TV studio in the previous interlude. Here, I was making choices that determined the content of a poem read out by one of the characters, and then I listened to Emily sing a song for the horses, as the scene was gradually filled with the black silhouettes encountered earlier in the act. The camera, which had until then been fixed in the middle of the town much like in *Un Pueblo De Nada*, moved upwards, remaining focused on the horses' grave but now showing a view from above. All of the characters gradually dispersed, and I was able to once again control the cat. When I had the cat run over to 5 Dogwood Drive, where Weaver seemed to be sitting on the steps and all the other main characters (except Conway, who disappeared at the end of Act IV) had gathered together with the antiques that Conway was originally tasked with delivering, the sun set, and the scene faded to a final title card, "The End."

If the player has made certain choices earlier in the game, namely returning to Equus Oils and talking to the character Carrington, then a final interlude will be available after the end of Act V, *The Death of the Hired*

Figure 5.19: Changing channels and listening to Carrington in *The Death of the Hired Man*.

Man. This interlude provides a final opportunity for defamiliarization, as almost all of the player's control is removed. All I could do was change the channels on a television above the bar in "The Lower Depths" and watch a wide range of seemingly unrelated programmes, while several characters, including Emily, talked about the failure of Carrington's play (see figure 5.19). This completely stripped away any sense that I was playing a game. Despite this, the conventions that were set up at the start of the game remain largely intact: the scene is presented continuously from a single camera angle, the dialogue is presented in black boxes sequentially on screen, and visually it still feels like a point-and-click adventure game. What is no longer present is any interaction beyond changing channels on the television.

So, what does this mean in terms of the dominant? As I have described, *Kentucky Route Zero* carefully sets up a range of conventions at the start, in terms of visual presentation, the use of the camera, audio and music, interaction, choices, the player's locus of control, and the linear presentation of the scenes in the game. Each of these is systematically foregrounded, and yet these foregrounded materials are then used consistently, and then once again defamiliarized. Despite this, at the core, the game has remained what it started as: a point-and-click adventure game that involves moving through a space, interacting through the use of dialogue, and as a result advancing the narrative. This is done over the course of roughly eight to ten hours of play time, for a game that was developed and gradually released over a period of eight years. This is very much in contrast to the games we have discussed earlier in this book, which have largely been short, and have often radically defamiliarized some aspects of the game in a way that could arguably not be sustained across a much longer play experience.

In *Kentucky Route Zero*, we have seen a constant need to renew, to push the boundaries and do so in a way that is, at the same time, continuous with the past. As Reed, Murray and Salter say in their discussion of *Kentucky Route Zero*, connecting the game to the larger history of adventure games:

> Adventure games are indeed, and always have been, awkward ... They get us lost and ask us to find our way out again, coming to a new understanding of the world, the way we think about it, or ourselves ... they centre the uncertain but tantalising sensation of encountering the unfamiliar (2020, 211).

Rather than trying to completely undermine the form of the game, what the creators of *Kentucky Route Zero* have been doing is to constantly show us the mystery and unfamiliarity in the familiar, so much so that we start to become familiar with it again, at which point they push us just a little bit further, once again making anew what we had started to take for granted. Perhaps it is this process itself that comes to be foregrounded, and acts as the dominant – the constant cycle of defamiliarization, refamiliarization, and once again defamiliarization.

In addition, it is this cycle of familiarity and unfamiliarity which suggests ways that the player may find to make sense of their aesthetic experience. The materials and devices encountered in *Kentucky Route Zero* connect not just to the history of adventure games, but more broadly to our experience of the world, and ourselves. The constant cycle of defamiliarization and refamiliarization mirrors the way that the modern world, while still seeming to be the same, also constantly seems to be becoming strange. Critics have often connected *Kentucky Route Zero* to the literary genre of magic realism, which does something similar. As Sheehan argues in their review of the game for NPR:

> It is a magical realist adventure, following in the traces of Gabriel Garcia Marquez (natch) and Neil Gaiman. It distorts reality and plays with surrealism like China Mieville and Haruki Murakami do, dropping references to Kafka and *100 Years of Solitude* and Appalachian myths, all seasoned with

a wicked, wry and weird sense of humor. [...] the power of magical realism as a genre – the thing that makes it so spooky, so off-putting and able to get at the particular crawling dread of this modern century – is that every injection of the surreal, the impossible, the magical is treated the same way we'd treat the wind blowing or a lamp switching on. It is not unusual. It is not remarkable. Magical realism, on the page, is a tacit acceptance of the fundamental brokenness of reality (or, alternately, the mundanity of unreality) and the lack of commentary IS the commentary (Sheehan 2021).

So, it is possible, and would be interesting, to focus on the specific connections that the game makes to the larger world, such as debt, the creeping power of nameless, faceless corporations, the importance of building community, and the fragmentary nature of memory and identify, each of which are indeed part of the formal structure of the work. However, my formalist analysis and identification of the dominant points to a boarder sense-making, that of the connection between the player's overall aesthetic experience of the game, and their experience of the simultaneous strangeness and mundanity of life beyond the game. Through their process of sense-making and finding meaningful connections between their play experience and the world, players can see their own lived experience in a new way, and in the process "recover the sensation of life" (Shklovsky 2012a, 26).

The Legend of Zelda: Breath of the Wild

Having applied a formalist analysis to *Kentucky Route Zero*, a game that seems to ideally fit the approach, we will now turn our focus to something more "mainstream," *The Legend of Zelda: Breath of the Wild* (Nintendo 2017), to demonstrate the flexibility of the toolkit provided by a formalist stance. This provides us with an opportunity to consider how a game that largely conforms to player expectations can still contain a range of different devices and materials that work together and in tension with each other to create broader aesthetic effects.

Given the focus of the approach and the academic tradition that we build on in this book, one would assume that videogame formalism is best applied to the study of art games like *Kentucky Route Zero*. After all, these games are the type of games that almost by definition do something unusual or unfamiliar when seen in relationship to the more conventional games whose materials function in such a way that our playing of them has become automatized. Furthermore, as Thompson notes, Russian formalist critics themselves, like most critics, "often singled out highly distinctive works" that provide interesting, unfamiliar devices to analyse whereby, in turn, difference or originality functions as "evaluative criteria of high quality" (1988, 49). Put differently, it is the games that clearly subvert conventions that actually give us something to write about, because what on earth would you write about the umpteenth game in a familiar AAA-franchise? Nevertheless, we argue that videogame formalism makes for a valuable analysis method that is also suitable to AAA-games, especially if we acknowledge that our aesthetic play experience does not solely concern the defamiliarization of abstract game material but also broader meaning-making processes.

Here, however, the critic's task is a slightly different one from the task of analysing an art game. Instead of departing from a more apparent aesthetic experience and then clarifying and interpreting the game's unfamiliar devices responsible, the critic now needs to lay bare a combination of materials and devices to show how these are in fact functioning in a way that is more complex and less ordinary than one would initially have thought. Or, as Thompson puts it when taking the "classical cinema" example of *Terror by Night* (Neill 1946) as a case study (a TV film in the Sherlock Holmes series that ran between 1939–46): "the critic's job could be to re-defamiliarize the film – indeed, to defamiliarize it more than it would have been on its first appearance" (1988, 51). By iteratively, but systematically, going through the game's different materials and devices and the way in which they function to evoke our aesthetic play responses, the critic can reveal how the combinations of these does in fact challenge specific conventions even if, on their own, they appeared not to or were hidden by more automatized materials with other more dominant motivations.

In this case we have opted for *The Legend of Zelda: Breath of the Wild* (*BotW*) as a case study to demonstrate the usefulness of the approach. *BoTW* is an interesting case study because it is both familiar and unfamiliar at the same time. As the nineteenth instalment in a risk-aversive AAA Zelda franchise (not counting the many spin-offs and remakes) the game comes in in familiar territory, continuing a long-existent storyline and building on familiar mechanics from earlier Zelda games as well as other (open world) games like *Shadow of the Colossus* (Team Ico 2005). On the other hand, it would be unfair to characterize *BotW* as just another ordinary AAA-game given the universal acclaim the game has received from critics and players alike. A quick Google search for *BotW* will pull up hundreds of reviews appraising the innovative open-world design of the game which shows that the game clearly also shattered conventions for many. While we wouldn't characterize *BotW* as an "art game" which purposefully subverts player expectations at multiple levels to stretch the medium's artistic potential beyond the conventional, the game still does something different with its open world design that draws our interest, and which provides a good starting point for our analysis below.

However, the open world design also raises challenges for the player critic. After all, little guidance from the game also means it is more difficult to follow the game's suggested path, potentially allowing for a great variety of possible playthroughs and thereby different readings within the game's architecture. This makes it all the more important to reflect on the player critic's background brought to the game and the choices made in it. While this does not make the analysis directly reproducible by another player critic, it at least makes all the steps transparent and traceable and provides insights into the way that the game, the player, and the context together shape the results of the analysis. So, it is a reflection on this situatedness that we will start with here.

The Player Critic: Playing *BotW* (Twice)

Analysing *BotW* can be a daunting exercise. With a total of fifteen main quests and seventy-seven side quests to complete, 120 Shrines to visit (forty-two of which only become available after completing a Shrine quest), and a wide variety of weapons, armour and materials to collect and foods to cook, the game is vast. When I (Jasper)[5] first decided to take up this game as a case study, I had already put in an excess of eighty-five hours of play which had only taken me through the main questline, twenty-three out of forty-two Shrine quests, and eighteen(!) out of seventy-seven side quests. While I had far from completed the game, I had considered it finished and hadn't touched it in over a year.

So, when picking up the game again for this analysis, I brought clearly established preconceptions on what the game was about and what its main experience consisted off. These preconceptions were of course also informed by experiences with other (Zelda) games which functioned as a comparative backdrop to help establish the game's most distinguishing features. At the time, these preconceptions would have read something like this:

> *BotW* is a wonderfully atmospheric open world game which provides the player with an unusual amount of freedom compared to other games in

5   In this section we use the first person when we are focusing on the second author's experiences.

the franchise while still structuring the play experience with familiar quest lines, environmental hazards (heat, cold, height) and enemies of different strengths. These characteristics allow the player to both freely bask in the natural beauty of Hyrule (the kingdom that most Zelda games take place in) and still engage in the familiar questing, grinding, and levelling up needed to progress through the game.

While these preconceptions again emphasize the dual nature of the game as both familiar and unfamiliar, I'll admit that my first playthrough was mostly focused on the familiar parts. This is because, as a player, I tend to align predominantly with what Bartle (2003) would characterize as the player category of "planners." I tend to set myself the goal of finishing a game and then quickly and systematically try to get to a point that could reasonably be considered an endpoint. In this case, my first playthrough had mostly focused on making my way through the main quest line and defeating the antagonist of the game, "Calamity Ganon." While I had spent hours roaming around Hyrule to climb and activate the different Sheikah towers, find different Shrines and complete the trials within them, and kill guardians (ancient machines under Ganon's control), all those actions were means to another end: completing the main questline and finishing the game. Climbing the Sheikah towers was needed to "open up" (make visible) the different areas of the map and find the locations of the main quests, and the grind of finishing the Shrine trials and killing guardians was needed to level up (stamina and health) and add a strong (ancient) armour to my inventory to withstand the more hazardous areas in the game. So, while I had certainly enjoyed the game (more than many other games), I was also of the opinion that much of the praise the game received about its innovative open-world character was exaggerated.

Picking up the game again for this book, my predisposition was therefore one of scepticism and curiosity. While I was keen to put more focus on the intriguing, unfamiliar elements of the game (in relationship to the familiar) using the framework of videogame formalism, I was also wary (and a little anxious) that the whole exercise could turn out to be a dud.

But when I started the game again, things flowed quite naturally. Having finished the game once before, I never felt my usual strong drive to make progress which in turn allowed me to see how the game actually affords (or, as I will show below, encourages) a more aimless loitering. Here, it shows how the aesthetic experience arises in the interplay of game, player, and context. Had I tried to analyse the game upon my first playthrough I may well have focused on different elements, made different in-game choices, and noticed different distinguishing features. But in this second playthrough, the goal of finishing the game made way for another goal of continuous digression, afforded by the game's lack of action-based design, its open world, the beauty of its natural landscape, and many other materials. While a desire for levelling up did kick in at some point, the increased health, stamina and stronger armour were never a means to progress but instead a means to a continuous wandering without being killed.

So, after acknowledging the role that situatedness played in this analysis, I will systematically go through the methodological considerations that make up the approach. I start by 1) asking what intrigues me about the game and explore aimless wandering as my initial aesthetic response. I then 2) reflect on the cooperative play strategy employed in relation to this wandering and continue to 3) move to establishing the dominant and the different materials and devices and their motivations. I finally 4) ask what makes this game's functioning meaningful, leading to my final conclusions about *BotW*.

The Aesthetic Experience of Wandering

When starting the game, Link, the main character, is seen waking up from a one-hundred-year sleep in the Shrine of Resurrection. After a brief moment of gameplay in which the player moves Link towards the exit of the Shrine, the game takes control, and the camera zooms out and tilts up to show a beautiful vista of the Great Plateau (a region in the Hyrule Kingdom) with Death Mountain looming in the background. This scene in which the player moves from indoors to outdoors is short but significant. While the indoor scene makes use of a single-point-perspective with the vanishing point indicating exactly where to go to, the outdoor scene provides a vista with no clear vanishing point, instead filling the screen with a range of points of interest in the landscape (see figure 5.20). None of these points of interest particularly stand out as clear goals, with even the prominent Death Mountain appearing just off-centre and the silhouette of Hyrule castle blending in with the mountains to the left and right of it.

While The Great Plateau is a relatively straightforward fenced-off starting/tutorial area in which certain quests need to be completed to acquire items and abilities (the Runes and the paraglider) and move on to other areas in the game, this opening scene already hints at the more open-ended rest of the game. As opposed to a game like *Journey* (thatgamecompany 2012) in which a single prominent mountain is nearly always visible in the background as a reminder of the game's endpoint, *BotW*'s landscape is characterized by obfuscation of a clear goal and multiple points of interest on the horizon.

Figure 5.20: Moving from indoor to outdoor in the opening scene of *BotW* (all screenshots from *BotW* are by the second author, unless otherwise indicated).

Figure 5.21: The triangle rule in the landscape design of *BotW*. Image taken from Schnaars (2021, 123), used by permission of Cornelia J. Schnaars.

Referencing a Nintendo talk at the Computer Entertainment Developers Conference in 2017 (Yang 2017; Matt Walker [@retroOtoko] 2017; Nishikawa 2017), Schnaars shows how *BotW*'s landscape is designed according to the "triangle rule," in which landscape features like mountains or rock formations are shaped like triangles (see figure 5.21). This design feature "ensures that the players' vision is constantly obstructed, and they must always decide whether to circumvent an obstacle or climb across it" (2021, 122). Scaling such a triangle presents the player with a new vista in which a new range of interesting points like mountaintops, Shrines, Sheikah towers, or other distinguishing features in the landscape present themselves. Consequently, the player keeps exploring the landscape and is rarely drawn to, or reminded of, one clear objective.

It is this exploration without clear objectives that characterizes the aesthetic experience I had on my second playthrough. After an hour or so in, this is what started to intrigue me about the game, and this is what consequently started to focus the analysis. This experience of playing without a clear guiding objective is highlighted from the get-go and the game keeps evoking it throughout, via a multitude of different rule-based, stylistic, and narrative materials functioning in different motivational categories (see below). While the game of course also has familiar features (main quests and side quests, a levelling system, a basic plot) which allow for a more conventional playthrough (like the one I had on my first go), the formalist framework helped to focus attention on the more unfamiliar devices (in their interplay with the more familiar materials) leading to this more distinguishing, intriguing experience with *BotW*.

This experience of aimless wandering in *BotW* has been noted by many others before, although most of the time, it is articulated in different ways. Most reviewers mention the game's innovative open-world character and unusual player freedom (Gray 2017) as its most distinguishing features. For example, Schnaars (2021) talks about the game's "airness" consisting of an optional non-sequential quest system, the already mentioned landscape design encouraging exploration, and the physics and chemistry system which allows for a plethora of creative manipulations of the environment and thereby experimental puzzle solving and different ways of progress.

However, where Schnaars and others emphasize how these design features provide players with reasons to do things in different ways (solving puzzles, discovering new routes, collecting objects etc.), I argue that many of these features are noteworthy because they actually allow players to digress or loiter. Instead of providing reasons to do things, *BotW* is okay with the player not doing much at all. Or, as an article in Medium.com from March 2018 puts it:

> While the game can lead you along a little bit, not only is the collar loose and easy to escape from – the game actively encourages its removal. In every direction of it's [sic] open world, beyond each mountain and over every rolling hill, there is something to discover. And between the things to discover, between the doing? Nothing, largely! While there are secrets to find and enemies to fight, there are many more spaces that are okay with just being spaces. Here, the action design of prior *Zelda* entries takes a backseat as the "breath" in *Breath of the Wild* takes the reigns – while the wind stirs the trees, a squirrel escapes into the brush: above, the clouds converge into a dark mass – looks like it'll rain soon (jace :) 2018).

Because the game's design features actively work against goal-directed play behaviour (see below), the aesthetic experience in this game shows similarities to the walking or wandering experienced in so-called "walking simulators." While walking is present in all games, it is usually a means to an end (following the storyline, completing a quest, solving a puzzle, etc.). However, in a lot of *BotW*, like in walking simulators, walking is the end. As Kagen puts it: "walking sims are often designed to retard activity and promote meandering, in a similar way that a wandering text works against quick reading" (2017, 280). In *BotW*, meandering is not an act of resistance against the game design, but instead it is explicitly afforded or even encouraged. Because, as I'll show below, *BotW* is not really that concerned with a clear guiding plot or even ludic objectives providing "movement impetus" (Davies 2009), "wandering is not wandering 'away' from the plot of the game [or ignoring the game's ludic functionalities]; wandering *is* the game" (Kagen 2017, 282).

Link the Flâneur: On Playing the "Right" Way

Because it is achieved through the strategy of cooperative play or playing the "right" way, I argue that wandering is not an act of resistance against the game's design. As we argued in chapter 4, this methodological play strategy involves taking note of the game's materials and devices in all motivational categories (ludic, compositional, realistic, transtextual, and artistic) and have these inform further actions in the game. In this case, the game encourages non-linearity by emphasizing different points of interest or possible objectives at the same time, which is also why many players of *BotW* will acknowledge that no one really plays this game in the same way. But more than that, the game provides players with reasons and means to loiter, to simply traverse the landscape.

This already becomes apparent in the opening hours of the game. Once the player has completed the four Great Plateau shrines and received a paraglider to leave the area, an old man, who has now revealed himself to be the ghost of King Rhoam (the last king of Hyrule), provides Link with the background story and the main objective of the game: go to Hyrule Castle and kill Calamity Ganon. However, as soon as the quest appears in Link's adventure log, the king immediately advices the player to digress from this main objective (see figure 5.22) and head elsewhere (in this case to Kakariko village to seek out the elder Impa). While minutes earlier, the voice of Zelda had urged Link to hurry and kill Ganon, that time pressure seems now to have gone out the window in favour of heading into the "wilderness." This first part of the game in which I was confronted with conflicting objectives (both of which can be strived for), opens the door to digression. Here, the

I believe it would be quite reckless for you to head directly to the castle at this point.

Figure 5.22: Cutscene with King Rhoam providing two conflicting quests.

game was basically telling me: "This is your objective! Now, ignore it and do something else."

From here on out, several materials and devices keep encouraging the player to digress. I will highlight a few here (and delve into several more below).

First, following King Rhoam's general directions on how to get to Kakariko village, will have the player come across different characters offering directions to other places around Hyrule as well. For example, the character Brigo, located on the bridge across the Hylia River, will provide directions back to the Great Plateau and Hyrule Castle, and the character Rensa, located at Dueling Peaks Station will add directions to Hateno Village (which, at that point, will certainly be in an undisclosed area on the map – see below). It is through these *helpful strangers*[6] that the game kept telling me about the range of other areas to explore and places to visit, in effect (again) luring me away from the quest that I was on (see figure 5.23).

Secondly, the *design of the landscape* (according to the above-mentioned triangle rule) in combination with the newly acquired paraglider, encourages the player to deviate from the trodden-path and scale mountains to paraglide down. In my case, this meant that (even on my first playthrough) my route to Kakariko village turned into a personal objective of continuously finding higher ground to be able to paraglide ever longer distances. Although *BotW* has a stamina mechanic that keeps players from climbing too high if their stamina is not levelled-up sufficiently, the highest mountains on the way

6   From here on, I will indicate relevant materials in *italics*.

Figure 5.23: The character Brigo providing directions to several places across Hyrule.

to Kakariko village are all scalable without levelling-up stamina. Climbing the Dueling Peaks, for instance, the two most tempting peaks in the area, is like scaling a stairstep construction whereby the mountains are designed in such a way that they provide flat services at exactly the right distance between vertical walls to allow the player to regain stamina to continue.

Thirdly, while the game offers a marker on the map for Kakariko Village, that part of the map has not been activated yet, in effect asking the player to traverse the landscape by orientating themself using landmarks. While the Sheikah tower is on the way to Kakariko village which would allow players to activate the map, sending the player off into unmapped territory happens throughout the game and is significant here. This attunes the player to the markers in and affordances of the environment and how to find their own path through it. Following de Certeau (1988, 117–22), I argue that, because of the lack of an objective set of spatial positions on a map, the player is encouraged to make sense of the environment by generating a personal spatial story within it, experiencing spatial relations from the point-of-view of the character (what de Certeau would call a "tour" rather than a "map"). Because that part of Hyrule has not yet been solidified within the static representation of the map, it remains open to whatever personal spatial relations the player constructs in there through their different actions. In other words, by sending the player into unchartered territory, the player is again encouraged to deviate from the objective and explore the landscape, to study its markers, and to make it their own.

So, if a player gives heed to these (and other) materials, loitering is not a deviant or transgressive act against the system, but one that is explicitly encouraged by it. Although this is by far the only set of actions and experiences encouraged by the game (it certainly also encourages more goal directed behaviour – see my first playthrough), meandering into the wild does not involve disobeying the game's guiding structure, nor does it require exceptional skills, let alone cheats. Instead, cooperating with this game system can quite easily lead to a variety of different and personal explorations of the game's natural environment whereby the player becomes more attuned to its landmarks and beauty. This means seeing its affordances for travel, but, as I will argue more below, also simply seeing it (unconditionally).

In anticipation of my conclusion, I see similarities here, between the game-player-relationship and the relationship between Haussmannized Paris of the nineteenth century and the flâneur. After Haussmann had renovated the city of Paris by order of Napoleon III, its new wide avenues and open spaces (parks and squares) provided Parisians with connecting routes to explore, and a new beauty and airiness to enjoy. This gave rise to the flâneur, whom Baudelaire describes as a "dandy" and a "passionate spectator" who mixes in with the crowd to traverse the city with no clear goal other than to watch "the river of life flow past him in all its splendour and majesty" (1964, 9–11). I argue that, just as Paris is modelled to play into this aimless wandering and scopophilia of the flâneur, so too is *BotW* designed for the player to simply walk around and enjoy its beauty. Its landscape is characterized by endless connecting routes, vast open spaces, and beautiful vistas for the player to appreciate. While in other games, aimless wandering often requires a more concerted effort against the system, similar to how the more structured aimless wandering practice of the Dérive was a political act of resistance against the city's guiding structure (Flanagan 2009, 194–97), in *BotW*, the game and the player work together. And, just as the flâneur becomes submerged in the stone jungle of the city, so too does the player become connected to (and overwhelmed by) the natural beauty of the represented land of Hyrule.

The Missing Link: Identifying (Some More) Materials and a Few Devices

Already in the abovementioned opening minutes of the game, we can identify a plethora of different materials such as landscape design, composition and framing of pre-established shots, lighting, camera perspectives, camera movement, player control (and lack thereof), the introduction of a few core mechanics, and the bare bones of a story introduction. As mentioned, many of these materials set the stage for an open world game without clear objective and the experience of aimless wandering. For example, inside the Shrine of Resurrection, a pre-established *camera position* directs the player in one clear direction in a perfectly symmetrical following shot, after which a long shot emphasizes the open landscape. The use of soft *lighting* further emphasizes the single player objective inside the dark confined Shrine which is juxtaposed by the harsh brighter backlighting of the Great Plateau creating the silhouettes of the mountains in the background, indicating multiple possible objectives. And, paradoxically, the promise of more freedom and contemplation outside of the Shrine is emphasized by taking *control* away from the player which forces Link to walk to the end of the cliff and allows the player to admire the view with its seemingly endless opportunities for action.

However, given that a few minutes of play already yield such a large number of materials, where do you start (and end) analysing a game that can easily take up more than one hundred hours of play? As we've noted in chapter 4, this is a matter of being selective in the in-game choices you make, the materials you focus on, and what you eventually decide to write up. In this case, I have not only let my play strategy (predominantly playing the "right" way) and focus (on the unfamiliar) be guided by the iterative process of establishing the dominant, but I also justify my selective write-up by acknowledging that this analysis serves to showcase the working of our formalist methodology. In that light, I select a few exemplary devices in the five motivational categories to show how they interrelate with other devices in cueing our aesthetic experience. I will start with the more obvious ludically motivated devices and make my way down to the less obvious artistically motivated ones.

Ludic Motivation

By the sheer definition of ludic motivations, it seems paradoxical (if not impossible) to highlight ludically motivated devices that serve a kind of aimlessness. After all, the whole point of ludically motivated materials is to provide incentives for, abilities to, and challenges towards progression towards a game's goal. And, as will be expected from a AAA-game like *BotW*, many of the ludically motivated materials indeed function rather conventionally, such as the already mentioned levelling system (stamina and health), the different armours (with different advantages), the enemies and environmental hazards, and the ability to carry different weapons in your inventory.

However, there are a few ways in which some of *BotW*'s ludically motivated devices do things differently. Most notably, the quests system in the game encourages a kind of "*non-sequentiallity.*" As opposed to a lot of other open-world games which tend to use bottle-neck structures and quest-bubbles to install a kind of order in the way the player moves around the game space and pursues quests, *BotW* allows players to traverse the world in a number of different ways and pursue quests in various orders or even at the same time (see above). On top of that, quests will often encourage idiosyncratic exploration of the environment by being enigmatic about where the player can find the location of the quest objective. As Schnaars puts it, comparing *BotW*'s quest structure to that in games employing the Ubisoft formula:[7]

> pre-defined quest markers on the map often only locate the character who is associated with the quest, not the location where it must be completed. The latter is often a puzzle in itself and requires thorough investigation of landscape structures in order to discover the desired location (118–19).

So, while quests are there to afford progress through the game world, the player is encouraged to decide when (if at all), in what order, and how to complete them. In that process, the player is encouraged to become more attuned to the environment and explore it (at their own pace and in their self-determined direction).

This non-sequentiality also shows in the ludic functionality of the game's *enemies* and *the map system*. New map areas do not "open up" as reward to ludic progression (e.g., defeating a boss), but are just there from the get-go for the player to traverse (and activate on the map if they decide to). Also, enemies of different strengths are not area-bound but just scale up when the player levels up, and most enemies can be easily outrun, in effect allowing the player to mostly ignore combat in the game and explore the landscape. This becomes especially apparent after several hours of play when the player has levelled-up significantly and acquired strong armour. At that point, the more widely scattered low-level enemies offer hardly any threat and killing them for (rather insignificant) loot is superfluous. This makes a lot of the environment in *BotW* (at that point) relatively unthreatening, allowing the player to traverse it freely without the continuous fear of getting killed.

These more unfamiliar ludically motivated devices stand out amongst, but are also supported by, a range of more familiar materials. The already

---

7   The Ubisoft formula is a design template which consists of an open world which gradually but linearly opens up by following the game's main storyline. This usually means engaging in a range of different quests in one area to then defeat the boss of that area and progress to/open up the next area with new quests.

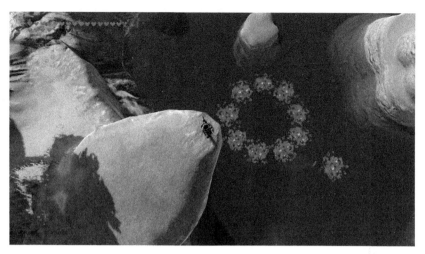

Figure 5.24: The unnatural arrangement of water lilies indicating the position of a Korok seed.

mentioned paraglider, for instance, offers the player a means to explore the open landscape from above and gives the player one more reason to keep searching for higher ground (with the bonus of beautiful vistas). Also, the familiar stamina system allows the player to climb up ever higher mountains and swim ever longer distances to also explore Hyrule's more difficult terrain. And finally, the game's collectable Korok seeds, which can be traded for more inventory space, are hidden throughout the natural landscape (a total of 900 of them) and require the player to pay close attention to the game's surroundings and identify the more unnatural or supernatural in the natural landscape (e.g., unnatural stone or water lily formations, or a conspicuously located flower or boulder) (see figure 5.24). While their ludic functionality as hidden treasure is familiar, the way in which they are embedded in the landscape again encourage exploration and studying of the game's environment.

Realistic Motivation

In *BotW*, realistically motivated materials encourage an aesthetic experience of aimless wandering in two specific ways. First of all, the design of the landscape has the player refer to the *beauty of the natural world* around them, making them contemplate their relationship to that environment (in-game and outside of it – see below), and encouraging them to explore its natural (looking) appeal. As Farca, Lehrer, and Navarro-Remesal put it:

> It [the experience of playing *BotW*] resensitises players to the beauty of the natural world, while granting them a different point of view on

Figure 5.25: Pro HUD mode (left) and normal HUD mode (right).

ecosystems and ecological issues that plague their contemporary surroundings (2020, 206).

Here, materials like the game's simulation of sunlight (and the way it reflects
off, and creates shadows in, the environment), its day-night cycle, its simulation of (wind-induced ripples in the) long grass, its awe-inspiring mountains,
and its serene vistas are all there to emphasize the game's natural beauty
for the player to bask in it. This is further emphasized if the player chooses
to play using the pro HUD-mode which hides all non-diegetic elements
(mini-map, weather information, time, direction towards equipped items)
from the Heads-Up-Display except for health and stamina information
(see figure 5.25). This effectively attunes the player even more towards the
environment and encourages spatial exploration without the use of a map
(also see De Certeau's idea of spatial stories discussed above). Finally, as
mentioned above, the triangle-rule employed in the design of the environment, encourages the player to keep exploring by drawing them towards
higher grounds (i.e., summits) and offering multiple points of interest on
the horizon.

The second way in which realistically motivated materials encourage
aimless wandering, is by discouraging ludic, goal-directed play behaviour.
For example, like in our real world, *tools and weapons* break after some
time, when used extensively. In *BotW*, this actually happens rather quickly,
with famous game critic Jim Sterling jokingly arguing that Hyrule's "swords
are made out of glass and wishes" (Sterling 2017). But while critics like
Sterling are highly critical of this durability system because it frustrates
the ludic functionality of weapons (in combat), I argue that this is exactly
what makes this an interesting unfamiliar device, contributing to the
overall aesthetic experience. Because weapons break so quickly, players are
encouraged to avoid using them in combat unless absolutely necessary. This
then creates opportunities for a different, more aimless way of exploring
the environment.

A similar argument can be made for *"cooking"* in *BotW*. This device also has clear realistic motivations (as well as ludic motivations – see hereafter), since it has players appeal to notions of cooking in the real world. Like real-world cooking, cooking in *BotW* allows players to throw together an immense range of different ingredients, and the dish can turn out good or bad. Although different combinations of ingredients offer different ludic benefits (increased health, strength, speed, warmth, stamina), *BotW* does not offer easy help in providing recipes, nor a way of saving them somewhere if you have found one. In fact, if the player is not keen on experimenting endlessly with different ingredients (or seek help from online walkthrough guides), the game really offers only two options: a) explore the environment to look for recipes on posters, in books, and through conversations with non-player characters, or b) (in my case) ignore cooking as much as possible and seek other ways (i.e., clothing, levelling-up) to increase health, stamina, heat/cold resistance etc. In other words, the device either encourages exploration to make use of its ludic benefits or encourages exploration through dismissal of this ludic function altogether.

Compositional and Transtextual Motivation

Where many contemporary games will have materials with strong compositional motivations, encouraging players to construct a causally related sequence of events in time and space (i.e., a narrative), *BotW* distinguishes itself from many other AAA-games in its genre (action-adventure) by its very *rudimental narrative*. In line with action-adventure films in the tradition of *Indiana Jones* (Spielberg 1981), the game genre tends to use strong narrative materials to make in-game actions meaningful and provide a movement impetus for the player. For instance, Richard Lemarchand, one of the two lead designers of the action-adventure game *Uncharted 2: Among Thieves* (Naughty Dog 2009) has indicated drawing extensively on "pulp adventure tropes" to "push both cinematic gameplay and character-driven storytelling" (Davidson and Lemarchand 2011, 75).

Yet, *BotW* is characterized by a narrative framework that is, as Schnaars has put it, "widely negligible and optionally accessible" (2021, 116). After waking up from his one-hundred-year slumber at the start of the game, the player character Link is quickly informed that he has lost all his memories, effectively making him an empty shell or a mere vehicle that the player enters into to be able to be present in the world of Hyrule. Link does not have any personal characteristics for the player to empathize with, other than his physical appearance and abilities, and Link's knowledge of the situation aligns completely with the player's knowledge who also has yet to discover what is going on in this world.[8] While the game will provide a few compositionally motivated cutscenes after completing the opening area of the Great Plateau and throughout some other parts of the game (most notably featuring the characters Impa in Kakariko Village and Purah in Hateno Village), the narrative remains highly generic and minimal: a story about a heroic warrior (Link) set out to free the land and the princess (Zelda) by slaying the main antagonist (Ganon). Link's memories remain missing throughout the game if the player does not actively pursue them in the main, but completely optional, quest "captured memories."

These compositionally motivated materials in *BotW*, again, encourage exploration of and an alertness to the game's environment in two interesting ways. First of all, as also Schnaars argues, the game's rudimentary narrative (with the "missing Link") encourages players to find their own ways through Hyrule because they are not guided by the discovery and activation of plot points anchored in specific places in the environment (2021, 118). This means that the order in which areas of the game are traversed will differ widely per player, with players thereby constructing highly personalized spatial stories in the game (De Certeau 1988). But it also means that, without the incentive of discovering the plot, players are encouraged to find other reasons for exploring the environment (e.g., discovering its natural beauty). Secondly, if the player does actively pursue the quest of finding the "memory inducing glows" in the landscape, the player is still encouraged to become familiar with the markers in and the perspectives on this landscape. This is because the positions of these memories are provided cryptically through photos of specific places in Hyrule which the player will only start recognizing after extensive exploration of and familiarization with the environment (unless they stumble upon them accidently).

This lack of narrative structure and narrative movement impetus is further emphasized by the transtextual functioning of the game's *boss fights*. After talking to the character Impa, Link is given the (main) quest of defeating the four so-called divine beasts to release them from Ganon's control and have them instead assist in fighting this main antagonist. These four divine beasts evoke clear references to the colossi in *Shadow of the Colossus* (Team Ico 2005) (see figure 5.26). Similar to how *BotW* offers the player a beautiful open world to explore and enormous mechanical animals to defeat, so too does *Shadow of the Colossus*, present the player

---

8   In fact, it could be argued that the player knows even more than Link does at that point, given their likely prior knowledge of some other Zelda games and the recurring story being told in them.

Figure 5.26: The divine beasts Vah Ruta (elephant) and Vah Naboris (camel) sticking out of the landscape of Hyrule.

with an overwhelming natural landscape to wander around in (the player character is even aptly called "Wander" or "The Wanderer") and large giant-like creatures to slay. And similar to how the colossi need to be slain by hitting (a specific order of) weak spots (sigils) on their bodies, so too are the divine beasts defeated by entering their bodies and activating specific terminals in puzzle-like challenges.

However, where in *Shadow of the Colossus*, the presumed heroic act of slaying the colossi eventually turns out to be an unfortunate villain-ous act (releasing the powers of the main antagonist Dormin and slowly deteriorating the physical appearance of the player character), slaying the divine beasts presents no such narrative twist. Instead, the divine beasts function in a much more familiar ludic and compositional way, offering the player a boss fight that, when won, will increase the player's chances of defeating the main antagonist of the game. It is exactly his familiarity that, when compared to the ludic and compositional unfamiliarity of the boss fights in *Shadow of the Colossus* (which frames winning as losing and good as evil – see chapter 3) foregrounds *BotW*'s lack of a clear guiding narrative. In *BotW* there is no mysterious, curiosity-inducing plot with a twist at the end, but simply the more conventional and optional (the quest of defeating these beasts can be ignored altogether) outlines of a story. This, I argue, makes Link in *BotW* more of a wanderer than the character Wander in *Shadow of the Colossus*.

Artistic Motivation

As we noted in chapter 2, artistic motivations of devices are often hard to identify in games since they tend to get overshadowed by more dominant ludic or compositional motivations. This is especially true for AAA-games which often shy away from too much experimentation in their design because (the assumption is) that risks turning away (parts of) their broad player base. So, these games generally rely on popular ludic and narrative

Figure 5.27: Sitting by the fire to pass the time in *BotW*.

tropes and do not include many elements that are there mostly for (the appreciation of) the game's overall artistic form. Nevertheless, there are a few devices in *BotW* which, in spite of some ludic motivation, show clear and interesting artistic motivations.

First of all, the game includes many *fires* that Link can sit by to pass the time (see figure 5.27), offering the player the opportunity to jump ahead to morning, afternoon, or night. However, where other games would often have the player character's health replenished after resting or sleeping, *BotW* has no such mechanic. There are one or two moments in the game where passing the time has ludic benefits (e.g., because a character or collectible may only be there during a specific time of day, or because the player is trying to scale a peak and wants the rain to stop), but mostly it appears to be a rather aimless exercise. Still, I found myself sitting by the fire numerous times during my second playthrough. This was because I was often keen to skip the night and enjoy the beauty of the natural landscape in the early hours of the morning. This is the time of day that photographers often refer to as the "golden hour," when the sun is low, lighting is soft and diffuse, and you might be able to catch the reflections of the rising sun on the calmly rippling grass of Hyrule. In other words, I would choose to sit by the fire simply to be able to admire the landscape.

Secondly, *BotW* offers the player the opportunity to become an in-game photographer, capturing nearly everything that Hyrule has to offer on film (creatures, monsters, objects, foods etc.) (see figure 5.28). While the *in-game camera* option has some ludic motivation once it is upgraded, since it can then help you track the location of some sought after objects (after

Figure 5.28: Photographing a blue-winged heron in *BotW*.

you've photographed one such object), it mostly remains an example of
what Möring and Mutiis (2019) call "photo mode." This is a type of in-game
photography that is largely "unrelated to the game's objectives and central
game mechanics" and therefore has the player step away from or "freeze the
flow of action" to instead "focus on the aesthetic quality of the game" (Möring
and de Mutiis 2019, 78). Here, photography really becomes part of virtual
tourism in which a player is incentivized to take in-game photographs "to
commemorate their travels, obtain a visual record of enjoyable experiences,
and show evidence of their experiences to friends and family" (Poremba
2007, 50).

Interestingly but unsurprisingly, the memorable moments captured on
film in the *BotW* community consist mostly of beautiful vistas rather than
player achievements or stunts.[9] And even online instructions about the use
of the in-game camera delve into tips and tricks to become a good (virtual)
nature photographer:

> Taking *good* pictures is a whole other matter – and it's one area where
> *Breath of the Wild* really shines. A photo that really captures the essence
> and soul of a creature or monster takes a little bit more work, care and
> (sometimes literal) pain (for Link, anyway). It's easy to take a picture of
> a heron, but catching a heron just as it takes off for flight requires some
> very good sneaking skills, and quick reflexes. A flock of Keese can easily
> be shot at a distance, but your photo will be a whole lot prettier if you wait

9   See for instance: https://www.tumblr.com/botw-photography.

until the flock is bearing down on you head-on, moments from hitting you, before taking the shot (Apolon 2017).

So, similar to the ability to sit by the fire and pass time, the in-game camera also encourages an engagement with the game that is focused on an appreciation of its beautifully represented natural landscape. This is an experience that is very close to the way in which we may appreciate natural landscapes in our real world, with the added difference that our admiration of an in-game landscape is also largely informed and motivated by us recognizing this landscape as the result of skilled craftsmanship from the game's designers. As such, these devices evoke what Perron (2005) and Frome (2006), following Tan (2000), would call a combination of artefact emotions (A-emotions) and represented world emotions (R-emotions). Where R-emotions are directed at the game's fictional world (and the characters and their stories in it), A-emotions are directed at the game as a purposefully crafted artefact and consist of things like an appreciation of a game's graphical style, interesting mechanics, or innovatively constructed story. My experience of *BotW*'s overall artistic shape is therefore both an unmediated engrossment in its fictional world as well as a heightened sense of that world's mediatedness.

A Link to Nature: Some Conclusions

In the sections above, I have identified a wide range of different familiar materials and more unfamiliar devices that stand out as doing things a little differently when compared to other open-world games, other action-adventure games, or other games in the Zelda franchise. Although the devices are not as clearly unfamiliar as some of the devices in *Kentucky Route Zero*, the combination of materials and devices certainly defamiliarizes our understanding of goal-directed, story-driven traversal through the game space by encouraging an aimless wandering (see figure 5.29). This wandering, while cooperative within the game system, is transtextually digressive and eventually leads me to the dominant.

The dominant boils down to the game's lack of action-based design, made up of things like a non-sequential quest structure, fully explorable open world, optional combat system, a largely superfluous narrative, and a landscape filled with characters and objects that continuously lure the player off path. Here, *BotW* does not just offer a plethora of different points of interest and a motivation and means to strive for them, the game also encourages the player to simply "pass the time" in Hyrule and capture its vistas on film and in memory. This "nothingness" encourages the aforementioned

Figure 5.29: The character Dantz tellingly asking Link if he's "some kinda wanderer."

"aimlessness" which in turn encourages a renewed appreciation of the game's environment.

Bogost explains this relationship between wandering and appreciation of the environment in his 2011 book *How to Do Things with Videogames*, where he compares travel by train or plane with travel in games. He argues that where train travel reduces space between points to fast moving summaries, and airplane travel removes the space entirely (replacing it with clouds), travel in games reinstates the "aura" of the experience of continuous space (2011, 45–51). This is especially the case for games (like *BotW*) that have players traverse in-game space at a slow walking speed, because in these games, as Bogost puts it, "the player develops an intuitive and continuous relationship with the [...] landscape" (2011, 49). Here, Bogost offers a perfect description of the aesthetic experience accompanying the aimless wandering in *BotW*. Because *BotW* encourages slow travel as an end in itself (rather than a means to another end), the player becomes attuned to, familiarized with, and appreciative of the space they are traversing. And because this space is relatively devoid of unavoidable ludic challenges (or unfolding plot) the player's experience of that space becomes closer to what Liboriussen (2008) has called an experience of the landscape as image, in which "the player develop[s] a general sense of the world's content and its distribution" rather than its "action and survival potentials" (2008, 148). Or, to put it in Shklovsky's (2012a, 26) terms, the player's perception is prolonged to become an aesthetic end in itself.

However, as we emphasized in chapter 2, Shklovsky's defamiliarization does not only concern the formal material of the work but extends towards the world that the work references to renew our habitualized perception of it. This, I argue, is where the aesthetic experience of wandering becomes meaningful to the player beyond the game. In the case of *BotW*, the player becomes more sensitized to and integrated in the (overwhelming beauty of the) natural in-game landscape of *BotW* to, in turn, gain a new appreciation of and relationship to real world natural landscapes and the ecological challenges plaguing them. This makes *BotW* effectively an eco-game (Holzbaur 2001) that frames (Lakoff 2010) the human-nature relationship in a way that is different from the player's daily experience of it. Following Bendor, *BotW* frames or, in his words, "refracts" "sustainability as felt embeddedness," as an issue that now resonates emotionally and becomes "personally meaningful" (Bendor 2018, 174–76) through the player's engagement with the viscerally overwhelming beauty of Hyrule. Compared to some other eco-games, *BotW* does not simplify sustainability into "small achievable actions" (which Bendor calls "sustainability as restored balance"), nor does it characterize sustainability as "a complex problem" (Bendor 2018, 170–74). Instead, *BotW*'s strength as an eco-game comes from its more offhand handling of the subject matter, presenting the player with a different, slowed-down relationship to the (fictional) natural world than the relationship to the (real) natural world the player is likely to be used to from their daily life.

Here, *BotW* leans towards a more "integrative worldview" in which humans stand on more equal footing with/are a part of nature and nature is intrinsically valuable (de Witt et al. 2016). However, in *BotW* the intrinsic value of nature concerns mostly, if not solely, its aesthetics, not its functionality. Even though the natural environment offers the player only limited ludic challenges (environmental hazards can generally be ignored and/or are easily overcome once the player has levelled up sufficiently), it does offer the conventional resources for exploitation like fruits, plants and critters for cooking or minerals for trading. Because these resources are endless, with vegetation growing back after a certain amount of time, the game appears to be communicating a more modernist worldview (de Witt et al. 2016) in which humans are above nature and can use nature for their own purpose without real consequences. This also shows in Westerlaken's interesting attempt at a vegan run of BotW, in which the game system (like the real world) resists a more integrative worldview, with non-player-characters asking her to "bring them the bodies of other animals for their own quests; [coming up] with challenges that would require [her] to abandon [her] values; and [trying] to convince [her] to hunt or bully other creatures for the sole reason to gain profit or to entertain [her]self" (Westerlaken 2017, 1).

But while *BotW* does not have us imagine a new, more sustainable world in which humans live as equals amongst/as part of nature (see Bendor's "sustainability as an imaginary" (2018, 176–78)), the player's slow and aimless experience of the beauty of the natural landscape is still meaningful beyond the game because it offers the player a renewed appreciation of and fear for the decline of the beauty of the real world natural environment. In other words, it offers the player an intimate reminder of what natural beauty is or could be, thereby making sustainability "less of a statistical phenomenon and more of a tangible state" (Bendor 2018, 175). A similar argument has been made before by Farca, Lehrer, and Navarro-Remesal who for instance state that "long hikes [in *BotW*] [...] have players gain respect for the land they traverse, offering them a sense of scale and the duration of time" (2020, 208), which in turn, as I quoted them above, grants players "a different point of view on ecosystems and ecological issues that plague their contemporary surroundings" (2020, 206). However, where Farca, Lehrer, and Navarro-Remesal arrive at this conclusion by analysing the game from an ecocritical perspective, focusing specifically on the game's story as a "hero's journey to restore ecological balance in Hyrule" (2020, 209), I hope to have shown here that taking a formalist (more bottom-up) approach helps to highlight a much broader range of unfamiliar devices and familiar materials at play.

Such a formalist analysis goes beyond the obvious (open world game design), and instead systematically highlights how devices and materials cue an appreciation of the beauty of the landscape and a depreciation of the game's ludic functionalities. So, even when a game does not evoke an immediately obvious aesthetic response, following the methodological considerations of our approach can still call attention to the complexity "under the hood." As noted at the start of this analysis, this complexifying or defamiliarizing is an important task for the formalist player critic, and one I hope to have delivered on in this case study.

References

Apolon. 2017. "'Legend of Zelda: Breath of the Wild' Camera Guide: Tips to Use the Camera Like a Pro." Player.One. March 3, 2017. https://www.player.one/legend-zelda-breath-wild-camera-guide-tips-use-camera-pro-587014.

Bartle, Richard. 2003. *Designing Virtual Worlds*. Indianapolis: New Riders.

Baudelaire, Charles. 1964. *The Painter of Modern Life and Other Essays*. Translated by Jonathan Mayne. London: Phaidon Press.

Bendor, Roy. 2018. *Interactive Media for Sustainability*. London: Palgrave MacMillan.

Bogost, Ian. 2011. *How to Do Things with Videogames*. Minneapolis: University of Minnesota Press.

Cardboard Computer. 2011. "Balloon Diaspora [MacOS Game]." Cardboard Computer.

Cardboard Computer. 2013. "Kentucky Route Zero [MacOS Game]." Annapurna Interactive.

Cardboard Computer, dir. 2016. *Junebug – "Static Between Stations."* https://www.youtube.com/watch?v=igvvC4I7v20.

Cardboard Computer. 2020. "Kentucky Route Zero." 2020. http://kentuckyroutezero.com/.

Cardboard Computer. n.d. "The Entertainment." Kentucky Route Zero. Accessed December 5, 2022. http://kentuckyroutezero.com/the-entertainment/.

Davidson, Drew, and Richard Lemarchand. 2011. "Uncharted 2: Among Thieves- Becoming a Hero." In *Well Played 3.0: Video Games, Value and Meaning*, edited by Drew Davidson, 77–112. Pittsburgh: ETC Press.

Davies, Mark. 2009. "Examining Game Pace: How Single-Player Levels Tick." *Game Developer*, May 12, 2009. https://www.gamedeveloper.com/design/examining-game-pace-how-single-player-levels-tick.

De Certeau, Michel. 1988. *The Practice of Everyday Life*. Translated by Steven Rendall. Los Angeles, CA: University of California Press.

Dontnod Entertainment. 2017. "Life Is Strange [MacOS Game]." Square Enix.

Elliot, Jake. 2011. "Kentucky Route Zero, a Magic Realist Adventure Game." Kickstarter. 2011. https://www.kickstarter.com/projects/149077132/kentucky-route-zero-a-magic-realist-adventure-game.

Farca, Gerald, Alexander Lehner, and Victor Navarro-Remesal. 2020. "Regenerative Play and the Experience of the Sublime: Breath of the Wild." In *Mythopoeic Narrative in The Legend of Zelda*, edited by Anthony Cirilla and Vincent Rone, 205–21. New York: Routledge.

Flanagan, Mary. 2009. *Critical Play: Radical Game Design*. Cambridge, MA: MIT Press.

Frome, Jonathan. 2006. "Why Films Make Us Cry but Videogames Don't: Emotions in Traditional and Interactive Media." PhD Thesis, The University of Wisconsin–Madison.

Genette, Gerard. 1997. *Paratexts: Thresholds of Interpretation*. Cambridge, MA: Cambridge University Press.

Gray, Kate. 2017. "Is The Legend of Zelda: Breath of the Wild the Best-Designed Game Ever?' *The Guardian*, May 30, 2017, sec. Games.

Holzbaur, Ulrich. 2001. "EcoGames – Simulation Games and Sustainable Development." In *Sustainability in the Information Society*, edited by Lorenz M. Hilty and Paul W. Gilgen, 971–78. Marburg: Metropolis Verlag.

jace :). 2018. "The Space Between Spaces: Breath of the Wild and Shadow of the Colossus." *Medium* (blog). 25 March 2018. https://medium.com/@pizzasheets/the-space-between-spaces-breath-of-the-wild-and-shadow-of-the-colossus-7a1182f0f502.

Jagoda, Patrick. 2018. "On Difficulty in Video Games: Mechanics, Interpretation, Affect." *Critical Inquiry* 45 (1): 199–233.

Junebug, and Ben Babbitt. 2020. *Too Late to Love You.*

Juul, Jesper. 2004. "Introduction to Game Time/Time to Play: An Examination of Game Temporality." In *First Person: New Media as Story, Performance, and Game*, edited by Noah Wardrip-Fruin and Pat Harrigan, 131–42. Cambridge, MA: MIT Press.

Kagen, Melissa. 2017. "Walking Sims, #gamergate, and the Gender of Wandering." In *The Year's Work in Nerds, Wonks, and Neo-Cons*, edited by Jonathan Eburne and Benjamin Schreier, 275–300. Bloomington, Indiana: Indiana University Press.

Lakoff, George. 2010. "Why It Matters How We Frame the Environment." *Environmental Communication* 4 (1): 70–81.

Liboriussen, Bjarke. 2008. "The Landscape Aesthetics of Computer Games." In *Conference Proceedings of the Philosophy of Computer Games 2008*, edited by Stephan Günzel, Michael Liebe, and Dieter Mersch, 2008. Potsdam University Press.

Magnuson, Jordan. 2019. "Playing and Making Poetic Videogames." MFA Thesis, University of California.

Magritte, René. 1965. *Le Blanc-Seing.*

Mitchell, Alex. 2014. "Defamiliarization and Poetic Interaction in Kentucky Route Zero." *Well Played: A Journal on Video Games, Value and Meaning* 3 (2): 161–78.

Mitchell, Alex. 2016. "Making the Familiar Unfamiliar: Techniques for Creating Poetic Gameplay." In *Proceedings of the First International Joint Conference of DiGRA and FDG 2016*. Dundee: Digital Games Research Association.

Mitchell, Alex, Liting Kway, Tiffany Neo, and Yuin Theng Sim. 2020. "A Preliminary Categorization of Techniques for Creating Poetic Gameplay." *Game Studies* 20 (2).

Möring, Sebastian, and Marco de Mutiis. 2019. "Camera Ludica: Reflections on Photography in Video Games." In *Intermedia Games—Games Inter Media: Video Games and Intermediality*, edited by Michael Fuchs and Jeff Thoss, 69–94. New York: Bloomsbury Academic.

Naughty Dog. 2009. "Uncharted 2: Among Thieves [PlayStation 3 Game]." Sony Computer Entertainment.

Neill, Roy William, dir. 1946. *Terror by Night.* Universal Pictures.

Nintendo. 2017. "The Legend of Zelda: Breath of the Wild [Nintendo Switch Game]." Nintendo.

Nishikawa Yoshiharu. 2017. "［CEDEC 2017］「ゼルダの伝説BotW」の完璧なゲーム世界は，任天堂の開発スタイルが変わったからこそ生まれた." *4Gamer.net*, September 2, 2017. https://www.4gamer.net/games/341/G034168/20170901120/.

Perron, Bernard. 2005. "A Cognitive Psychological Approach to Gameplay Emotions." In *Proceedings of the 2005 DiGRA International Conference: Changing Views–Worlds in Play*.

Poremba, Cindy. 2007. "Point and Shoot: Remediating Photography in Gamespace." *Games and Culture* 2 (1): 49–58.

Reed, Aaron A., John Murray, and Anastasia Salter. 2020. *Adventure Games: Playing the Outsider*. New York: Bloomsbury Publishing USA.

Schnaars, Cornelia J. 2021. "Taking a Breath of the Wild: The Concept of Airness in Nintendo's Take on Open World Games." *Game| World| Architectonics*, 115.

Sharp, John. 2015. *Works of Game: On the Aesthetics of Games and Art*. Cambridge, MA: MIT Press.

Sheehan, Jason. 2021. "Reading the Game: Kentucky Route Zero." *NPR*, February 11, 2021, sec. Reading the Game. https://www.npr.org/2021/02/11/966499158/reading-the-game-kentucky-route-zero.

Shklovsky, Victor. 2012a. "Art as Technique." In *Russian Formalist Criticism: Four Essays*, edited by Lee T. Lemon and Marion J. Reis, 2nd ed., 21–34. Lincoln: University of Nebraska Press.

Spielberg, Steven, dir. 1981. *Raiders of the Lost Ark*. Paramount Pictures.

Sterling, James Stephanie. 2017. "The Legend of Zelda: Breath of the Wild Review – Broken Sword." The Jimquisition. March 12, 2017. https://www.thejimquisition.com/post/the-legend-of-zelda-breath-of-the-wild-review-broken-sword.

Švelch, Jan. 2020. "Paratextuality in Game Studies: A Theoretical Review and Citation Analysis." *Game Studies* 20 (2).

Tan, Ed S. 2000. "Emotion, Art, and the Humanities." In *Handbook of Emotions*, edited by Michael Lewis and Jeanette M. Haviland-Jones, 2nd ed., 116–34. New York: Guildford Press.

Team Ico. 2005. "Shadow of the Colossus [Playstation 2 Game]." Sony Computer Entertainment.

Telltale Games. 2012. "The Walking Dead: Season 1 [MacOS Game]." Telltale Games.

thatgamecompany. 2012. "Journey [Playstation 3 Game]." Sony Computer Entertainment.

Thompson, Kristin. 1988. *Breaking the Glass Armor: Neoformalist Film Analysis*. Princeton, New Jersey: Princeton University Press.

Tusman, Lee. 2013. "Limits and Demonstrations Exhibition." 2013. http://leetusman.com/projects/limits_and_demonstrations.html.

Walker, Matt [@retroOtoko]. 2017. "Got around to Reading Some of the BotW CEDEC Articles. Interesting Fact – https://T.Co/494TwAuYxi." Tweet. *Twitter.* https://twitter.com/retroOtoko/status/915037635663425536.

Westerlaken, Michelle. 2017. "Self-Fashioning in Action: Zelda's Breath of the Wild Vegan Run." Kraków: Game Philosophy Network.

Witt, Annick de, Joop de Boer, Nicholas Hedlund, and Patricia Osseweijer. 2016. "A New Tool to Map the Major Worldviews in the Netherlands and USA, and Explore How They Relate to Climate Change." *Environmental Science and Policy* 63: 101–12.

Yang, Robert. 2017. "Open World Level Design: Spatial Composition and Flow in Breath of the Wild." *Radiator* (blog). October 4, 2017. https://www.blog.radiator.debacle.us/2017/10/open-world-level-design-spatial.html.

6.   Conclusion

We end this book with a (familiar) thought experiment. Consider the game *Stray* (BlueTwelve Studio 2022) described in the introductory chapter. Now, after you have successfully made your way through the roughly 200 pages of this book, imagine analysing *Stray* using a formalist approach. How would you start? What would you focus on? How would you play? What games or other cultural artefacts would you compare it to so as to recognize where the game challenges your expectations? What would be the game's dominant and your resulting aesthetic experience?

At this point (or hopefully already well before this point), you may be realizing that we have not actually offered you a blueprint to give clear-cut definitive answers to these questions at all. Instead, as we already quoted from Bordwell (1989) in the introduction, we have only offered you some guiding and structuring "hollow analytical categories" (e.g., defamiliarization, the dominant, and motivations) and some methodological considerations (e.g., on the role of the player critic, choice of reading strategies and the importance of context). This is because every game and every new (historical) context will require its own focus. And even though the formalist approach anchors any claims in the characteristics of the work itself (rather than relying on authorial intent or studying player effects), a single game can still be activated in numerous ways, which can potentially result in finding different dominant structures. This can be seen in both of our extended case studies in chapter 5: the analysis of *Kentucky Route Zero* (Cardboard Computer 2013) by Alex draws from but also diverges significantly from his earlier analysis (Mitchell 2014), and Jasper's analysis of *Breath of the Wild* (Nintendo 2017) shows how it is possible to play the same game in very different ways, depending on what you attend to (upon replay). This suggests that there is no one-size-fits-all formula for a formalist analysis of a videogame. In other words, while we can offer some guidelines for doing the analysis, you still need to do the heavy lifting yourself, drawing from (your own knowledge of) other cultural artefacts in your time and your own playthrough of the game.

Nevertheless, by sticking to these guidelines, your analysis should become (more) focused and (more) systematic and rigorous, and thereby eventually

Mitchell, A. and J. van Vught, *Videogame Formalism: On Form, Aesthetic Experience, and Methodology*. Amsterdam: Amsterdam University Press, 2024
DOI 10.5117/9789463720663_CH06

(more) convincing. This is because these guidelines offer a set of epistemo-logical and methodological assumptions that have been well-established and heavily scrutinized in long running academic traditions in adjacent fields. As we argued in the introductory chapter, no one starts analysing a game as a tabula rasa, and the wide range of unspoken starting positions out there risk making an analysis unverifiable and idiosyncratic at best and inconsistent or self-contradictory at worst. So, it is always good practice to be upfront about your guiding assumptions and explore how these are impacting your analysis, but it is even better to rely on a set of consistent assumptions drawn from a clear, robust, and guiding approach.

By having anchored our videogame formalism in the tradition of Russian Formalism and Neoformalism, we have offered such an approach. The player analyst following this videogame formalism starts off with their aesthetic experience of play. This experience is the result of the game's devices which defamiliarize the way the player expects games (and the world around them) to "do things" (e.g., provide opportunities for action, offer (ludic) challenges, and communicate meaning). The player then uses a heuristic and iterative methodological strategy to focus on the interplay of a specific set of these devices (and some more familiar materials) and establish the game's dominant structure. This means that this approach positions this player first and foremost as a player critic, offering a broad but systematic way of thinking about, analysing, and reporting on what is interesting about a specific game under investigation.

Given the fact that methodological steps in game studies papers are often broad or implicit, providing students with little in the way of concrete guidelines on how to actually do a game analysis (van Vught and Glas 2018), this formalist approach provides a significant contribution to a field that, as Daneels et al. (2022) put it, has seen a "lack of methodological consensus and standardization on how to conduct a game analysis and subsequently report on the analysis in a transparent manner." Although our approach offers only one way of analysing games (with its own focus on defamiliarizing form and identification of the dominant), its considerations are detailed and clearly articulated. This makes this approach specifically interesting for students getting to grips with game analysis procedures for the first time, but also useful for game journalists looking to systemically highlight the more interesting parts of a game to cast a value judgement over them.

In the case of *Stray*, taking note of our formalist considerations could look something like this. Upon initially encountering the game, the most likely source of intrigue for the player critic is the use of a cat as the play-able character. It would be tempting to simply focus on this one distinct characteristic. However, following our approach, the player critic should first play through the game and consider the accompanying aesthetic experience, then begin to notice how the various materials in the game work to create that experience. In this case, the game creates a very realistic set of behaviours for the cat protagonist, placing this character in a dystopian cyberpunk-esque world that is seen from the perspective of a cat. Much of the gameplay focuses on relatively simple puzzles and platforming, making good use of the cat's physical characteristics. There are moments where the initial clarity of design seems to be lost, with the introduction of a drone companion, B-12, and the ensuing narrative related to the robots trapped in the dystopian city and what happened to all the humans. Most likely by first playing for continuation, and then replaying to play the right way, or possibly even to play playfully, the player critic can examine how these various materials work together and begin to identify the dominant. A first suggestion of this might be the tension between the realistic depiction of the cat protagonist and the resulting identification with the protagonist that this encourages in the player, and the eventual revelation that the game is really about humans, and how their civilization came to an untimely end.[1] This set of tensions can be considered against the backdrop of a time that has seen the release of a wide range of games, from oddities such as *PowerWash Simulator* (FuturLab 2021), genre-bending games like *Inscryption* (Daniel Mullins Games 2021), masterful storytelling in *Norco* (Geography of Robots 2022) and *Citizen Sleeper* (Jump Over The Age 2022), and punishing difficulty combined with freeform exploration in *Elden Ring* (FromSoftware Inc. 2022), using this to keep in mind what the player's expectations would be, and how this would impact what may or may not be foregrounded. While player critics with different gameplay experiences and different backgrounds and training may come to different conclusions as to the devices and the dominant present within *Stray*, by following our formalist approach, they would be able to clearly articulate how they went about doing the analysis, and how that led to their conclusions. This should help to provide the analysis, and the accompanying reporting of that analysis, with the type of clarity and accessibility that Daneels et al. (2022) are calling for.

In addition, drawing from the tradition of Russian Formalism and Neoformalism has another clear benefit: it has allowed our videogame formalism to avoid the many pitfalls that earlier videogame formalisms have fallen into, which should also make it of interest to game scholars who are willing

---

1   We encourage you to analyze the game yourself and see what you identify as the devices and dominant.

to give the approach another try. As we noted at the beginning of this book, formalisms have had a reputation in game studies for being conservative. As a practitioner's mantra, advocated by people like Koster (2012; 2014) and Lantz (2015a; 2015b), formalism has been criticized for gatekeeping against a specific type of games (narrative driven games like those made in *Twine* (Klimas 2009)) and thereby against a specific type of player who would likely prefer to play these types of games. Similarly, scholarly formalisms advocated by people like Aarseth (2004) or Eskelinen (2001) have been accused of normatively driven boundary work that devalues or even excludes a specific type of scholarship (e.g., cultural studies, feminism, narratology) and by extension certain scholars working in those areas. And finally, formalists like Bogost (2007) have been accused of methodological barrenness for ignoring the creative (and emancipatory) characteristic of play (Sicart 2011).

Our videogame formalism tackles these (very valid) criticisms in a number of ways. First of all, the approach shies away from normative statements about what makes good, real, or even interesting games. Although the approach has the player critic focus on what is interesting or intriguing about one specific game, it has no ambition to extend this into a model for all games. Or, to put it differently, more defamiliarization does not make a better game. Instead, it simply serves as the methodological focus of the analysis. Secondly, our videogame formalism sees all game material (rule-based, narrative or stylistic) as equally capable of making things unfamiliar in all five of the motivational categories (ludic, compositional, realistic, transtextual and artistic) described in this book. This means our formalism does not favour form over content or mechanics over story but considers all of these as formal devices of equal interest to the critic. It is only through the iterative methodological strategy of finding the dominant that certain devices become foregrounded as the more interesting ones for that particular analytic context. Thirdly, and finally, our videogame formalism does not ignore the role of the player in analysing the functioning of the game but instead sees the player's particular play experience as both the methodological starting point (the "what intrigues me" question) as well as the methodological means (the "reading" strategy) to focus on the game's defamiliarizing devices. Here, we do not see the player as merely an activator of an objectively existent game but instead we see the game as existent in the (intersubjective) lived experience of play in a particular context.

Historicizing our videogame formalism in line with earlier formalisms in other fields and taking on board the many criticisms voiced against earlier videogame formalisms, contributes significantly to an understanding of formalism in our field and hopefully removes it from the doghouse of game analysis methodologies. Here we specifically aim to ignite interest from our game studies colleagues, whose opinion on the value of formalism may well align with one or more of the anti-formalist sentiments outlined in chapter 1. To those of you we say: while it's perfectly fine to ignore this approach because its selective focus (on defamiliarizing form) doesn't fit your research interest, it should not be shunned for a presumed tendency towards conservative gatekeeping or methodological inadequacy.

We have attempted to demonstrate the applicability of our proposed approach to students of game studies, those who are working in game journalism, and game studies scholars through the use of two detailed case studies, and a number of illustrative examples throughout the book. The examples in chapter 3, focusing on the games *Lim* (k 2012), *Getting Over It with Bennett Foddy* (Foddy 2017), *Akrasia* (Team Aha! 2008), and *Shadow of the Colossus* (Team Ico 2005), serve to clarify some of the concepts introduced in chapters 2 and 3, and show the relationship between specific devices and the player's aesthetic experience. These examples also show how the consideration of a range of motivations, beyond the ludic, allows us to expand on Mitchell's (2016; 2020) earlier poetic gameplay patterns. We also use these examples to begin to show how the various materials and devices in the games should not be considered in isolation, but instead should be seen as working together, and at times in tension with each other, to create the overall player experience, forming the dominant. This will provide solid examples of the concepts for students and those less familiar with the academic terminology being used. For established scholars, these examples will help to clarify our approach and the underlying concepts and help to demonstrate how the formalist perspective can be productively applied to a range of games.

In chapter 4, we make use of two recurring examples, *Paratopic* (Arbitrary Metric 2018) and *A Short Hike* (Robinson-Yu 2019), to more specifically demonstrate the steps in the formalist approach. By showing how a player critic can clearly identify a starting point of interest for these two games, and then use that as a way to focus the iterative process of playing and replaying the game and uncovering materials and devices, this provides a concrete demonstration of the approach for those new to formalist analysis. By also discussing the need to carefully choose a reading strategy, reflect on your position as player critic, and keep the context of play in mind during analysis, we again show how our approach avoids some of the issues for which formalism is often critiqued.

Finally, in chapter 5 we have shared two more detailed case studies, *Kentucky Route Zero* and *Breath of the Wild*. In addition to demonstrating how to apply our formalist approach to longer games, these case studies provide some interesting insights into how a formalist approach can surface particular aspects of a game. In the case of *Kentucky Route Zero*, by considering the game as it has developed and changed over eight years of development, and how a player is exposed to multiple variations of devices across both the time of the game's development, and the eight to ten hours of play time, it becomes clear that these devices are repeatedly re-defamiliarized, allowing for sustained foregrounding without disrupting the coherence of the play experience. In *Breath of the Wild*, we can see how the defamiliarization occurs in the interplay of many different materials and devices, even though the materials by themselves are often not as unfamiliar as those in art games. This shows how an otherwise typically mainstream, AAA title can also allow, or even encourage, space for exploration and wandering, bringing a new perspective to the "open world" game genre.

Possible Future Directions

These examples show the range of application of our videogame formalism. Having said that, the games discussed in this book of course do not cover the wide range of different types of games out there. We have chosen to focus mostly on so-called indie-games, art-games or anti-games because those games simply offer the more obviously defamiliarizing devices and thus the clearest examples to illustrate how our approach works. Although we have gone some way in showing the usefulness of applying the formalist approach beyond these indie-games (by taking a AAA-game as a case study), we certainly acknowledge there are many types of games not covered. Some of these games, like abstract or non-narrative games, would likely have fit with the approach outlined, although there may be specific considerations to keep in mind here. It would be worthwhile to examine in more detail whether, for example, the lack of an explicit narrative requires possible reconsideration of the various motivational categories, and whether the current set of categories are sufficient and appropriate to analyse this type of game. However, other types of games like multiplayer games or VR-games would certainly have required a reworking, refocusing, or expanding of the tenets of the approach.

Also, as mentioned in a footnote in chapter 1, we have deliberately labelled our approach as a *videogame* formalism. It would be worth considering whether, for example, it would make sense to conduct a formalist analysis of a board game or a card game. Does the focus on the player's aesthetic experience allow us to extend our approach to games that are not represented in a digital, computational medium? After all, is there anything in our approach that assumes this type of medium? What about games that are not represented in any concrete medium, such as a tabletop roleplaying game? Knowing where the approach can be extended, and where it simply is no longer relevant (sports, or gambling, perhaps?), would help to strengthen our understanding of the formalist approach and its limitations. We don't have the answers to these questions at present. For our future work, we have therefore taken it upon ourselves to explore a wider range of games to see where these games challenge the usefulness of our approach and where it thus needs changing or refining (recall Eichenbaum's (2012) notion of formalism as a flexible toolkit discussed in chapter 1).

Aside from challenging the approach with other case materials, we are also interested in exploring how the approach could inform other types of research methodologies, and also potentially inform practice. In terms of using our approach to inform other methodologies, one perspective would be to think about a textual, close reading analysis as forming part of a larger research programme, possibly providing the initial insights into a game which could then be used as the starting point for an empirical, observational study of player response to a game or games. As an example of this approach, Mitchell's (2016) analysis of *Thirty Flights of Loving* (Blendo Games 2012) provided the initial set of poetic gameplay patterns and the initial insights into the use of defamiliarization in games, which was then used as the starting point for an observational study of player response (Mitchell, Sim, and Kway 2017) to three games: *The Graveyard* (Tale of Tales 2008), *Thirty Flights of Loving*, and *The Stanley Parable* (Galactic Cafe 2013). This study focused on the question of whether the assumption that the concepts of defamiliarization and foregrounding, taken as they are from the study of non-interactive forms such as poetry, literary fiction, and film, actually create an aesthetic response in players. This approach was inspired by empirical studies of literature, such as those undertaken by Miall and Kuiken (1994). It is worth noting that, in addition to determining whether the devices identified in a close reading seem to surface and impact the actual experience of a group of players, this type of study also shows that using our theoretical framing of the player's aesthetic experience as emerging from their encounter with devices can be a productive way to similarly frame an empirical study of player response to gameplay. Here, the formalist focus comes through in terms of what the study is attending to – player aesthetic experience, the associated devices, and how they work together to create the experience in the form of the dominant.

Following on from this, and as suggested by Mitchell et al. (2017), it is worth considering whether, and in what sense, our videogame formalism could be of use to practitioners. Would it make sense to consider a formalist analysis as a "first step towards identifying actionable design knowledge to support artists and designers who want to create poetic gameplay" with the aim being to find "ways to communicate these techniques to artists and designers" (Mitchell, Sim, and Kway 2017)? This might, for example, take the form of formulating "design patterns" (Björk and Holopainen 2005; Alexander, Ishikawa, and Silverstein 1977) based on devices that have been identified through a combination of close readings and empirical studies. Would this be in conflict with our earlier emphasis on a formalist analysis not being an attempt to generalize beyond one game, with the findings not making any claim to be applicable across other games? Or would our formalist approach, which acknowledges the importance of context and a focus on the player experience, bring such an attempt perhaps closer to the original approach advocated by Alexander (1979), which involves closely observing what creates "life" in a building, and then developing a flexible but clear set of patterns, what he calls a "pattern language," that when taken together balance the forces at work in a particular context? One way to start doing this might be to consider reformulating Mitchell's (2020) poetic gameplay devices as a set of design patterns, and seeing whether designers might find this a useful resource for their own practice. This is a clear possible next step beyond this book if the intention might be to explore ways to make our approach useful to practitioners.

Another approach to making our approach applicable to practitioners might be, rather than focusing on the specific devices, to think about the underlying concepts we have introduced, namely the notions of defamiliarization, foregrounding, and the dominant, as a way to focus creative practice. While this may sound dangerously like some of the issues we raised in chapter 1, such as the notion of formalism as an art movement or a practitioners' mantra, and the possibility of (game) formalism focusing too much on game design to the detriment of the player, there have been examples of works created with this focus in mind. For example, Bogost's collection of "game poems," *A Slow Year* (2010b), are deliberately designed to be "about the experience of observing things. These games are neither action nor strategy: each of them requires a different kind of sedate observation and methodical input" (Bogost 2010a). Similarly, Magnuson's "game poems" (2009) take a deliberately poetic approach, something that Magnuson has reflected on at length (2019; 2023), and has articulated in terms of what he calls a "personal, subjectively-grounded *praxis* of poetic intervention" (emphasis in original) for "videogame creators seeking to engage with videogames as a medium of poetic expression" (2019, 84). Magnuson suggests that the videogame creator carefully consider that "the core material of the videogame poet is the *language* of videogames" (emphasis in original) which has become "established and prosaic," and that the videogame poet's key concern is to consider "how one might intervene [in that language] to question or recast that meaning" (2019, 103). He connects this to, for example, Shelley's argument that poetry "lifts the veil from the hidden beauty of the world, and makes familiar objects be as if they were not familiar" (Shelley et al. 1969, 50, quoted in Magnuson 2019, 106). This is, of course, very similar to how we have been viewing the process of defamiliarization and foregrounding. It would be worth considering whether providing advice for designers and artists that parallels what we have laid out as an analytical methodology would be useful for practitioners. This could involve, for example, providing a number of suggestions for practitioners to consider, such as:

– How can you consider form and content as equal devices at your disposal to trigger an aesthetic experience?
– Where do you challenge conventions (unfamiliar) and where do you embrace them (familiar)?
– Where (in relationship to which norms) do you place your work in time and over time?
– How can or do you consider your devices to be working in different motivational categories (ludic, compositional, realistic, transtextual, artistic)?
– How do you aim for and stick to a dominant design principle aiming to evoke an overall aesthetic response?

Possible future work in this direction could involve formalizing this advice, and then working with practitioners to see whether this set of suggestions, possibly together with a set of "poetic gameplay design patterns," would be of interest and use to them as they develop games.

Limitations and Final Thoughts

Coming back to our formalist game analysis, there are a number of possible limitations that we have experienced as we have applied this approach in the case studies in chapter 5. This includes the tendency to fix on a particular idea of what the dominant might be from the start of an analysis, and the difficulty of avoiding being overly influenced by other analyses of the same game.

Although we suggest that the player critic first consider what it is that intrigues them about the game, and then gradually and iteratively uncover the materials and foregrounded devices, eventually seeing how these work together and in tension with each other to form the dominant, it was very tempting to simply latch on to an idea as to what the dominant might be from the start, and be influenced by this throughout the process. There is no guaranteed way to avoid this. Instead, what we tried to do in our analyses was to constantly remind ourselves of the need to remain open to the discovery of new devices, connecting this to our deliberate choice of play strategy. It is also helpful to make sure to continue to take notes and journal your thoughts after each play session, as this reflective process allows you to think through and articulate the direction of your thoughts as you begin to work through your analysis. This will also help to provide you with the material you need to back up your argument as you actually write the analysis. This essentially involves maintaining a constant focus on the player experience and the context, even as you engage with the game as object. As with any process, our approach requires not just rigour and focus, but also practice. As you repeatedly make use of the process, you will find that it is easier to remember to check your analysis against the three pillars of the approach, object, process/experience and context, and use this to try to avoid fixating on one possible outcome.

Similarly, it is almost impossible to avoid reading other analyses of the game you are analysing, so it is worth considering how you deal with this during your own analysis. Is it possible that you are just looking for a gap in the previous readings of the game, hoping that you will be able to make a contribution, and see the game in a way that has not been articulated by previous critics? While this is a valid ambition, the danger here is that, as with our earlier point about fixating on the dominant from the start, you may be predetermining what you are looking for, or in this case not looking for, and as a result miss out some interesting aspect of the work. As with the above issue, one possible way to avoid this is to constantly reflect on your observations and findings, always making sure that you connect them back to the game, the player, and the context of play.

Finally, having begun this book by providing an overview of the (many) various formalisms, both outside of and within game studies, it is worth ending by looking back over what we have presented, particularly the various areas we have touched upon in this chapter, and consider where we have got to, and whether we have successfully laid out a videogame formalism that manages to move forward while avoiding the pitfalls of the past. In spite of some new pitfalls identified above, we believe that our discussion of the core tenets of the approach in terms of form, aesthetic experience, and context has avoided a slip into, for example, elitism or gatekeeping, and has also maintained a balance between the role of the game itself and the player's experience. We have also maintained a connection to historical context in terms of both when the game was created and when it was and is played, without having to rely on, for example, authorial intention. Although we have positioned our formalism as an analytical approach, consisting of methodological considerations for carrying out a textual analysis, we have also suggested ways that the focus on the player's aesthetic experience and the notions of foregrounding and the dominant could perhaps be productively applied in other areas, such as by practitioners or by those engaging in empirical, observational research.

In the end, our main intention in this book is to articulate a videogame formalism that provides a historically grounded, theoretically justified set of methodological considerations for carrying out a textual analysis of a videogame. By making the ontological, epistemological, and methodological assumptions underlying this approach clear, we hope that those who are considering taking up this approach will be able to make that decision based on an understanding of what types of questions this approach can answer, and whether it fits with their overall approach to game studies. As this is a flexible set of considerations rather than a prescriptive approach (Eikhenbaum 2012), we hope that those of you who do choose to take up this method as part of your toolkit will share your experiences, challenge our assumptions, extend what we have done here, and work together to help build up a stronger and more robust field of game studies.

References

Aarseth, Espen. 2004. "Genre Trouble: Narrativism and the Art of Simulation." In *First Person: New Media as Story, Performance, and Game*, edited by Noah Wardrip-Fruin and Pat Harrigan, 45–55. Cambridge, MA: MIT Press.

Alexander, Christopher. 1979. *The Timeless Way of Building*. New York: Oxford University Press.

Alexander, Christopher, Sara Ishikawa, and Murray Silverstein. 1977. *A Pattern Language: Towns, Buildings, Construction*. New York: Oxford University Press.

Arbitrary Metric. 2018. "Paratopic [MacOS Game]." Arbitrary Metric.

Björk, Staffan, and Jussi Holopainen. 2005. *Patterns in Game Design*. Boston, MA: Charles River Media.

Blendo Games. 2012. "Thirty Flights of Loving [MacOS Game]." Blendo Games.

BlueTwelve Studio. 2022. "Stray [Microsoft Windows Game]." Annapurna Interactive.

Bogost, Ian. 2007. *Persuasive Games*. Cambridge, MA: The MIT Press.

Bogost, Ian. 2010a. "A Slow Year." Bogost.Com. 2010. http://bogost.com/games/aslowyear/.

Bogost, Ian. 2010b. *A Slow Year: Game Poems*. Louisville, KY: Open Texture.

Bordwell, David. 1989. "Historical Poetics of Cinema." In *The Cinematic Text: Methods and Approaches*, edited by R. Barton Palmer, 369–98. Cambridge, MA: Harvard University Press.

Cardboard Computer. 2013. "Kentucky Route Zero [MacOS Game]." Annapurna Interactive.

Daneels, Rowan, Maarten Denoo, Alexander Vandewalle, Bruno Dupont, and Steven Malliet. 2022. "The Digital Game Analysis Protocol (DiGAP): Introducing a Guide for Reflexive and Transparent Game Analyses." *Game Studies* 22 (2).

Daniel Mullins Games. 2021. "Inscryption [Microsoft Windows Game]." Devolver Digital.

Eikhenbaum, Boris. 2012. "The Theory of the 'Formal Method'." In *Russian Formalist Criticism: Four Essays*, edited by Lee T. Lemon and Marion J. Reis, 2nd ed., 78–104. Lincoln: University of Nebraska Press.

Eskelinen, Markku. 2001. "The Gaming Situation." *Game Studies* 1 (1).

Foddy, Bennett. 2017. "Getting Over It with Bennett Foddy [Microsoft Windows Game]." Bennet Foddy.

FromSoftware Inc. 2022. "Elden Ring [Microsoft Windows Game]." Bandai Namco Entertainment Inc.

FuturLab. 2021. "PowerWash Simulator [Microsoft Windows Game]." Square Enix.

Galactic Cafe. 2013. "The Stanley Parable [MacOS Game]." Galactic Cafe.

Geography of Robots. 2022. "Norco [MacOS Game]." Raw Fury.

Jump Over The Age. 2022. "Citizen Sleeper [MacOS Game]." Fellow Traveller.

k, merritt. 2012. "Lim [Browser Game]." merritt k.

Klimas, Chris. 2009. "Twine [Computer Software]." Chris Klimas.

Koster, Raph. 2012. "Two Cultures and Games." *Raph's Website* (blog). July 6, 2012. https://www.raphkoster.com/2012/07/06/two-cultures-and-games/.

Koster, Raph. 2014. "A New Formalism." *Critical Proximity* (blog). March 16, 2014. https://critical-proximity.com/2014/03/16/a-new-formalism/.

Lantz, Frank. 2015a. "TwitLonger – When You Talk Too Much for Twitter." January 13, 2015. http://www.twitlonger.com/show/n_1sjugos.

Lantz, Frank. 2015b. "More Thoughts on Formalism." *Game Developer* (blog). January 20, 2015. https://www.gamedeveloper.com/design/more-thoughts-on-formalism.

Magnuson, Jordan. 2009. "Necessary Games | Games Considered for Meaning and Significance." 2009. https://www.necessarygames.com/.

Magnuson, Jordan. 2019. "Playing and Making Poetic Videogames." MFA Thesis, University of California.

Magnuson, Jordan. 2023. *Game Poems: Videogame Design as Lyric Practice*. Electronic Communities of Making. Amherst, MA: Amherst College Press.

Miall, David S., and Don Kuiken. 1994. "Foregrounding, Defamiliarization, and Affect: Response to Literary Stories." *Poetics* 22 (5): 389–407.

Mitchell, Alex. 2014. "Defamiliarization and Poetic Interaction in Kentucky Route Zero." *Well Played: A Journal on Video Games, Value and Meaning* 3 (2): 161–78.

Mitchell, Alex. 2016. "Making the Familiar Unfamiliar: Techniques for Creating Poetic Gameplay." In *Proceedings of the First International Joint Conference of DiGRA and FDG 2016*. Dundee: Digital Games Research Association.

Mitchell, Alex, Liting Kway, Tiffany Neo, and Yuin Theng Sim. 2020. "A Preliminary Categorization of Techniques for Creating Poetic Gameplay." *Game Studies* 20 (2).

Mitchell, Alex, Yuin Theng Sim, and Liting Kway. 2017. "Making It Unfamiliar in the "Right" Way: An Empirical Study of Poetic Gameplay." In *Proceedings of the 2017 DiGRA International Conference*. Melbourne, Australia: Digital Games Research Association.

Nintendo. 2017. "The Legend of Zelda: Breath of the Wild [Nintendo Switch Game]." Nintendo.

Robinson-Yu, Adam. 2019. "A Short Hike [MacOS Game]." Adam Robinson-Yu.

Shelley, Percy Bysshe, Patrick Garland, Richard Marquard, and Gary Watson. 1969. *A Defence of Poetry*. Haldeman-Julius.

Sicart, Miguel. 2011. "Against Procedurality." *Game Studies* 11 (3).

Tale of Tales. 2008. "The Graveyard [MacOS Game]." Tale of Tales.

Team Aha! 2008. "Akrasia [Microsoft Windows Game]." Singapore-MIT GAMBIT Game Lab.

Team Ico. 2005. "Shadow of the Colossus [Playstation 2 Game]." Sony Computer Entertainment.

Vught, Jasper van, and René Glas. 2018. "Considering Play: From Method to Analysis." *Transactions of the Digital Games Research Association* 4 (2).

Bibliography

2K Boston. 2007. "BioShock [Xbox360 Game]." 2K Games.

2K Marin. 2010. "Bioshock 2 [Xbox360 Game]." 2K Games.

Aarseth, Espen. 1997. *Cybertext: Perspectives on Ergodic Literature*. London: The Johns Hopkins University Press.

Aarseth, Espen. 2003. "Playing Research: Methodological Approaches to Game Analysis." In *MelbourneDAC, Proceedings of the 5th International Digital Arts and Culture Conference*. Melbourne, Australia: RMIT University.

Aarseth, Espen. 2004. "Genre Trouble: Narrativism and the Art of Simulation." In *First Person: New Media as Story, Performance, and Game*, edited by Noah Wardrip-Fruin and Pat Harrigan, 45–55. Cambridge, MA: MIT Press.

Aarseth, Espen. 2014. "I Fought the Law: Transgressive Play and the Implied Player." In *From Literature to Cultural Literacy*, edited by Naomi Segal and Daniela Koleva, 180–88. London: Springer.

Aarseth, Espen. 2017. "Against 'Videogames': Epistemic Blindness in (Video) Game Studies." In *Extended Abstract Presented at DiGRA 2017 International Conference*.

Aarseth, Espen. 2019. "Game Studies: How to Play – Ten Play-Tips for the Aspiring Game-Studies Scholar." *Game Studies* 19 (2).

Aarseth, Espen, and Sebastian Möring. 2020. "The Game Itself? Towards a Hermeneutics of Computer Games." In *Proceedings of the 15th International Conference on the Foundations of Digital Games*, 1–8. New York: ACM.

Academy of American Poets. 2014. "A Brief Guide to New Formalism | Academy of American Poets." 2014. https://poets.org/text/brief-guide-new-formalism.

Ainsworth, Thomas. 2020. "Form vs. Matter." In *Stanford Encyclopedia of Philosophy*. https://plato.stanford.edu/entries/form-matter/.

Alber, Jan. 2013. "Unnatural Narratology: The Systematic Study of Anti-Mimeticism." *Literature Compass* 10 (5): 449–60.

Alber, Jan. 2014. "Unnatural Narrative." In *Handbook of Narratology*, edited by Peter Hühn, Jan Christoph Meister, John Pier and Wolf Schmid, 887–95. New York: de Gruyter.

Alber, Jan, Stefan Iversen, Henrik Skov Nielsen, and Brian Richardson. 2010. "Unnatural Narratives, Unnatural Narratology: Beyond Mimetic Models." *Narrative* 18 (2): 113–36.

Alexander, Christopher. 1979. *The Timeless Way of Building*. New York: Oxford University Press.

Alexander, Christopher, Sara Ishikawa, and Murray Silverstein. 1977. *A Pattern Language: Towns, Buildings, Construction*. New York: Oxford University Press.

Anable, Aubrey. 2018. *Playing with Feelings: Video Games and Affect*. Minneapolis: University of Minnesota Press.

Anthropy, Anna. 2012. "Dys4ia [Flash Game]." Newgrounds.

Apolon. 2017. ""Legend of Zelda: Breath of the Wild" Camera Guide: Tips to Use the Camera Like a Pro." Player.One. March 3, 2017. https://www.player.one/legend-zelda-breath-wild-camera-guide-tips-use-camera-pro-587014.

Arbitrary Metric. 2018a. "Paratopic." Steam. 2018. https://store.steampowered.com/app/897030/Paratopic/.

Arbitrary Metric. 2018b. "Paratopic [MacOS Game]." Arbitrary Metric.

Bálint, Katalin, Frank Hakemulder, Moniek M. Kuijpers, Miruna M. Doicaru, and Ed S. Tan. 2016. "Reconceptualizing Foregrounding." *Scientific Study of Literature* 6 (2): 176–207.

Bartle, Richard. 2003. *Designing Virtual Worlds*. Indianapolis: New Riders.

Baudelaire, Charles. 1964. *The Painter of Modern Life and Other Essays*. Translated by Jonathan Mayne. London: Phaidon Press.

Beirne, Stephen. 2015. "Why I Said Ludo-Fundamentalism and Not Something Else." *Normally Rascal* (blog). January 13, 2015. https://normallyrascal.wordpress.com/2015/01/13/why-i-said-ludo-fundamentalism/.

Bendor, Roy. 2018. *Interactive Media for Sustainability*. London: Palgrave MacMillan.

Bennett, Tony, and Janet Woollacott. 1987. *Bond and beyond: The Political Career of a Popular Hero*. London: Macmillan International Higher Education.

Bioware. 2007. "Mass Effect [Microsoft Windows Game]." Electronic Arts.

Bizzocchi, Jim, and Teresa Jean Tanenbaum. 2011. "Well Read: Applying Close Reading Techniques to Gameplay Experiences." In *Well Played 3.0. Video Games, Value and Meaning*, edited by Drew Davidson, 262–90. Pittsburgh: ETC Press.

Bizzocchi, Jim, and Theresa Jean Tanenbaum. 2012. "Mass Effect 2: A Case Study in the Design of Game Narrative." *Bulletin of Science, Technology & Society* 32 (5): 393–404.

Björk, Staffan, and Jussi Holopainen. 2003. "Describing Games: An Interaction-Centric Structural Framework." In *Proceedings of the 2003 DiGRA International Conference: Level Up*, edited by Marinka Copier and Joost Raessens. Utrecht: Utrecht University.

Björk, Staffan, and Jussi Holopainen. 2005. *Patterns in Game Design*. Boston, MA: Charles River Media.

Blendo Games. 2012. "Thirty Flights of Loving [MacOS Game]." Blendo Games.

BlueTwelve Studio. 2022a. "A Spoiler-Free Introduction to Stray." PlayStation. 2022. https://www.playstation.com/en-sg/games/stray/a-spoiler-free-introduction-to-stray/.

BlueTwelve Studio. 2022b. "Stray." PlayStation Store. 2022. https://www.playstation.com/en-sg/games/stray-englishchinesekoreanjapanese-ver.

BlueTwelve Studio. 2022c. "Stray [Microsoft Windows Game]." Annapurna Interactive.

Bogost, Ian. 2006. *Unit Operations: An Approach to Videogame Criticism*. Cambridge, MA: The MIT Press.

Bogost, Ian. 2007. *Persuasive Games*. Cambridge, MA: The MIT Press.

Bogost, Ian. 2010a. "A Slow Year." Bogost.Com. 2010. http://bogost.com/games/aslowyear/.

Bogost, Ian. 2010b. *A Slow Year: Game Poems*. Louisville, KY: Open Texture.

Bogost, Ian. 2011. *How to Do Things with Videogames*. Minneapolis: University of Minnesota Press.

Bopp, Julia Ayumi. 2020. "Aesthetic Emotions in Digital Games: The Appeal of Moving, Challenging, and Thought-Provoking Player Experiences." PhD Thesis, Aalto University.

Bopp, Julia Ayumi, Elisa D. Mekler, and Klaus Opwis. 2016. "Negative Emotion, Positive Experience?: Emotionally Moving Moments in Digital Games." In *Proceedings of the 2016 CHI Conference on Human Factors in Computing Systems*, 2996–3006. New York: ACM.

Bordwell, David. 1985. *Narration in the Fiction Film*. Madison, Wisconsin: University of Wisconsin Press.

Bordwell, David. 1989. "Historical Poetics of Cinema." In *The Cinematic Text: Methods and Approaches*, edited by R. Barton Palmer, 369–98. Cambridge, MA: Harvard University Press.

Bordwell, David. 1991. *Making Meaning: Inference and Rhetoric in the Interpretation of Cinema*. Cambridge, MA: Harvard University Press.

Bordwell, David. 2008. *Poetics of Cinema*. New York: Routledge.

Bordwell, David. 2013. *Narration in the Fiction Film*. New York: Routledge.

Bordwell, David, and Kristin Thompson. 2010. *Film Art: An Introduction*. 9th ed. New York: McGraw-Hill.

Bradford, Clare. 2009. "Playing at Bullying: The Postmodern Ethic of Bully (Canis Canem Edit)." *Digital Culture and Education* 1 (1): 67–82.

Brewer, Christopher G. 2017. "Born to Run: A Grounded Theory Study of Cheating in the Online Speedrunning Community." MA Thesis, The University of Southern Mississippi.

Brinkema, Eugenie. 2020. "Form." In *A Concise Companion to Visual Culture*, 259–75. Hoboken, New Jersey: John Wiley & Sons, Ltd.

Burford, Doc. 2018. "How I Attempted to Redefine the 'Walking Sim' with Paratopic." *USgamer*, September 6, 2018. https://www.usgamer.net/articles/how-i-attempted-to-redefine-the-walking-sim-with-paratopic.

Calleja, Gordon. 2007. "Digital Games as Designed Experience: Reframing the Concept of Immersion." PhD Thesis, Victoria University of Wellington.

Cardboard Computer. 2011. "Balloon Diaspora [MacOS Game]." Cardboard Computer.

Cardboard Computer. 2013. "Kentucky Route Zero [MacOS Game]." Annapurna Interactive.

Cardboard Computer, dir. 2016. *Junebug – "Static Between Stations."* https://www. youtube.com/watch?v=igvvC4I7v2o.

Cardboard Computer. 2020. "Kentucky Route Zero." 2020. http://kentuckyroutezero. com/.

Cardboard Computer. n.d. "The Entertainment." Kentucky Route Zero. Accessed December 5, 2022. http://kentuckyroutezero.com/the-entertainment/.

Carr, Diane. 2009. "Textual Analysis, Digital Games, Zombies.' In *Proceedings of the 2009 DiGRA International Conference: Breaking New Ground – Innovation in Games, Play, Practice and Theory*. London: Digital Games Research Association.

Carr, Diane. 2014. "Ability, Disability and Dead Space." *Game Studies* 14 (2).

Carr, Diane. 2019. "Methodology, Representation, and Games." *Games and Culture* 14 (7–8): 707–23.

Carroll, Lewis. 1865. *Alice's Adventures in Wonderland*. London: MacMillan.

Central Committee of the All-Union Communist Party. 1948. "Against Formalistic Tendencies in Soviet Music." *Sovetskaia Muzyka* 1: 3–8.

Chew, Evelyn C., and Alex Mitchell. 2020. "Bringing Art to Life: Examining Poetic Gameplay Devices in Interactive Life Stories." *Games and Culture* 15 (8): 874–901.

Chew, Evelyn, and Alex Mitchell. 2016. "'As Only a Game Can': Re-Creating Subjective Lived Experiences through Interactivity in Non-Fictional Video Games." In *Subjectivity across Media: Interdisciplinary and Transmedial Perspectives*, edited by Maike Sarah Reinerth and Jan Noël Thon, 214–32. New York: Routledge.

Chew, Evelyn, and Alex Mitchell. 2019. "Multimodality and Interactivity in 'Natively' Digital Life Stories." *POETICS TODAY* 40 (2): 319–53.

The Chinese Room. 2012. "Dear Esther [MacOS Game]." The Chinese Room.

Clark, Naomi. 2017. "What Is Queerness in Games, Anyway?' In *Queer Game Studies*, edited by Bonnie Ruberg and Adrienne Shaw, 3–14. Minneapolis: University of Minnesota Press.

Cogan, John. n.d. "The Phenomenological Reduction." In *Internet Encyclopedia of Philosophy*. Accessed June 13, 2023. https://iep.utm.edu/phen-red/.

Cohen, Ethan, dir. 2008. *No Country for Old Men*. Paramount Pictures.

Consalvo, Mia. 2009. *Cheating: Gaining Advantage in Videogames*. Cambridge, MA: MIT Press.

Consalvo, Mia, and Christopher A. Paul. 2019. *Real Games: What's Legitimate and What's Not in Contemporary Videogames*. Cambridge, MA: MIT Press.

Copier, Marinka. 2003. "The Other Game Researcher. Participating in and Watching the Construction of Boundaries in Game Studies." In *Proceedings of the 2003*

DiGRA International Conference: Level Up, edited by Marinka Copier and Joost Raessens, 404–19. Utrecht: Utrecht University.

Costikyan, Greg. 2002. "I Have No Words & I Must Design: Toward a Critical Vocabulary for Games." In *Proceedings of the Computer Games and Digital Cultures Conference, Finland*, edited by Frans Mäyrä, 9–33. Tampere: Tampere University Press.

Csikszentmihályi, Mihály. 1990. *Flow: The Psychology of Optimal Experience*. New York: Harper and Row.

Culler, Jonathan. 1997. *Literary Theory: A Very Short Introduction*. New York: Oxford University Press.

Daneels, Rowan, Maarten Denoo, Alexander Vandewalle, Bruno Dupont, and Steven Malliet. 2022. "The Digital Game Analysis Protocol (DiGAP): Introducing a Guide for Reflexive and Transparent Game Analyses." *Game Studies* 22 (2).

Daniel Mullins Games. 2021. "Inscryption [Microsoft Windows Game]." Devolver Digital.

Davidson, Drew, and Richard Lemarchand. 2011. "Uncharted 2: Among Thieves-Becoming a Hero." In *Well Played 3.0: Video Games, Value and Meaning*, edited by Drew Davidson, 77–112. Pittsburgh: ETC Press.

Davies, Mark. 2009. "Examining Game Pace: How Single-Player Levels Tick." *Game Developer*, May 12, 2009. https://www.gamedeveloper.com/design/examining-game-pace-how-single-player-levels-tick.

De Certeau, Michel. 1988. *The Practice of Everyday Life*. Translated by Steven Rendall. Los Angeles, CA: University of California Press.

Dinosaur Games. 2017. "Desert Bus VR [Microsoft Windows Game]." Gearbox Software, LLC.

Dontnod Entertainment. 2017. "Life Is Strange [MacOS Game]." Square Enix.

Dowling, Christopher. n.d. "Aesthetic Formalism." In *Internet Encyclopedia of Philosophy*. Accessed December 7, 2022. https://iep.utm.edu/aesthetic-formalism/.

Eco, Umberto. 1990. *The Limits of Interpretation*. Bloomington, Indiana: Indiana University Press.

Eikhenbaum, Boris. 2012. "The Theory of the 'Formal Method'." In *Russian Formalist Criticism: Four Essays*, edited by Lee T. Lemon and Marion J. Reis, 2nd ed., 78–104. Lincoln: University of Nebraska Press.

Eisenstein, Sergei, dir. 1944. *Ivan the Terrible*. Mosfilm.

Elliot, Jake. 2011. "Kentucky Route Zero, a Magic Realist Adventure Game." Kickstarter. 2011. https://www.kickstarter.com/projects/149077132/kentucky-route-zero-a-magic-realist-adventure-game.

Ensslin, Astrid. 2015. "Video Games as Unnatural Narratives." *Diversity of Play*, 41–72.

Ensslin, Astrid, and Isabel Balteiro, eds. 2019. *Approaches to Videogame Discourse: Lexis, Interaction, Textuality*. New York: Bloomsbury Academic.

Ericsson, Karl Anders, and Herbert Alexander Simon. 1993. *Protocol Analysis: Verbal Reports as Data*. Revised Edition. Cambridge, MA: MIT Press.

Erlich, Victor. 1980. *Russian Formalism: History, Doctrine*. 4th ed. The Hague: Mouton & Co.

Ermi, Laura, and Frans Mäyrä. 2005. "Fundamental Components of the Gameplay Experience: Analysing Immersion." In *Proceedings of the 2005 DiGRA International Conference: Changing Views – Worlds in Play*. Vancouver, BC, Canada: Digital Games Research Association.

Errant Signal, dir. 2015. *Errant Signal – The Debate That Never Took Place*. https://www.youtube.com/watch?v=xBN3Rom31bA.

Eskelinen, Markku. 2001. "The Gaming Situation." *Game Studies* 1 (1).

Fabricatore, Carlo, Miguel Nussbaum, and Ricardo Rosas. 2002. "Playability in Action Videogames: A Qualitative Design Model." *Human-Computer Interaction* 17 (4): 311–68.

Farca, Gerald, Alexander Lehner, and Victor Navarro-Remesal. 2020. "Regenerative Play and the Experience of the Sublime: Breath of the Wild." In *Mythopoeic Narrative in The Legend of Zelda*, edited by Anthony Cirilla and Vincent Rone, 205–21. New York: Routledge.

Fernández-Vara, Clara. 2019. *Introduction to Game Analysis*. 2nd ed. New York: Routledge.

Fialho, Olivia da Costa. 2007. "Foregrounding and Refamiliarization: Understanding Readers' Response to Literary Texts." *Language and Literature* 16 (2): 105–23.

Flanagan, Mary. 2009. *Critical Play: Radical Game Design*. Cambridge, MA: MIT Press.

Foddy, Bennett. 2017. "Getting Over It with Bennett Foddy [Microsoft Windows Game]." Bennet Foddy.

Foddy, Bennett. n.d. "Getting Over It with Bennett Foddy." Steam. Accessed June 24, 2021. https://store.steampowered.com/app/240720/Getting_Over_It_with_Bennett_Foddy/.

Folkerts, Jef. 2010. "Playing Games as an Art Experience: How Videogames Produce Meaning through Narrative and Play.' *At the Interface / Probing the Boundaries* 69 (October): 99–117.

Frasca, Gonzalo. 2003. "Ludologists Love Stories, Too: Notes from a Debate That Never Took Place." In *Proceedings of the 2003 DiGRA International Conference: Level Up*, edited by Marinka Copier and Joost Raessens, 92–99. Utrecht: Utrecht University.

Frasca, Gonzalo. 2007. "Play the Message: Play, Game and Videogame Rhetoric." PhD Thesis, IT University of Copenhagen.

Frome, Jonathan. 2006. "Why Films Make Us Cry but Videogames Don't: Emotions in Traditional and Interactive Media." PhD Thesis, The University of Wisconsin–Madison.

FromSoftware Inc. 2022. "Elden Ring [Microsoft Windows Game]." Bandai Namco Entertainment Inc.

Fullerton, Tracy. 2019. *Game Design Workshop: A Playcentric Approach to Creating Innovative Games*. 4th ed. New York: CRC Press (Taylor and Francis).

FuturLab. 2021. "PowerWash Simulator [Microsoft Windows Game]." Square Enix.

Galactic Cafe. 2013. "The Stanley Parable [MacOS Game]." Galactic Cafe.

Games for Change. 2013. "Play | Lim." Games for Change. June 5, 2013. http://legacy. gamesforchange.org/play/lim/.

Gasque, Terra M, Kevin Tang, Brad Rittenhouse, and Janet H. Murray. 2020. "Gated Story Structure and Dramatic Agency in Sam Barlow's Telling Lies BT – Interactive Storytelling." In *Interactive Storytelling: 13th International Conference on Interactive Digital Storytelling – ICIDS*, edited by Anne-Gwenn Bosser, David E. Millard, and Charlie Hargood, 314–26. Cham: Springer International Publishing.

Genette, Gerard. 1997. *Paratexts: Thresholds of Interpretation*. Cambridge, MA: Cambridge University Press.

Geography of Robots. 2022. "Norco [MacOS Game]." Raw Fury.

Gioia, Dana. 1987. "Notes on the New Formalism." *The Hudson Review* 40 (3): 395–408.

Gray, Kate. 2017. "Is The Legend of Zelda: Breath of the Wild the Best-Designed Game Ever?" *The Guardian*, 30 May 2017, sec. Games.

Greenberg, Clement. 1971. "Necessity of 'Formalism'." *New Literary History* 3 (1): 171–75.

Heidegger, Martin. 1962. *Being and Time*. Translated by John Macquarrie and Edward Robinson. 1st English ed. Malden, MA: Blackwell.

Hernandez, Patricia. 2013. "It's Time We Put the Bald Space Marine Away. It's Time to Make Games for More People." *Kotaku*, January 8, 2013. https://kotaku.com/ its-time-we-put-the-bald-space-marine-away-its-time-to-5973806.

Holbrook, Morris B., Robert W. Chestnut, Terence A. Oliva, and Eric A. Greenleaf. 1984. "Play as a Consumption Experience: The Roles of Emotions, Performance, and Personality in the Enjoyment of Games." *The Journal of Consumer Research* 11 (2): 728–39.

Holzbaur, Ulrich. 2001. "EcoGames – Simulation Games and Sustainable Development." In *Sustainability in the Information Society*, edited by Lorenz M. Hilty and Paul W. Gilgen, 971–78. Marburg: Metropolis Verlag.

Howe, Austin C. 2015. "Haptic Feedback: On the Ghost of Formalism." *Haptic Feedback* (blog). January 31, 2015. http://hapticfeedbackgames.blogspot.com/2015/01/ on-ghost-of-formalism_62.html.

Hu, Junyao, and Tao Xi. 2019. "The Relationship between Game Elements and Player Emotions by Comparing Game Frameworks." In *HCI International 2019 – Late Breaking Papers*, edited by Constantine Stephanidis, 320–29. Cham: Springer International Publishing.

Hughes, John, dir. 1985. *The Breakfast Club*. Universal Pictures.

Hughes, John, dir. 1986. *Ferris Bueller's Day Off*. Paramount Pictures.

Hughes, Thomas. 1857. *Tom Brown's Schooldays*. London: MacMillan.

Hunicke, Robin, Marc LeBlanc, and Robert Zubek. 2004. "MDA: A Formal Approach to Game Design and Game Research." In *Proceedings of the Challenges in Game AI Workshop, Nineteenth National Conference on Artificial Intelligence*. San Jose, CA.

Imagineering. unreleased. "Penn & Teller's Smoke and Mirrors [Sega Genesis Game]." Absolute Entertainment.

Independent Games Festival. 2019. "IGF 2019." Independent Games Festival (IGF). July 19, 2019. https://igf.com/2019.

Isbister, Katherine. 2016. *How Games Move Us: Emotion by Design*. Cambridge, MA: MIT Press.

Iser, Wolfgang. 1980. *The Act of Reading: A Theory of Aesthetic Response*. London: The Johns Hopkins University Press.

Iwatani, Toru. 1980. "Pac-Man [Arcade Game]." Bandai Namco Entertainment.

jace :). 2018. "The Space Between Spaces: Breath of the Wild and Shadow of the Colossus." *Medium* (blog). March 25, 2018. https://medium.com/@pizzasheets/the-space-between-spaces-breath-of-the-wild-and-shadow-of-the-colossus-7a1182f0f502.

Jagoda, Patrick. 2018. "On Difficulty in Video Games: Mechanics, Interpretation, Affect." *Critical Inquiry* 45 (1): 199–233.

Jakobson, Roman. 1921. *Noveĭshaia Russkaia Poeziia*. Tip. "Politika."

Jakobson, Roman. 1987. *Language in Literature*. Edited by Krystyna Pomorska and Stephen Rudy. Cambridge, MA: Harvard University Press.

Järvinen, Aki. 2007. "Introducing Applied Ludology: Hands-on Methods for Game Studies." In *Proceedings of the 2007 DiGRA International Conference: Situated Play*, 134–44. Tokyo: The University of Tokyo.

Jayemanne, Darshana. 2017. *Performativity in Art, Literature, and Videogames*. Cham: Palgrave MacMillan.

Jayemanne, Darshana. 2020. "Chronotypology: A Comparative Method for Analyzing Game Time." *Games and Culture* 15 (7): 809–24.

Jazzuo. 2002. "Sexy Hiking [Microsoft Windows Game]." Jazzuo.

Jiang, Sisi. 2022. "Stray Falls into the Usual Orientalism Pitfalls of the Cyberpunk Genre." *Kotaku*, July 25, 2022. https://kotaku.com/stray-game-annapurna-interactive-cat-cyberpunk-1849328820.

Jump Over The Age. 2022. "Citizen Sleeper [MacOS Game]." Fellow Traveller.

Junebug, and Ben Babbitt. 2020. *Too Late to Love You*.

Juul, Jesper. 2003. "The Game, the Player, the World: Looking for a Heart of Gameness." In *Level Up: Digital Games Research Conference Proceedings*, 30–45. Utrecht: Utrecht University.

Juul, Jesper. 2004. "Introduction to Game Time/Time to Play: An Examination of Game Temporality." In *First Person: New Media as Story, Performance, and Game*, edited by Noah Wardrip-Fruin and Pat Harrigan, 131–42. Cambridge, MA: MIT Press.

Juul, Jesper. 2005. *Half-Real: Video Games between Real Rules and Fictional Worlds*. Cambridge, MA: MIT Press.

Juul, Jesper. 2008. "Who Made the Magic Circle? Seeking the Solvable Part of the Game Player Problem." In *Philosophy of Computer Games Conference 2008*. Potsdam.

Juul, Jesper. 2009. "Fear of Failing? The Many Meanings of Difficulty in Video Games." In *The Video Game Theory Reader*, edited by Bernard Perron and Mark J. P. Wolf, 237–52. New York: Routledge.

Juul, Jesper. 2010. *A Casual Revolution: Reinventing Video Games and Their Players*. Cambridge, MA: MIT Press.

Juul, Jesper. 2013. *The Art of Failure: An Essay on the Pain of Playing Video Games*. Cambridge, MA: The MIT Press.

Juul, Jesper. 2015a. "A Brief History of Anti-formalism in Video Games." *The Ludologist* (blog). February 11, 2015. https://www.jesperjuul.net/ludologist/2015/02/11/a-brief-history-of-anti-formalism-in-video-games/.

Juul, Jesper. 2015b. "What Is a Game Redux." *The Ludologist* (blog). June 10, 2015. https://www.jesperjuul.net/ludologist/2015/06/10/what-is-a-game-redux/.

k, merritt. 2012. "Lim [Browser Game]." merritt k.

k, merritt. 2023. "LIM by Merritt k." Itch.Io. January 7, 2023. https://merrittk.itch.io/lim.

Kagen, Melissa. 2017. "Walking Sims, #gamergate, and the Gender of Wandering." In *The Year's Work in Nerds, Wonks, and Neo-Cons*, edited by Jonathan Eburne and Benjamin Schreier, 275–300. Bloomington, Indiana: Indiana University Press.

Karhulahti, Veli-Matti. 2015. "An Ontological Theory of Narrative Works: Storygame as Postclassical Literature." *Storyworlds: A Journal of Narrative Studies* 7 (1): 39–73.

Keogh, Brendan. 2015a. "A Play of Bodies: A Phenomenology of Videogame Experience." PhD Thesis, RMIT University.

Keogh, Brendan. 2015b. "Some Quick Thoughts on Videogame Form off the Top of My Head." Tumblr. *Tumblr* (blog). January 13, 2015. https://ungaming.tumblr.com/post/107969280935/some-quick-thoughts-on-videogame-form-off-the-top.

Keogh, Brendan. 2018. *A Play of Bodies: How We Perceive Videogames*. Cambridge, MA: MIT Press.

King, Geoff, and Tanya Krzywinska. 2002. *Screenplay: Cinema/Videogames/Interfaces*. London: Wallflower Press.

King, Geoff, and Tanya Krzywinska. 2006a. "Film Studies and Digital Games." *Understanding Digital Games*, 112–28.

King, Geoff, and Tanya Krzywinska. 2006b. *Tomb Raiders and Space Invaders: Videogame Forms and Contexts*. London: IB Tauris.

Klimas, Chris. 2009. "Twine [Computer Software]." Chris Klimas.

Knickmeyer, Rachel Lee, and Michael Mateas. 2005. "Preliminary Evaluation of the Interactive Drama Facade." In *CHI '05 Extended Abstracts*, 1549–52. New York: ACM.

Konzack, Lars. 2002. "Computer Game Criticism: A Method for Computer Game Analysis.' In *Proceedings of the Computer Games and Digital Cultures Conference, Finland*, edited by Frans Mäyrä, 89–100. Tampere: Tampere University Press.

Koschmann, Timothy, Kari Kuutti, and Larry Hickman. 1998. "The Concept of Breakdown in Heidegger, Leont'ev, and Dewey and Its Implications for Education." *Mind, Culture, and Activity* 5 (1): 25–41.

Koster, Raph. 2012. "Two Cultures and Games." *Raph's Website* (blog). July 6, 2012. https://www.raphkoster.com/2012/07/06/two-cultures-and-games/.

Koster, Raph. 2014. "A New Formalism." *Critical Proximity* (blog). March 16, 2014. https://critical-proximity.com/2014/03/16/a-new-formalism/.

Kuijpers, Moniek. 2014. "Absorbing Stories: The Effects of Textual Devices on Absorption and Evaluative Responses." PhD Thesis, University Utrecht.

kunzelman. 2015. "On Video Games, Content, and Expression." *This Cage Is Worms* (blog). January 22, 2015. https://thiscageisworms.com/2015/01/22/on-video-games-content-and-expression/.

Lachmann, Renate. 1984. "'Die Verfremdung' Und Das 'Neue Sehen' Bei Viktor Sklovskij." In *Verfremdung in Der Literatur*, edited by H. Helmers, 321–51. Darmstadt: Wissenschaftliche Buchgesellschaft.

Lakoff, George. 2010. "Why It Matters How We Frame the Environment." *Environmental Communication* 4 (1): 70–81.

Lankoski, Petri, and Staffan Björk. 2015. "Formal Analysis of Gameplay." In *Game Research Methods: An Overview*, edited by Petri Lankoski and Staffan Björk, 23–36. Pittsburgh: ETC Press.

Lantz, Frank. 2009. "Drop7 [Mobile Game]." Zynga.

Lantz, Frank. 2015a. "Parley." *Game Design Advance* (blog). January 1, 2015. https://gamedesignadvance.com/?p=2794.

Lantz, Frank. 2015b. "TwitLonger – When You Talk Too Much for Twitter." January 13, 2015. http://www.twitlonger.com/show/n_1sjugos.

Lantz, Frank. 2015c. "More Thoughts on Formalism." *Game Developer* (blog). January 20, 2015. https://www.gamedeveloper.com/design/more-thoughts-on-formalism.

Leech, Geoffrey N., and Mick Short. 2007. *Style in Fiction: A Linguistic Introduction to English Fictional Prose*. 2nd ed. Harlow: Pearson Education.

Leino, Olli Tapio. 2010. "Emotions in Play: On the Constitution of Emotion in Solitary Computer Game Play." PhD Thesis, IT University of Copenhagen, Innovative Communication.

Liboriussen, Bjarke. 2008. "The Landscape Aesthetics of Computer Games." In *Conference Proceedings of the Philosophy of Computer Games 2008*, edited by Stephan Günzel, Michael Liebe, and Dieter Mersch, 2008. Potsdam University Press.

Lindley, Craig A. 2002. "The Gameplay Gestalt, Narrative, and Interactive Storytelling." In *Proceedings of the Computer Games and Digital Cultures Conference*, edited by Frans Mäyrä, 203–15. Tampere: Tampere University Press.

Lynch, David, dir. 1990. "Twin Peaks."

Macgregor, Jody. 2018. "The Creators of Spelunky and Getting Over It Talk about Sexy Hiking and 'B-Games'." *PC Gamer*, April 11, 2018. https://www.pcgamer.com/the-creators-of-spelunky-and-getting-over-it-with-bennett-foddy-on-sexy-hiking-and-b-games/.

Magnuson, Jordan. 2009. "Necessary Games | Games Considered for Meaning and Significance." 2009. https://www.necessarygames.com/.

Magnuson, Jordan. 2019. "Playing and Making Poetic Videogames." MFA Thesis, University of California.

Magnuson, Jordan. 2023. *Game Poems: Videogame Design as Lyric Practice*. Electronic Communities of Making. Amherst, MA: Amherst College Press.

Magritte, René. 1965. *Le Blanc-Seing*.

Malaby, Thomas M. 2007. "Beyond Play: A New Approach to Games." *Games and Culture* 2 (2): 95–113.

Mäyrä, Frans. 2020. "Game Culture Studies and the Politics of Scholarship: The Opposites and the Dialectic." *G|A|M|E Games as Art, Media, Entertainment* 1 (9). https://www.gamejournal.it/game-culture/.

McGee, American. 2000. "American McGee's Alice [MacOS Game]." Electronic Arts.

McMillan, Edmund, and Tommy Refenes. 2010. "Super Meat Boy [MacOS Game]." Team Meat.

Medvedev, Pavel N. 1928. *Formal'nyj Metod v Literaturovedenii: Kritieskoe Vvedenie v Sociologieskuju Poetiku*. Leningrad: Proboj.

Mejia, Robert, Jaime Banks, and Aubrie Adams. 2017. *100 Greatest Video Game Franchises*. Lanham: Rowman & Littlefield.

Meretzky, Steve, and Douglas Adams. 1984. "The Hitchhiker's Guide to the Galaxy [MS DOS Game]." Infocom.

Miall, David S. 1992. "Response to Poetry: Studies of Language and Structure." In *Reader Response to Literature: The Empirical Dimension*, edited by Elaine F. Nardocchio, 153–70. The Hague: Mouton de Gruyter.

Miall, David S., and Don Kuiken. 1994. "Foregrounding, Defamiliarization, and Affect: Response to Literary Stories." *Poetics* 22 (5): 389–407.

Midway Games. 1992. "Mortal Kombat [Arcade Game]." Midway Games.

Mitchell, Alex. 2014. "Defamiliarization and Poetic Interaction in Kentucky Route Zero." *Well Played: A Journal on Video Games, Value and Meaning* 3 (2): 161–78.

Mitchell, Alex. 2016. "Making the Familiar Unfamiliar: Techniques for Creating Poetic Gameplay." In *Proceedings of the First International Joint Conference of DiGRA and FDG 2016*. Dundee: Digital Games Research Association.

Mitchell, Alex, and Liting Kway. 2020. "'How Do I Restart This Thing?' Repeat Experience and Resistance to Closure in Rewind Storygames." In *Interactive Storytelling: Proceedings of ICIDS 2020*, edited by Anne-Gwenn Bosser, David E. Millard, and Charlie Hargood, 164–77. Cham: Springer International Publishing.

Mitchell, Alex, Liting Kway, and Brandon Junhui Lee. 2020. "Storygameness: Understanding Repeat Experience and the Desire for Closure in Storygames." In *Proceedings of the 2020 DiGRA International Conference: Play Everywhere*. Tampere: Digital Games Research Association.

Mitchell, Alex, Liting Kway, Tiffany Neo, and Yuin Theng Sim. 2020. "A Preliminary Categorization of Techniques for Creating Poetic Gameplay." *Game Studies* 20 (2).

Mitchell, Alex, Yuin Theng Sim, and Liting Kway. 2017. "Making It Unfamiliar in the 'Right' Way: An Empirical Study of Poetic Gameplay." In *Proceedings of the 2017 DiGRA International Conference*. Melbourne, Australia: Digital Games Research Association.

Miyazaki, Hidetaka. 2011. "Dark Souls [Microsoft Windows Game]." Namco Bandai Games.

Montembeault, Hugo, and Maxime Deslongchamps-Gagnon. 2019. "The Walking Simulator's Generic Experiences." *Press Start* 5 (2): 1–28.

Möring, Sebastian, and Marco de Mutiis. 2019. "Camera Ludica: Reflections on Photography in Video Games." In *Intermedia Games–Games Inter Media: Video Games and Intermediality*, edited by Michael Fuchs and Jeff Thoss, 69–94. New York: Bloomsbury Academic.

Mortensen, Torill Elvira, and Kristine Jørgensen. 2020. *The Paradox of Transgression in Games*. New York: Routledge.

Mukařovský, Jan, and Jan Chovanec. 2014. "Standard Language and Poetic Language." In *Chapters from the History of Czech Functional Linguistics*. Brno: Masarykova univerzita.

Murray, Janet H. 1998. *Hamlet on the Holodeck: The Future of Narrative in Cyberspace*. Cambridge, MA: MIT Press.

Murray, Janet H. 2013. "The Last Word on Ludology v Narratology (2005)." *Janet H. Murray* (blog). June 28, 2013. https://inventingthemedium.com/2013/06/28/the-last-word-on-ludology-v-narratology-2005/.

Myers, David. 2009. "The Video Game Aesthetic: Play as Form." In *The Video Game Theory Reader 2*, edited by Bernard Perron and Mark J. P. Wolf, 45–64. New York: Routledge.

Myers, David. 2010. *Play Redux: The Form of Computer Games*. Ann Arbor: University of Michigan Press.

Nacke, Lennart, and Anders Drachen. 2011. "Towards a Framework of Player Experience Research." In *Proceedings of the Second International Workshop on Evaluating Player Experience in Games at FDG*. Bordeaux.

Naughty Dog. 2009. "Uncharted 2: Among Thieves [PlayStation 3 Game]." Sony Computer Entertainment.

Neill, Roy William, dir. 1946. *Terror by Night*. Universal Pictures.

Neo, Tiffany, and Alex Mitchell. 2019. "Expanding Comics Theory to Account for Interactivity: A Preliminary Study." *Studies in Comics2* 10 (2): 189–213.

Nijman, Jan Willem, Kitty Calis, Jukio Kalio, and Dominik Johann. 2018. "Minit [MacOS Game]." Devolver Digital.

Nintendo. 2017. "The Legend of Zelda: Breath of the Wild [Nintendo Switch Game]." Nintendo.

Nishikawa, Trizette Zenji. 2005. "3Dゲームファンのための「ワンダと巨像」グラフィックス講座." *GAME Watch Impress*, December 7, 2005. https://game.watch.impress.co.jp/docs/20051207/3dwa.htm.

Nishikawa Yoshiharu. 2017. "[CEDEC 2017]「ゼルダの伝説BotW」の完璧なゲーム世界は，任天堂の開発スタイルが変わったからこそ生まれた." *4Gamer.net*, September 2, 2017. https://www.4gamer.net/games/341/G034168/20170901120/.

Numinous Games. 2016. "That Dragon, Cancer [MacOS Game]." Numinous Games.

O'Connor, Alice. 2018. "Paratopic Is Some Fine Low-Fi Vignette-y Horror." *RockPaperShotgun*, March 15, 2018. https://www.rockpapershotgun.com/paratopic-vignette-horror-game-released.

O'Donnell, Mike. 2010. *Structure and Agency*. London: Sage Publications.

Pajitnov, Alexey. 1988. "Tetris [MS DOS Game]." Spectrum Holobyte.

Perron, Bernard. 2005. "A Cognitive Psychological Approach to Gameplay Emotions." In *Proceedings of the 2005 DiGRA International Conference: Changing Views–Worlds in Play*.

Perron, Bernard. 2018. *The World of Scary Video Games: A Study in Videoludic Horror*. New York: Bloomsbury Publishing USA.

Perron, Bernard, Dominic Arsenault, Martin Picard, and Carl Therrien. 2008. "Methodological Questions in 'Interactive Film Studies'." *New Review of Film and Television Studies* 6 (13): 233–52.

Piering, Julie. n.d. "Diogenes of Sinope." In *Internet Encyclopedia of Philosophy*. Accessed November 15, 2022. https://iep.utm.edu/diogenes-of-sinope/.

Pitkänen, Jori. 2015. "Studying Thoughts: Stimulated Recall as a Game Research Method." In *Game Research Methods: An Overview*, edited by Petri Lankoski and Staffan Björk, 117–32. Pittsburgh: ETC Press.

Pope, Lucas. 2018. "Return of the Obra Dinn [MacOS Game]." 3909 LLC.

Poremba, Cindy. 2007. "Point and Shoot: Remediating Photography in Gamespace." *Games and Culture* 2 (1): 49–58.

Pötzsch, Holger. 2017. "Playing Games with Shklovsky, Brecht, and Boal: Ostranenie, V-Effect, and Spect-Actors as Analytical Tools for Game Studies." *Game Studies* 17 (2).

Pötzsch, Holger. 2019. "From a New Seeing to a New Acting: Viktor Shklovsky's Ostranenie and Analyses of Games and Play." In *Viktor Shklovsky's Heritage in Literature, Arts, and Philosophy*, edited by Slav N. Gratchev and Howard Mancing, 235–51. Lanham: Rowman & Littlefield.

Quantic Dream. 2010. "Heavy Rain [Playstation 3 Game]." Sony Computer Entertainment.

Reed, Aaron A., John Murray, and Anastasia Salter. 2020. *Adventure Games: Playing the Outsider*. New York: Bloomsbury Publishing USA.

Richardson, Brian. 2011. "What Is Unnatural Narrative Theory?' In *Unnatural Narratives, Unnatural Narratology*, edited by Jan Alber and Rüdiger Heinze, 23–40. Berlin: Walter de Gruyter.

Richardson, Brian. 2015. *Unnatural Narrative: Theory, History, and Practice*. Columbus, Ohio: The Ohio State University Press.

Ritchie, Stuart. 2021. "Why Are Gamers So Much Better Than Scientists at Catching Fraud?' *The Atlantic*, July 2, 2021. https://www.theatlantic.com/science/archive/2021/07/gamers-are-better-scientists-catching-fraud/619324/.

Robertson, Adi. 2018. "Paratopic Is a Short, Grimy Horror Game with a Style Straight out of 1998." *The Verge*, April 29, 2018. https://www.theverge.com/2018/4/29/17228744/paratopic-horror-exploration-game-tapes-review.

Robinson-Yu, Adam. 2019. "A Short Hike [MacOS Game]." Adam Robinson-Yu.

Robinson-yu, Adam. n.d. "A Short Hike." Accessed June 28, 2022. https://ashorthike.com/.

Rockstar Studios. 2019. "Red Dead Redemption 2 [Playstation 4 Game]." Rockstar Games.

Rockstar Vancouver. 2006. "Bully [Playstation 2 Game]." Rockstar Games.

Rohrer, Jason. 2007. "Passage [Microsoft Windows Game]." Jason Rohrer.

Roth, Christian, Tom van Nuenen, and Hartmut Koenitz. 2018. "Ludonarrative Hermeneutics: A Way Out and the Narrative Paradox." In *International Conference on Interactive Digital Storytelling*, 93–106. Cham: Springer.

Ruberg, Bonnie. 2020. "Empathy and Its Alternatives: Deconstructing the Rhetoric of "Empathy" in Video Games." *Communication, Culture & Critique* 13 (1): 54–71.

Salen, Katie, and Eric Zimmerman. 2004. *Rules of Play: Game Design Fundamentals*. Cambridge, MA: MIT Press.

Sawicki, Marianne. n.d. "Phenomenology." In *Internet Encyclopedia of Philosophy*. Accessed June 13, 2023. https://iep.utm.edu/phenom/.

Schmierbach, Mike. 2009. "Content Analysis of Video Games: Challenges and Potential Solutions." *Communication Methods and Measures* 3 (3): 147–72.

Schnaars, Cornelia J. 2021. "Taking a Breath of the Wild: The Concept of Airness in Nintendo's Take on Open World Games." *Game| World| Architectonics*, 115.

Seiferle, Rebecca. 2012. "Formalism in Modern Art: Definition Overview and Analysis." The Art Story. 2012. https://www.theartstory.org/definition/formalism/.

Sekhavat, Yoones A., Samad Roohi, Hesam Sakian Mohammadi, and Georgios N. Yannakakis. 2020. "Play with One's Feelings: A Study on Emotion Awareness for Player Experience." *IEEE Transactions on Games*, 1–10.

Sharp, John. 2010. "The Purpose and Meaning of Drop 7." In *Well Played 2.0: Video Games, Value and Meaning*, edited by Drew Davidson, 48–55. Pittsburgh: ETC Press.

Sharp, John. 2015. *Works of Game: On the Aesthetics of Games and Art*. Cambridge, MA: MIT Press.

Sheehan, Jason. 2021. "Reading the Game: Kentucky Route Zero." *NPR*, February 11, 2021, sec. Reading the Game. https://www.npr.org/2021/02/11/966499158/reading-the-game-kentucky-route-zero.

Shelley, Percy Bysshe, Patrick Garland, Richard Marquard, and Gary Watson. 1969. *A Defence of Poetry*. Haldeman-Julius.

Shklovsky, Victor. 2012a. "Art as Technique." In *Russian Formalist Criticism: Four Essays*, edited by Lee T. Lemon and Marion J. Reis, 2nd ed., 21–34. Lincoln: University of Nebraska Press.

Shklovsky, Victor. 2012b. "Sterne's *Tristam Shandy:* Stylistic Commentary." In *Russian Formalist Criticism: Four Essays*, edited by Lee T. Lemon and Marion J. Reis, 2nd ed., 35–54. Lincoln: University of Nebraska Press.

Sicart, Miguel. 2008. "Defining Game Mechanics." *Game Studies* 8 (2).

Sicart, Miguel. 2011. "Against Procedurality." *Game Studies* 11 (3).

Silverman, David, and Amir Marvasti. 2008. *Doing Qualitative Research: A Comprehensive Guide*. London: Sage Publications.

Smith, Joel. n.d. "Edmund Husserl (1859–1938)." In *Internet Encyclopedia of Philosophy*. Accessed June 13, 2023. https://iep.utm.edu/husserl/.

Smith, Jonas Heide. 2006. "Plans and Purposes How Videogame Goals Shape Player Behaviour." PhD Thesis, The IT University of Copenhagen.

Snyder, David. 2017. *Speedrunning: Interviews with the Quickest Gamers*. McFarland.

Soderman, Braxton. 2021. *Against Flow: Video Games and the Flowing Subject*. Cambridge, MA: MIT Press.

Spiegel, Amy Rose. 2017. "Merritt k on Changing Your Path." *The Creative Independent*, March 28, 2017. https://thecreativeindependent.com/people/merritt-k-on-changing-your-path/.

Spielberg, Steven, dir. 1981. *Raiders of the Lost Ark*. Paramount Pictures.

Stang, Sarah. 2022. "Too Close, Too Intimate, and Too Vulnerable: Close Reading Methodology and the Future of Feminist Game Studies." *Critical Studies in Media Communication* 39 (3): 230–38.

Steiner, Peter. 2014. *Russian Formalism: A Metapoetics*. Geneva: Sdvig Press.

Sterling, James Stephanie. 2017. "The Legend of Zelda: Breath of the Wild Review – Broken Sword." The Jimquisition. March 12, 2017. https://www.thejimquisition. com/post/the-legend-of-zelda-breath-of-the-wild-review-broken-sword.

Sudnow, David. 1983. *Pilgrim in the Microworld*. New York: Warner Books.

Švelch, Jan. 2020. "Paratextuality in Game Studies: A Theoretical Review and Citation Analysis." *Game Studies* 20 (2).

Swink, Steve. 2008. *Game Feel: A Game Designer's Guide to Virtual Sensation*. London: CRC Press.

Szabó, Judit. 2022. "Fear and Agency in Survival Horror." In *Negative Emotions in the Reception of Fictional Narratives*, 43–62. Paderborn: Brill | mentis.

Tale of Tales. 2008. "The Graveyard [MacOS Game]." Tale of Tales.

Tan, Ed S. 2000. "Emotion, Art, and the Humanities." In *Handbook of Emotions*, edited by Michael Lewis and Jeanette M. Haveland-Jones, 2nd ed., 116–34. New York: Guildford Press.

Tanenbaum, Teresa Jean. 2015. "Identity Transformation and Agency in Digital Narratives and Story Based Games." PhD Thesis, Simon Fraser University.

Tavinor, Grant. 2008. "Definition of Videogames." *Contemporary Aesthetics* (*Journal Archive*) 6 (1).

Team Aha! 2008. "Akrasia [Microsoft Windows Game]." Singapore-MIT GAMBIT Game Lab.

Team Ico. 2001. "Ico [Playstation 2 Game]." Sony Computer Entertainment.

Team Ico. 2005. "Shadow of the Colossus [Playstation 2 Game]." Sony Computer Entertainment.

Telltale Games. 2012. "The Walking Dead: Season 1 [MacOS Game]." Telltale Games.

thatgamecompany. 2012. "Journey [Playstation 3 Game]." Sony Computer Entertainment.

Tholen, Jay, Mike Lasch, Xalavier Nelson Jr., and Corey Cochran. 2019. "Hypnospace Outlaw [MacOS Game]." No More Robots.

Thomashevsky, Boris. 2012. "Thematics." In *Russian Formalist Criticism: Four Essays*, edited by Lee T. Lemon and Marion J. Reis, 2nd ed., 55–77. Lincoln: University of Nebraska Press.

Thompson, Kristin. 1981. *Eisenstein's "Ivan the Terrible": A Neoformalist Analysis*. Princeton, New Jersey: Princeton University Press.

Thompson, Kristin. 1988. *Breaking the Glass Armor: Neoformalist Film Analysis*. Princeton, New Jersey: Princeton University Press.

Thomson-Jones, Katherine. 2008. "Formalism." In *The Routledge Companion to Philosophy and Film*, edited by Paisley Livingston and Carl Plantinga, 131–41. New York: Routledge.

Thorson, Maddy. 2018. "Celeste [MacOS Game]." Maddy Makes Games.

Tracy, Sarah J. 2020. *Qualitative Research Methods: Collecting Evidence, Crafting Analysis, Communicating Impact*. 2nd ed. Hoboken, New Jersey: John Wiley & Sons.

Treanor, Mike. 2013. "Investigating Procedural Expression and Interpretation in Videogames." PhD Thesis, UC Santa Cruz.

Treanor, Mike, Bobby Schweizer, Ian Bogost, and Michael Mateas. 2011. "Proceduralist Readings: How to Find Meaning in Games with Graphical Logics." In *Proceedings of Foundations of Digital Games (FDG 2011)*, 115–22. New York: ACM.

Trotsky, Leon. 2005. *Literature and Revolution*. Chicago: Haymarket Books.

Tsur, Reuven. 2008. *Towards a Theory of Cognitive Poetics*. 2nd ed. Eastbourne: Sussex Academic Press.

Tusman, Lee. 2013. "Limits and Demonstrations Exhibition." 2013. http://leetusman. com/projects/limits_and_demonstrations.html.

Tyack, April, and Elisa D. Mekler. 2021. "Off-Peak: An Examination of Ordinary Player Experience." In *Proceedings of the 2021 CHI Conference on Human Factors in Computing Systems*, 1–12. New York: ACM.

Tynianov, Yuri. 2019. "On Literary Evolution (1927)." In *Permanent Evolution: Selected Essays on Literature, Theory and Film*, edited by Morse Ainsley and Philip Redko, 267–82. Boston, MA: Academic Studies Press.

Ungvári, Tamás. 1979. "The Origins of the Theory of Verfremdung." *Neohelicon* 7 (1): 171–232.

Vella, Daniel. 2015. "The Ludic Subject and the Ludic Self: Analyzing the 'I-in-the-Gameworld'." PhD Thesis, IT University of Copenhagen.

Vossen, Emma. 2018. "On the Cultural Inaccessibility of Gaming: Invading, Creating, and Reclaiming the Cultural Clubhouse." PhD Thesis, University of Waterloo.

Vught, Jasper van. 2016. "Neoformalist Game Analysis: A Methodological Exploration of Single-Player Game Violence." PhD Thesis, University of Waikato.

Vught, Jasper van, and René Glas. 2018. "Considering Play: From Method to Analysis." *Transactions of the Digital Games Research Association* 4 (2).

Waern, Annika. 2012. "Framing Games." In *Proceedings of the 2012 Nordic DiGRA*. Tampere: Digital Games Research Association.

Walker, Austin. 2015. "The Long Game: Subterfuge, Formalism and Interactivity." *Pastemagazine.Com*, January 28, 2015. https://www.pastemagazine.com/games/ the-long-game-subterfuge-formalism-and-interactivi/.

Walker, Matt [@retroOtoko]. 2017. "Got around to Reading Some of the BotW CEDEC Articles. Interesting Fact – https://T.Co/494TwAuYxi." Tweet. *Twitter*. https://twitter.com/retroOtoko/status/915037635663425536.

Wardrip-Fruin, Noah. 2009. *Expressive Processing: Digital Fictions, Computer Games, and Software Studies*. Cambridge, MA: MIT Press.

Westerlaken, Michelle. 2017. "Self-Fashioning in Action: Zelda's Breath of the Wild Vegan Run." Kraków: Game Philosophy Network.

Willumsen, Ea Christina. 2018a. "Source Code and Formal Analysis: A Reading of Passage." *Transactions of the Digital Games Research Association* 3 (2).

Willumsen, Ea Christina. 2018b. "The Form of Game Formalism." *Media and Communication* 6 (2): 137–44.

Wimsatt, William K., and Monroe C. Beardsley. 1946. "The Intentional Fallacy." *The Sewanee Review* 54 (3): 468–88.

Wimsatt, William K., and Monroe C. Beardsley. 1949. "The Affective Fallacy." *The Sewanee Review* 57 (1): 31–55.

Winograd, Terry, and Fernando Flores. 1986. *Understanding Computers and Cognition: A New Foundation for Design*. Norwood, New Jersey: Alex Publishing.

WIRED Staff. 2006. "Behind the Shadow: Fumito Ueda." *Wired*, 2006. https://www.wired.com/2006/03/behind-the-shadow-fumito-ueda/.

Witt, Annick de, Joop de Boer, Nicholas Hedlund, and Patricia Osseweijer. 2016. "A New Tool to Map the Major Worldviews in the Netherlands and USA, and Explore How They Relate to Climate Change." *Environmental Science and Policy* 63: 101–12.

Wolf, Mark J. P., ed. 2002. *The Medium of the Video Game*. Austin: University of Texas Press.

Wolfinger, Nicholas H. 2002. "On Writing Fieldnotes: Collection Strategies and Background Expectancies." *Qualitative Research* 2 (1): 85–93.

Wright, Peter C., Jayne Wallace, and Jack C. McCarthy. 2008. "Aesthetics and Experience-Centered Design." *ACM Transactions on Computer-Human Interaction (TOCHI)* 15 (4): 1–21.

Yang, Robert. 2017. "Open World Level Design: Spatial Composition and Flow in Breath of the Wild." *Radiator* (blog). October 4, 2017. https://www.blog.radiator.debacle.us/2017/10/open-world-level-design-spatial.html.

Zagal, José P., Michael Mateas, Clara Fernández-Vara, Brian Hochhalter, and Nolan Lichti. 2007. "Towards an Ontological Language for Game Analysis." In *Worlds in Play: International Perspectives on Digital Games Research*, edited by Suzanne de Castell and Jennifer Jenson, 25–36. New York: Peter Lang.

Zirmunsky (Zhirmunskij), Viktor. 1928. "K Voprosu o Formal'nom Metode." In *Voprosy Teorii Literatury* [*Literature Theory Questions*]. Leningrad.

About the Authors

Alex Mitchell teaches in the Department of Communications and New Media, National University of Singapore. His research investigates defamiliarization in gameplay, motivations for replaying story-focused games, authoring tools, and collaborative storytelling. He is a founding member of the executive board of the Association for Research in Interactive Digital Narratives (ARDIN).

Jasper van Vught is assistant professor in the department of Media and Culture Studies at Utrecht University (Netherlands). His research includes methodological challenges to studying games as texts and pedagogical challenges to teaching about them. He's a core member of the Utrecht Centre for Game Research.

Index

Page numbers in *italics* refer to images.